DK EYEWITNESS TOP 10 TRAVEL GUIDES

PARIS

MIKE GERRARD & DONNA DAILEY

Left **Glass Pyramid, Musée du Louvre** Right **Crypt vaults, Sacré-Coeur**

LONDON, NEW YORK,
MELBOURNE, MUNICH AND DELHI
www.dk.com

Produced by
Book Creation Services, Ltd, London

Reproduced by Colourscan, Singapore
Printed and bound in China by
Leo Paper Products Ltd

First published in Great Britain in 2002
by Dorling Kindersley Limited
80 Strand, London WC2R 0RL
A Penguin Company

Reprinted with revisions 2003, 2004, 2005, 2006

A CIP catalogue record is available from the British Library.

ISBN 13: 978-1-40531-241-7
ISBN 10: 1-40531-241-6

Within each Top 10 list in this book, no hierarchy of quality or popularity is implied. All 10 are, in the editor's opinion, of roughly equal merit.

Contents

Paris Top 10

The information in this DK Eyewitness Top 10 Travel Guide is checked regularly.
Every effort has been made to ensure that this book is as up-to-date as possible at the time of going to press. Some details, however, such as telephone numbers, opening hours, prices, gallery hanging arrangements and travel information are liable to change. The publishers cannot accept responsibility for any consequences arising from the use of this book, nor for any material on third party websites, and cannot guarantee that any website address in this book will be a suitable source of travel information. We value the views and suggestions of our readers very highly. Please write to: Publisher, DK Eyewitness Travel Guides, Dorling Kindersley, 80 Strand, London, Great Britain WC2R 0RL.

Cover: All photographs specially commissioned except: Front – **Corbis**: Paul Steel main; Robert Holmes bl; **DK Images**: cl. Back – **DK Images**: Max Alexander tc; Michael Crockett tl; Steven Wooster tr. Spine – **DK Images**: Max Alexander.

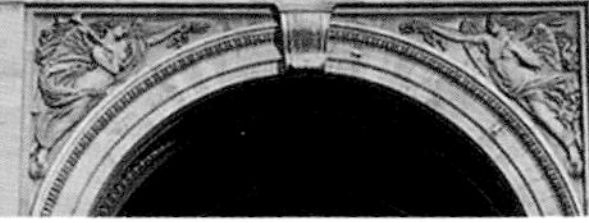

Left Rose window, Notre-Dame Right Stone carvings, Arc de Triomphe

Left Bois de Boulogne Right Montmartre

PARIS TOP 10

TOP 10 Paris Highlights

From Notre-Dame to the Eiffel Tower, Paris holds some of the world's most famous sights and these ten attractions should be top of the list for any first-time visitor. With the exception of the overtly modern Pompidou Centre, they have been landmarks of this elegant and romantic capital for centuries and remain awe-inspiring sights, no matter how often you visit the city.

1 Musée du Louvre

The world's largest museum unsurprisingly also contains one of the world's most important collections of art and antiquities. To complete the superlatives, the building was once France's largest royal palace *(see pp8–11)*.

2 Musée d'Orsay

This remarkable conversion has turned a former railway station into one of the world's leading art galleries *(above)* and is, for many, reason alone to visit Paris *(see pp12–15)*.

3 Eiffel Tower

Some six million visitors a year ascend to the top of this most famous Paris landmark for the spectacular views. It was erected for the Universal Exhibition of 1889 *(see pp16–17)*.

4 Notre-Dame

This great Gothic cathedral, founded on the site of a Roman temple, was completed in 1334 and is a repository of French art and history. It also represents the geographical heart of France *(see pp18–21)*.

5 Sacré-Coeur
The terrace in front of this monumental white-domed basilica in Montmartre affords one of the finest free views over Paris *(see pp22–3)*.

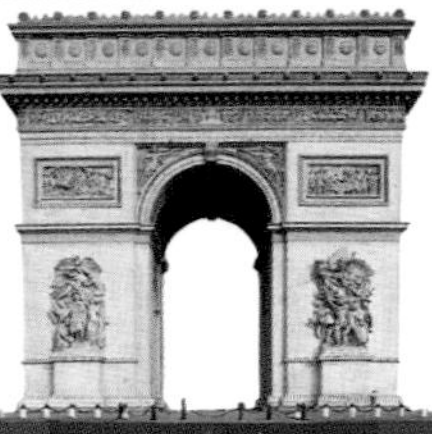

6 Arc de Triomphe
Napoleon's triumphal arch, celebrating battle victories, stands proudly at the top of the Champs-Elysées and, along with the Eiffel Tower, is one of the city's most enduring images *(see pp24–5)*.

7 Centre Georges Pompidou
Home to the Paris Museum of Modern Art, the design of the Pompidou Centre makes it a distinctive exhibition in itself. The Centre also has extensive research facilities *(see pp26–7)*.

8 Panthéon
The great and the good of France are buried in the Panthéon *(above)*, including Voltaire and Victor Hugo *(see pp28–9)*.

9 Sainte-Chapelle
Called "a gateway to heaven", this splendid medieval church *(left)* was built to house the relics collected by St Louis on his many Crusades *(see pp30–31)*.

10 Hôtel des Invalides
The glowing golden dome of the Hôtel des Invalides church *(right)* is unmistakable across the rooftops of Paris *(see pp32–3)*.

For guided tours in Paris **See p165**

TOP 10 Musée du Louvre

One of the world's most impressive museums, the Louvre contains more than 350,000 priceless objects. Built as a fortress by King Philippe-Auguste in 1190, Charles V (1364–80) was the first king to make it his home. In the 16th century François I replaced it with a Renaissance-style palace and founded the royal art collection with 12 paintings looted from Italy. Revolutionaries opened the collection to the public in 1793. Shortly after, Napoleon renovated the Louvre as a museum.

Musée du Louvre façade

Le Café Marly in the Richelieu Wing has a superb location overlooking the pyramid, but the food is average. Other options are Le Grand Louvre, serving top cuisine beneath the pyramid, or the fast-food hall in Carrousel du Louvre.

Beat the queues by arriving 20 minutes before opening time. Or visit on one of the evening openings.

34 quai du Louvre, 75001
• Map L2
• 01 40 20 50 50 (for advance booking)
• www.louvre.fr
• Open 9am–6pm Wed, Thu, Sat & Sun, 9am–9:45pm Fri & Mon; closed Tue & public hols
• Admission €8.50 (reduced price of €6.00 after 3pm and Sun; free 1st Sun of month)
• Partial disabled access

Top 10 Exhibits

1. Venus de Milo
2. Mona Lisa
3. Glass Pyramid
4. Marly Horses
5. The Raft of the Medusa
6. The Winged Victory of Samothrace
7. The Lacemaker
8. Slaves
9. Medieval Moats
10. Perrault's Colonnade

1 Venus de Milo

The positioning of this Hellenistic statue, dramatically lit at the end of a long hallway, enhances its feminine beauty. It dates from the end of the 2nd century BC and was discovered on the Greek island of Milos in 1820.

2 Mona Lisa

Arguably the most famous painting in the world, Leonardo's portrait of the woman with the enigmatic smile *(see p11)* was encased in glass after a knife attack. Visit early or late in the day.

3 Glass Pyramid

The unmistakable pyramid, designed by I.M. Pei, became the Louvre's new entrance in 1989. Stainless steel tubes form the 21-m-high (69-ft) frame *(below)*.

4 Marly Horses

Coustou's rearing horses being restrained by horse-tamers were sculpted in 1745 for Louis XIV's Château de Marly. Replicas stand near the Place de la Concorde.

For more Paris museums **See pp34–5**

5 The Raft of the Medusa

A shipwreck three years earlier inspired this early Romantic painting *(right)* by Théodore Géricault (1791–1824) in 1819. The work depicts a moment when the survivors spot a sail on the horizon.

6 The Winged Victory of Samothrace

This Hellenistic treasure (3rd–2nd century BC) stands atop a stone ship radiating grace and power. It commemorates a naval triumph at Rhodes.

7 The Lacemaker

Jan Vermeer's masterpiece *(below)*, painted around 1665 gives a simple but beautiful rendering of everyday life and is the highlight of the Louvre's Dutch collection.

8 Slaves

Michelangelo sculpted these two slaves (1513–20) for the tomb of Pope Julius II in Rome. He purposely left parts unfinished to symbolize the figures emerging from "prisons" of stone.

9 Medieval Moats

An excavation in the 1980s uncovered the remains of the medieval fortress. You can see the base of the towers and the drawbridge support.

10 Perrault's Colonnade

The majestic east façade by Claude Perrault (1613–88), with its columns *(below)*, was part of an extension plan commissioned by Louis XIV.

6

9

1

10

Key

Ground Floor

First Floor

Second Floor

Gallery Guide

The main entrance is beneath the glass pyramid, but you can also enter through the Carrousel du Louvre shopping mall on Rue de Rivoli. From the ticket hall, corridors radiate out to each of the three wings – the Sully, Denon and Richelieu – set around several courtyards. The works are displayed on four floors, with paintings and sculpture collections arranged by country of origin. There are separate areas for *objets d'art*, antiquities, prints and drawings.

Above **Sleeping Hermaphrodite, Greek Antiquities**

Top 10 Louvre Collections

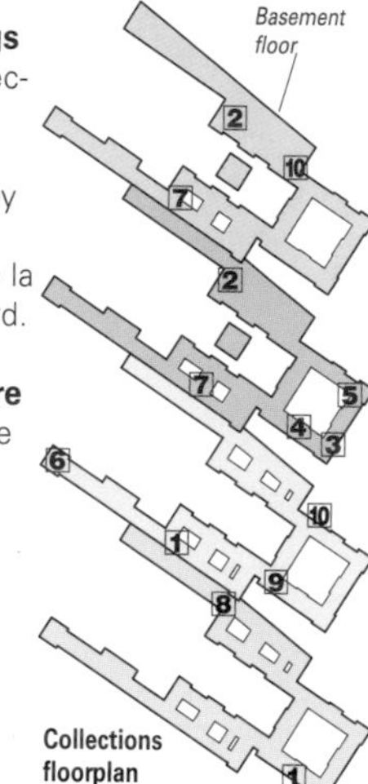

Collections floorplan

1 French Paintings

This superb collection ranges from the 14th century to 1848 and includes works by such artists as Jean Watteau, Georges de la Tour and JH Fragonard.

2 French Sculpture

Highlights include the Tomb of Philippe Pot by Antoine le Moiturier, the Marly Horses *(see p8)* and the works by Pierre Puget in the glass-covered courtyards.

3 Egyptian Antiquities

The finest collection outside Cairo, featuring a Sphinx in the crypt, the Seated Scribe of Sakkara, huge sarcophagi, mummified animals, funerary objects and intricate carvings depicting everyday life in Ancient Egypt.

Akhenaton and Nefertiti, Egypt

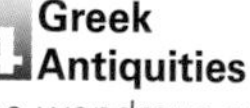

4 Greek Antiquities

The wondrous art of Ancient Greece here ranges from a Cycladic idol from the third millennium BC to Classical Greek marble statues (*c*.5th century BC) to Hellenistic works (late 3rd–2nd century BC).

5 Oriental Antiquities

A stunning collection includes a re-created temple of an Assyrian king and the Codex of Hammurabi (18th century BC), mankind's oldest written laws.

6 Italian Paintings

French royalty adored the art of Italy and amassed much of this collection (1200–1800). There are many works by da Vinci including the *Mona Lisa*.

7 Italian Sculpture

Highlights of this collection, dating from the early Renaissance, include a 15th-century *Madonna and Child* by Donatello and Michelangelo's *Slaves (see p9)*.

8 Dutch Paintings

Rembrandt works take pride of place in this section, along with domestic scenes by Vermeer and portraits by Frans Hals.

9 Objets d'Art

This collection of ceramics, jewellery and other items spans many countries and centuries.

10 Islamic Art

An exquisite collection ranging from a 7th-century silver dish to treasures from the Ottoman Empire (14th–19th centuries).

For more Paris museums **See pp34–5**

Top 10 Louvre Residents

1. Charles V (1364–80)
2. Henri II (1547–49)
3. Catherine de' Medici (1519–89)
4. Henri IV (1589–1610)
5. Louis XIII (1610–43)
6. Louis XIV (1643–1715)
7. Anne of Austria (1601–66)
8. Guillaume Coustou, sculptor (1677–1746)
9. Edmé Bouchardon, sculptor (1698–1762)
10. François Boucher, artist (1703–70)

Leonardo da Vinci and the Mona Lisa

***Mona Lisa*, Leonardo da Vinci's enigmatic portrait**

Leonardo da Vinci

A Renaissance man extraordinaire, Leonardo was not only an artist but a sculptor, engineer, architect and scientist. His many achievements included the study of anatomy and aerodynamics.

Born in Vinci to a wealthy family, Leonardo da Vinci (1452–1519) first took up an apprenticeship under the Florentine artist Andrea del Verrocchio, then served the Duke of Milan as an architect and military engineer, during which time he painted the acclaimed Last Supper *mural (1495). On his return to Florence, to work as architect to Cesare Borgia, he painted his most celebrated portrait, the* Mona Lisa *(1503–06). It is also known as* La Gioconda*, allegedly the name of the model's aristocratic husband, although recent speculation suggests that da Vinci himself could be the subject. The masterpiece, particularly the sitter's mysterious smile, shows mastery of two techniques:* chiaroscuro*, the contrast of light and shadow, and* sfumato*, subtle transitions between colours. It was the artist's own favourite painting and he took it with him everywhere. In 1516 François I brought them both to France, giving da Vinci the use of Château de Cloux, near Amboise in the Loire Valley, where he died three years later. The* Mona Lisa *is the Renaissance master's only known surviving work of portraiture.*

Musée d'Orsay

This wonderful collection covers a variety of art forms from the 1848–1914 period, including a superb Impressionists section. Its setting, in a converted railway station, is equally impressive. Built in 1900, in time for the Paris Exposition, the station was in use until 1939, when it was closed and largely ignored, bar its use as the location for Orson Welles' 1962 film, The Trial. *It was later used as a theatre and as auction rooms, and in the mid-1970s was considered for demolition. In 1977, the Paris authorities decided to save the imposing station building by converting it into this striking museum.*

Musée d'Orsay façade

The museum restaurant serves an excellent lunch during the day but arrive early, as long queues form. For a snack or a drink it is easier to go to the café on the upper level.

1 rue de la Légion-d'Honneur, 75007
• Map J2
• 01 40 49 48 14
• www.musee-orsay.fr
• Open summer: 9am–6pm Tue–Sun (Thu till 9:45pm); winter: 10am–6pm Tue–Sat, 9am–6pm Sun; closed 1 Jan, 1 May, 25 Dec
• Admission €7.50 (€5.50 Sun)

Top 10 Features

1. The Building
2. Van Gogh Paintings
3. Le Déjeuner sur l'Herbe
4. Olympia
5. Blue Waterlilies
6. Degas' Statues of Dancers
7. Jane Avril Dancing
8. Dancing at the Moulin de la Galette
9. La Belle Angèle
10. Café des Hauteurs

1 The Building

The former railway station which houses this museum is almost as stunning as the exhibits. The light and spacious feel when one first steps inside, after admiring the magnificent old façade, takes one's breath away.

2 Van Gogh Paintings

The star of a star collection is Vincent Van Gogh (1853–90) and perhaps the most striking of the several canvases on display is the 1889 work showing the artist's *Bedroom at Arles (below)*. Also on display are self-portraits, painted with the artist's familiar intensity.

3 Le Déjeuner sur l'Herbe

Edouard Manet's (1832–83) controversial painting (1863) was first shown in an "Exhibition of Rejected Works". Its bold portrayal of a classically nude woman *(below)* enjoying the company of 19th-century men in suits brought about a wave of virulent criticism.

For more Paris museums **See pp34–5**

4 Olympia

Another Manet portrayal (1865) of a naked courtesan, receiving flowers sent by an admirer, was also regarded as indecent and shocked public and critics alike, but it was a great influence on later artists.

5 Blue Waterlilies

Claude Monet (1840–1926) painted this stunning canvas (1919) on one of his favourite themes. His love of waterlilies led him to create his own garden at Giverney to enable him to paint them in a natural setting. This experimental work *(below)* inspired many abstract painters later in the 20th century.

6 Degas' Statues of Dancers

Edgar Degas' (1834–1917) sculpted dancers range from the innocent to the erotic. *Young Dancer of Fourteen* (1881) is one of the most striking and the only one exhibited in the artist's lifetime *(left)*.

7 Jane Avril Dancing

Toulouse-Lautrec's (1864–1901) paintings define Paris's *belle époque*. Jane Avril was a Moulin Rouge dancer and featured in several of his works, including this 1895 canvas *(below)*.

8 Dancing at the Moulin de la Galette

One of the best-known paintings of the Impressionist era (1876), the exuberance of Renoir's (1841–1919) work captures the look and mood of Montmartre.

9 La Belle Angèle

This portrait of a Brittany beauty (1889) by Paul Gauguin (1848–1903) shows the influence of Japanese art on the artist. It was bought by Degas, to finance Gauguin's first trip to Polynesia.

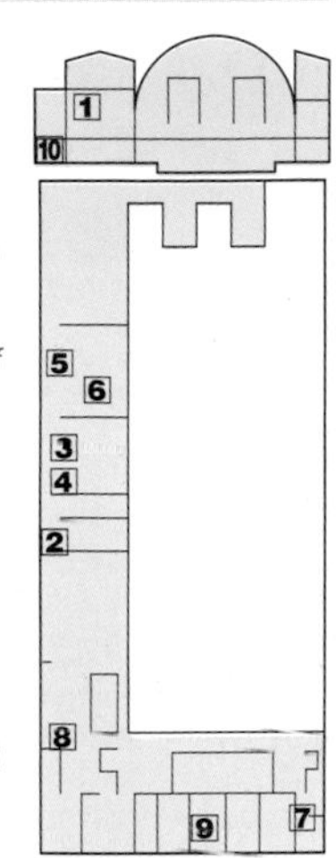

Musée d'Orsay Upper Level

10 Café des Hauteurs

As a rest from all the art, the Musée d'Orsay's café is delightfully situated behind one of the former station's huge clocks, making a break here an experience in itself. The food is good too.

Gallery Guide

As soon as you enter the gallery, collect a map of its layout. Escalators near the entrance lead to all three floors. The ground floor houses fine works from the early to mid-19th century, as well as striking Oriental works, decorative arts and a book shop. The middle level includes Naturalist and Symbolist paintings and sculpture terraces. The upper level is home to the Impressionist and Post-Impressionist galleries, which contain the collection's most popular paintings.

For more Paris art galleries **See pp36–7**

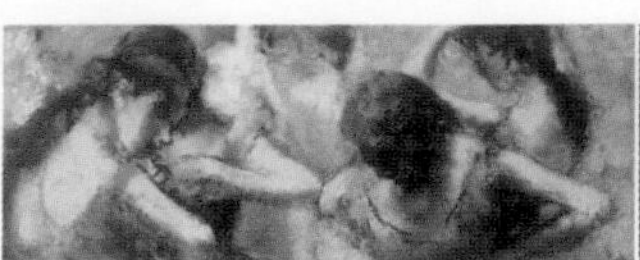

Left ***Blue Dancers* (1890), Degas** Right ***La Belle Angèle* (1889), Gauguin**

Musée d'Orsay Collections

1 The Impressionists
One of the best Impressionist collections in the world. Admirers of Manet, Monet and Renoir will not be disappointed.

2 The Post-Impressionists
The artists who moved on to a newer interpretation of Impressionism are equally well represented, including Matisse, Toulouse-Lautrec and the towering figure of Van Gogh.

3 School of Pont-Aven
Paul Gauguin *(see p13)* was at the centre of the group of artists associated with Pont-Aven in Brittany. His work here includes the carved door panels known as the *House of Pleasure* (1901).

4 Art Nouveau
Art Nouveau is synonymous with Paris, with many metro stations retaining entrances built in that style. Pendants and bottles by René-Jules Lalique (1860–1945) are among the examples.

5 Symbolism
This vast collection includes works by Gustav Klimt (1862–1918), Edvard Munch (1863–1944) and James Whistler's (1834–1903) 1871 portrait of his mother.

6 Romanticism
The Romantics wanted to heighten awareness of the spiritual world. One striking work is *The Tiger Hunt* (1854) by Eugène Delacroix (1798–1863).

Floorplan: the collections

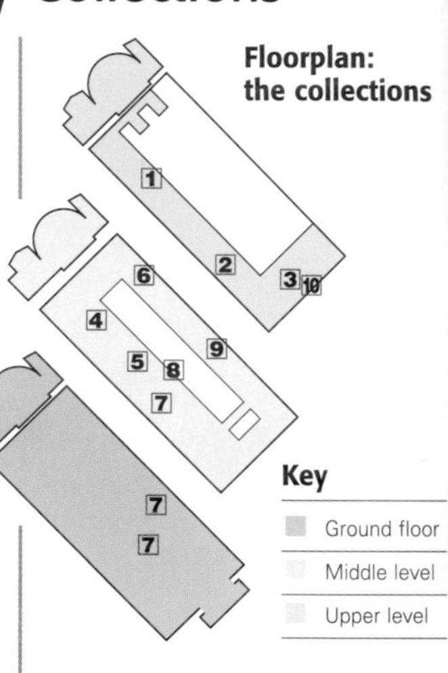

7 Sculpture
The collection includes pieces by Rodin *(see p111)* and satirical carvings of politicians by Honoré Daumier (1808–79).

8 Naturalism
Naturalist painters intensified nature in their work. *Haymaking* (1877) by Jules Bastien-Lepage (1848–84) is a fine example.

9 Nabis
The Nabis Movement moved art into a more decorative form. Pierre Bonnard (1867–1947) is one of its exponents.

10 Photography Collection
Some 10,000 early photographs include work by Bonnard, Degas and photographer Julia Margaret Cameron (1815–79).

Top 10 Impressionists

1. Claude Monet (1840–1926)
2. Edouard Manet (1832–83)
3. Auguste Renoir (1841–1919)
4. Edgar Degas (1834–1917
5. Camille Pissarro (1830–1903)
6. Alfred Sisley (1839–99)
7. James Whistler (1834–1903)
8. Walter Sickert (1860–1942)
9. Mary Cassatt (1845–1926)
10. Berthe Morisot (1841–95)

(Prices for Impressionist paintings at auction are considered a financial barometer for the art world. One of Monet's Waterlily paintings fetched US$22.6 million.)

The Impressionist Movement

Regarded as the starting point of modern art, the Impressionist Movement is probably the best-known and best-loved art movement in the world – certainly if prices at auction and the crowds in the Musée d'Orsay's galleries are anything to go by. The movement started in France, and almost all its leading figures were French, including the Parisian-born British artist Alfred Sisley. Impressionism was a reaction against the formality and Classicism insisted upon by the Académie des Beaux-Arts in Paris, who were very much the art establishment and decided what would or would not be exhibited at the all-important Paris Salon. The term "impressionism" was actually coined by a critic of the style, who dismissed the 1872 Monet painting Impression: Sunrise *in a magazine. The artists themselves then adopted the term. The style profoundly influenced painters such as Van Gogh and was to have a lasting influence on 19th- and 20th-century art.*

Cathedral at Rouen (1892–3), Claude Monet

Dancing at the Moulin de la Galette (1876), Renoir

TOP 10 Eiffel Tower

The most distinctive symbol of Paris, the Eiffel Tower (Tour Eiffel) was much maligned by critics when it rose on the city's skyline in 1889 as part of the Universal Exhibition, but its graceful symmetry soon made it the star attraction. At 320 m (1,050 ft) high, it was the world's tallest building until it was surpassed by New York's Empire State Building in 1931. Despite its delicate appearance, it weighs 10,100 metric tons and engineer Gustave Eiffel's construction was so sound that it never sways more than 7 cm (2.5 in) in strong winds.

Eiffel Tower from the Trocadéro

In addition to the restaurants on levels 1 and 2, vendors sell snacks at the base of tower.

Try and visit the tower at night, when it is beautifully floodlit and the queues are shorter.

Champ-de-Mars, 7e
• Map B4
• 01 44 11 23 23
• www.tour-eiffel.fr
• Open 9:30am–11:45pm daily (last adm for top: 10.30pm) (mid-Jun–Aug: 9am–12:45am; last adm for top: 11pm)
• Admission: €4.10 (stairs); €3.70–€10.70 (lift, depending on level)
• Disabled access first and second levels only

Top 10 Features

1. Viewing Gallery
2. Ironwork
3. Lighting
4. View from the Trocadéro
5. Cinémax
6. First Level
7. Second Level
8. Hydraulic Lift Mechanism
9. Bust of Gustave Eiffel
10. Champ de Mars

1 Viewing Gallery

At 274 m (899 ft), the view is stupendous from the third-level viewing gallery, stretching for 80 km (50 miles) on a clear day. You can also see Gustave Eiffel's sitting room on this level.

2 Ironwork

The complex pattern of the girders, held together by 2.5 million rivets, stabilizes the tower in high winds. The 18,000 metal parts can expand up to 15 cm (6 in) on hot days.

For more on the Eiffel Tower Quarter **See pp110–17**

3 Lighting
A 292,000-watt lighting system makes the Eiffel Tower the most spectacular night-time sight in Paris. Illuminated for 10 minutes every hour, it forms a golden filigree against the dark sky.

4 View from the Trocadéro
Day or night, the best approach for a first-time view of the tower is from the Trocadéro *(see p136)*, which affords a monumental vista from the terrace across the Seine.

5 Cinémax
Located on the first level, this small museum tells the history of the tower through an audio-visual show. It includes footage of famous visitors to the tower, from Charlie Chaplin to Adolf Hitler.

6 First Level
You can walk the 360 steps to the 57 m (187 ft) high first level, or jump the lift queue by booking a table at the Altitude 95 restaurant *(see p117)*. Mail your postcards at the post office.

7 Second Level
At 115 m (377 ft) high, this is the location of the Jules Verne Restaurant, one of the finest in Paris for both food and views *(see p117)*. The walk up from the first level is 700 steps.

8 Hydraulic Lift Mechanism
The 1889 lift mechanism is still in operation and travels some 100,000 km (62,000 miles) a year. The lifts have limited capacity, so on busy days allow two hours to the top.

9 Bust of Gustave Eiffel
This bust of the tower's creator, by Antoine Bourdelle, was placed below his remarkable achievement, by the north pillar, in 1930.

10 Champ-de-Mars
The long gardens of this former parade ground *(right)* stretch from the base of the tower to the École Militaire (military school).

Caricature of Gustave Eiffel with his tower

The Life of Gustave Eiffel

Born in Paris, Gustave Eiffel (1832–1923) was an engineer and builder who made his name building bridges and viaducts. Eiffel was famous for the graceful designs and master craftsmanship of his wrought-iron constructions. He once remarked that his famous tower was "formed by the wind itself". In 1890 he became immersed in the study of aerodynamics, and kept an office in the tower until his death, using it for experiments. In 1889, when the Eiffel Tower was erected, its creator was awarded the Légion d'Honneur for the achievement.

TOP 10 Notre-Dame

The heart of the country, both geographically and spiritually, the Cathedral of Notre-Dame (Our Lady) stands majestic on the Ile de la Cité. After Pope Alexander III laid the foundation stone in 1163, an army of craftsmen toiled for 170 years to realize Bishop Maurice de Sully's magnificent design. Almost destroyed during the Revolution, the Gothic masterpiece was restored in 1841–64 by architect Viollet-le-Duc. Some 130 m (430 ft) in length with a high-vaulted nave and double side aisles, it also contains France's largest organ.

3 Flying Buttresses

The striking buttresses supporting the cathedral's east façade are by Jean Ravy and have a span of 15 m (50 ft). The best view is from Square Jean XXIII.

Notre-Dame seen from the River Seine

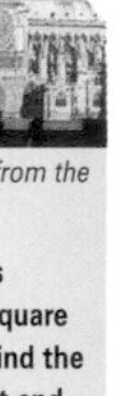

There are cafés opposite the Square Jean XXIII behind the cathedral's east end.

Free recitals on the great organ take place every Sunday afternoon.

6 pl du Parvis-de-Notre-Dame, 75004
• Map N4
• 01 53 10 07 00 (towers)
• Open Apr–Jun & Sep: 9:30am–7:30pm daily; Jul– Aug: 9am–7:30pm Mon– Fri, 9am–11pm Sat–Sun; Oct–Mar: 10am–7:30pm daily
• Admission towers: €7.00 (€4.50 18–25s, under-18s free)

Top 10 Features

1. West Front
2. Portal of the Virgin
3. Flying Buttresses
4. The Towers
5. Galerie des Chimières
6. The Spire
7. Rose Windows
8. Statue of the Virgin and Child
9. Carved Choir Stalls
10. Treasury

1 West Front

The glorious entrance to the cathedral *(right)* is through three elaborately carved portals. Biblical scenes, painted in the Middle Ages, represent the life of the Virgin, the Last Judgment and the Life of St Anne. Above is the Gallery of Kings of Judaea and Israel.

2 Portal of the Virgin

The splendid stone tympanum *(left)* was carved in the 13th century and shows the Virgin Mary's death and glorious coronation in heaven. However, the Virgin and Child carving seen between the doors is a modern work of art.

4 The Towers

The twin towers are 69 m (226 ft) high: visitors can climb the 387 steps of the north tower for splendid vistas over Paris. The south tower houses the Emmanuel Bell, weighing 13 tonnes.

For more Paris churches **See pp40–41**

5 Galerie des Chimères

Lurking between the towers are the famous gargoyles *(chimères)*, placed here by Viollet-le-Duc to ward off evil.

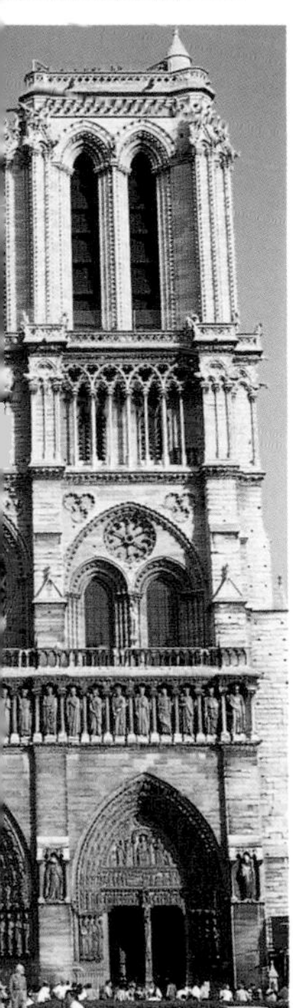

6 The Spire

The 90-m (295-ft) spire was added by Viollet-le-Duc. Next to the Apostles statues on the roof is one of the architect, admiring his work.

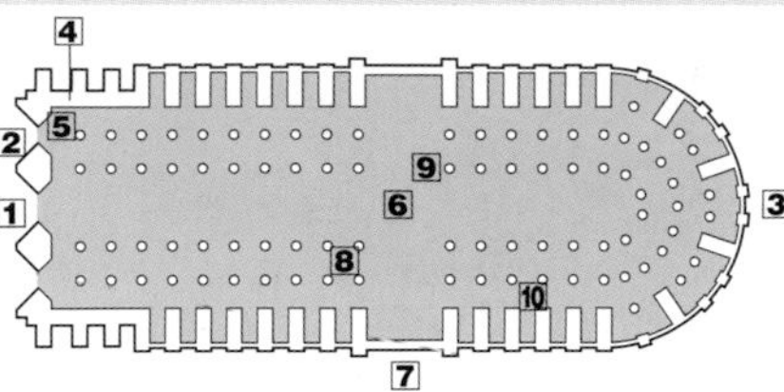

Floorplan of the Cathedral

7 Rose Windows

Three great rose windows adorn the north, south and west façades, but only the north window *(below)* retains its 13th-century stained glass, depicting the Virgin surrounded by figures from the Old Testament. The south window shows Christ encircled by the Apostles.

8 Statue of the Virgin and Child

Also known as Notre-Dame de Paris (Our Lady of Paris), this beautiful 14th-century statue was brought to the cathedral from the chapel of St Aignan. It stands against the southeast pillar of the transept, at the entrance to the chancel.

9 Choir Stalls

More than half of the original stalls commissioned by Louis XIV survive. Among the beautifully carved work on the 78 stalls are scenes from the Life of the Virgin.

10 Treasury

Ancient manuscripts, reliquaries and religious garments are housed in the sacristy. The crown of thorns and a piece of the True Cross are on public view every Good Friday.

Cathedral Guide

Enter through the West Front. The stairs to the towers are outside to your left. Ahead, the central nave soars to a height of 35 m (115 ft), while 37 side chapels line the walls. These contain the "May" paintings by Charles le Brun, donated by the goldsmiths' guild each May in the 17th–18th centuries. The fine transept across the nave is the best place to admire the three rose windows. Remnants of the 14th-century stone screen can be seen on the north and south bays of the chancel. Nicolas Coustou's *Pietà* stands behind the high altar, flanked by statues of Louis XIII by Coustou and Louis XIV by Antoine Coysevox.

Left **Joan of Arc** Centre **Empress Josephine** Right **King Charles I**

Top 10 Famous Visitors to Notre-Dame

1 Joan of Arc

The French patriot Jeanne d'Arc (1412–31), who defended her country against the invading English, had a posthumous trial here in 1455, despite having been burnt at the stake 24 years earlier. At the re-trial she was found to be innocent of heresy.

2 François II and Mary Stuart

Mary Stuart (1542–87) (Mary Queen of Scots) had been raised in France and married the Dauphin in 1558. He ascended the throne as François II in 1559 and the king and queen were crowned in Notre-Dame.

3 Napoleon

The coronation of Napoleon (1769–1821) in Notre-Dame in 1804 saw the eager general seize the crown from Pope Pius VII and crown himself emperor and his wife Josephine, empress.

4 Josephine

Josephine's (1763–1814) reign as Empress of France lasted only five years; Napoleon divorced her in 1809.

5 Pope Pius VII

In 1809 Pope Pius VII (1742–1823), who oversaw the Notre-Dame coronation, was taken captive when the emperor declared the Papal States to be part of France. The pope was imprisoned at Fontainebleau, outside Paris, for a time.

6 Philip the Fair

In 1302 the first States General parliament was formally opened at Notre-Dame by Philip IV (1268–1314), otherwise known as Philip the Fair. He greatly increased the governing power of the French royalty.

7 Henry VI of England

Henry VI (1421–71) became King of England at the age of one. Like his father, Henry V, he also claimed France and was crowned in Notre-Dame in 1430.

8 Marguerite of Valois

In August 1572, Marguerite (1553–1589), sister of the French king Charles IX, stood in the Notre-Dame chancel during her marriage to Henri of Navarre (1553–1610), while he stood alone by the door.

9 Henri of Navarre

As a Protestant Huguenot, Henri's marriage to the Catholic Marguerite resulted in uprising and massacres. In 1589 he became Henri IV, the first Bourbon king of France, and converted to Catholicism, declaring that "Paris is well worth a mass".

10 Charles de Gaulle

On 26 August 1944, Charles de Gaulle entered Paris and attended a Te Deum mass to celebrate the liberation of Paris, despite the fact that hostile snipers were still at large both inside and outside the cathedral.

For more historic events in Paris **See pp44–5**

Top 10 Events in Notre-Dame History

1 Construction on the cathedral begins (1163)
2 St Louis places the Crown of Thorns here temporarily (1239)
3 Construction is completed (1334)
4 Re-trial of Joan of Arc (1455)
5 Crowning of Emperor Napoleon (1804)
6 Publication of Hugo's novel *The Hunchback of Notre-Dame* (1831)
7 Completion of 23-year restoration programme (1864)
8 Assassination attempt on Charles de Gaulle (1944)
9 De Gaulle's Requiem Mass is held (1970)
10 De Gaulle Special Memorial Service (1996)

The Man Who Saved Notre-Dame

Novelist Victor Hugo

By 1831, when Victor Hugo's novel Notre-Dame de Paris (The Hunchback of Notre-Dame) *was published, the cathedral was in a sorry state of decay. Even for the crowning of Emperor Napoleon in 1804, the setting for such ceremonious state occasions was crumbling and had to be disguised with wall hangings and ornamentation. During the Revolution, the cathedral was even sold to a scrap dealer, but was never actually demolished. Hugo was determined to save the country's spiritual heart and helped mount a successful campaign to restore Notre-Dame before it was too late; the man chosen to design and oversee the restoration was Eugène Emmanuel Viollet-le-Duc (1814–1879). Paris-born, Viollet-le-Duc had already proved his skill in restoration work, as evidenced by the cathedrals in Amiens and Laon, and on the spectacular walled city of Carcassone in southern France. Work began in 1841 and continued for 23 years until the building was finished more or less as we see it today. Viollet-le-Duc later went on to restore the chapel of Ste-Chapelle* (see pp30–31).

The Hunchback of Notre-Dame

Hugo's 1831 novel tells the story of Quasimodo, a hunchbacked bell-ringer at Notre-Dame, who falls in love with gypsy girl Esmeralda.

For more novels set in Paris **See pp46–7**

Sacré-Coeur

One of the most photographed images of the city, the spectacular white outline of Sacré-Coeur (Sacred Heart) watches over Paris from its highest point. The basilica was built as a memorial to the 58,000 French soldiers killed during the Franco-Prussian War (1870–71) and took 46 years to build, finally completed in 1923 at a cost of 40 million francs (6 million euros). Priests still pray for the souls of the dead here 24 hours a day. Although the interior is less impressive than many other churches in the city, people flock here for the panoramic views – at sunset, in particular, there are few sights in Paris more memorable.

Sacré-Coeur dome

Le Gastelier, at Place St-Pierre at the base of the funicular, is a great spot for breakfast, lunch, ice cream or just afternoon tea (closed Mon).

An evocative sung Mass takes place on Sundays at 11am.

Parvis du Sacré-Coeur, 75018
• Map F1
• 01 53 41 89 00
• www.sacre-coeur-montmartre.com
• Open 6am–11pm (basilica), 9:15am–5:30pm (dome and crypt) daily
• Admission €5.00 (dome and crypt only)
• No disabled access

Top 10 Features

1. Great Mosaic of Christ
2. Crypt Vaults
3. Bronze Doors
4. Dome
5. Statue of Christ
6. Bell Tower
7. Equestrian Statues
8. Stained-Glass Gallery
9. Façade
10. The Funicular

1 Great Mosaic of Christ

A glittering Byzantine mosaic of Christ *(right)*, created by Luc Olivier Merson between 1912–22, decorates the vault over the chancel. It represents France's devotion to the Sacred Heart.

2 Crypt Vaults

The most interesting feature of the interior is the arched vaults of the crypt. A chapel contains the heart of Alexandre Legentil, one of the advocates of Sacré-Coeur.

3 Bronze Doors

The doors of the portico entrance are beautifully decorated with bronze relief sculptures depicting the Last Supper *(right)* and other scenes from the life of Christ.

For more Paris churches **See pp40–41**

4 The Dome

The distinctive egg-shaped dome of the basilica is the second-highest viewpoint in Paris after the Eiffel Tower. Reached via a spiral staircase, vistas can stretch as far as 48 km (30 miles) on a clear day.

5 Statue of Christ

The basilica's most important statue shows Christ giving a blessing. It is symbolically placed in a niche over the main entrance, above the two equestrian statues.

6 Bell Tower

The beautiful *campanile*, designed by Lucien Magne and added in 1904, is 80 m (262 ft) high. One of the heaviest bells in the world, the 19-ton La Savoyarde hangs in the belfry. Cast in Annecy in 1895, it was donated by the dioceses of Savoy.

7 Equestrian Statues

Two striking bronze statues of French saints stand on the portico above the main entrance, cast by H Lefèbvre *(below)*. One is of Joan of Arc, the other of Saint Louis.

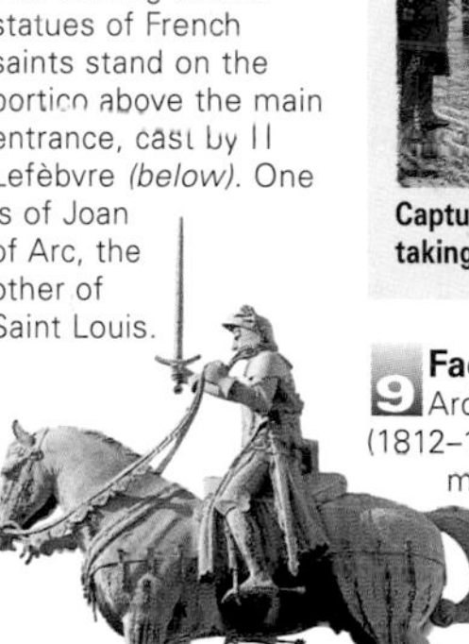

8 Stained-Glass Gallery

One level of the great dome is encircled by stained-glass windows. From here there is a grand view over the whole interior.

The Franco-Prussian War

In 1870, as Prussia made moves to take over Germany, France was also threatened by its military power. Two Catholic businessmen in Paris vowed to build a church dedicated to the Sacred Heart if France were spared the Prussian onslaught. France declared war on Prussia in July, but she was ill-prepared and in September Napoleon III was captured. Parisians held fast, however, defending their city with home-made weapons and eating dogs, cats and rats. But by January 1871 they surrendered.

Captured French soldier taking leave of his wife

9 Façade

Architect Paul Abadie (1812–1884) employed a mix of domes, turrets and Classical features in his design. The Château-Landon stone secretes calcite when wet and bleaches the façade white.

10 The Funicular

To avoid the steep climb up to Sacré-Coeur, take the *funiculaire* cable railway and enjoy the views at leisure. It runs from the end of rue Foyatier, near Square Willette.

Top 10 Arc de Triomphe

The best day to visit the world's most familiar triumphal arch is 2 December, the date that marks Napoleon's victory at the Battle of Austerlitz in 1805, when the sun sets in line with the Champs-Elysées and the Arc de Triomphe, creating a spectacular halo around the building. Work began on the 50-m (164-ft) arch in 1806 but was not completed until 1836, due, in part, to Napoleon's fall from power. Four years later, Napoleon's funeral procession passed beneath it, on its way to his burial in Les Invalides (see pp32–3). *Today the arch is a focal point for rallies and public events.*

Arc de Triomphe pediment

Try to get here early, as the morning light shows the golden tone of the stone-work at its best.

Enjoy a coffee and the old-world charm of Le Fouquet (99 Champs-Elysées) – expensive, but worth the treat.

- *Place du Général-de-Gaulle, 75008*
- *Map B2*
- *Open Apr–Sep: 10am–11pm daily; Oct–Mar: 10am–10:30pm daily; closed 1 Jan, 1 May, 25 Dec and for major events*
- *Admission €8.00*

Top 10 Features

1. Viewing Platform
2. Tomb of the Unknown Soldier
3. Museum
4. Departure of the Volunteers in 1792
5. Frieze
6. Triumph of Napoleon
7. Battle of Austerlitz
8. Battle of Aboukir
9. General Marceau's Funeral
10. Thirty Shields

1 Viewing Platform

Taking the elevator or climbing the 284 steps to the top of the Arc de Triomphe *(below)* gives visitors a sublime and unique view of Paris. To the east is the Champs-Elysées *(see p103)*, one of the world's most famous avenues, and to the west, slightly out of line, is the Grande Arche of La Défense *(see p151)*.

2 Tomb of the Unknown Soldier

In the centre of the arch flickers the eternal flame on the Tomb of the Unknown Soldier, a victim of World War I buried on 11 November 1920. It is symbolically re-ignited every day at 6:30pm.

For more historic buildings in Paris **See pp42–3**

3 Museum
Within the [a]rch is a small but [in]teresting [m]useum which [t]ells the history [o]f its construction and [g]ives details of various [c]elebrations and funerals [t]hat the arch has seen [o]ver the years. The more [r]ecent of these are [s]hown in a short video.

6 Triumph of Napoleon
As you look at the arch from the Champs-Elysées, the relief on the left base shows the *Triumph of Napoleon*. This celebrates the Treaty of Vienna peace agreement signed in 1810, when Napoleon's empire was in its heyday.

7 Battle of Austerlitz
Another battle victory is shown on a frieze *(above)* on the arch's northern side. It depicts Napoleon's heavily outnumbered troops breaking the ice on Lake Satschan in Austria, a tactic which drowned thousands of enemy troops and helped France to victory.

8 Battle of Aboukir
Above the *Triumph of Napoleon* carving is this scene showing Napoleonic victory over the Turks in 1799. The same victory was commemorated on canvas in 1806 by the French painter Antoine Gros and is now on display at the palace of Versailles *(see p151)*.

9 General Marceau's Funeral
Marceau died in battle against the Austrian army in 1796, after a famous victory against them only the previous year. His funeral is depicted in this frieze *(right)*, located above the *Departure of the Volunteers in 1792* sculpture.

4 Departure of the Volunteers in 1792
One of the most striking sculptures is on the front right base *(right)*. It shows French citizens going to defend their nation against Austria and Prussia.

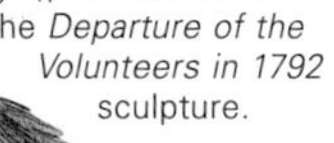

10 Thirty Shields
Immediately below the top of the arch runs a row of 30 shields, each carrying the name of a Napoleonic victory.

5 Frieze
A frieze running around the arch shows French troops departing for battle (east) and their victorious return (west).

The Great Axis

The Arc de Triomphe is at the centre of three arches and together they create a grand vision of which even Napoleon would have been proud. The emperor was responsible for the first two, placing the Arc de Triomphe directly in line with the Arc de Triomphe du Carrousel in front of the Louvre *(see pp8–11)*, which also celebrates the 1805 victory. As late as 1989, the trio was completed with the erection of the Grande Arche at La Défense. The 8km-long (5-mile) *Grand Axe* (Great Axis) runs from here to the Glass Pyramid at the Louvre.

TOP 10 Centre Georges Pompidou

Today one of the world's most famous pieces of modern architecture, the Pompidou Centre opened in 1977, when architects Richard Rogers and Renzo Piano startled everyone by turning the building "inside out", with brightly coloured pipes displayed on the façade. Designed as a cross-cultural arts complex, it houses the excellent Musée National d'Art Moderne (Modern Art Museum) as well as a cinema, library, shops and performance space. The outside forecourt is a popular gathering-spot for tourists and locals alike.

Centre Georges Pompidou façade

Le Cavalier Bleu, on the junction of rue Rambuteau and rue St-Martin, is a great brasserie for a snack and cheaper than the Centre's café.

For reasonably priced postcards to send home visit the Centre's bookshop.

- *Place Georges Pompidou 75004*
- *Map P2*
- *www.centrepompidou.fr*
- *01 44 78 12 33*
- *Open 11am–10pm Wed–Mon; closed 1 May*
- *Adm (museum) €7.00*

Top 10 Features

1. Escalator
2. Top-Floor View
3. Buskers
4. Place Igor Stravinsky Fountains
5. Pipes
6. Bookshop
7. Brancusi's Studio
8. Man with a Guitar
9. Sorrow of the King
10. Blues

1 Escalator

One of the building's most striking and popular features is the external escalator *(right)*, which climbs, snake-like, up the front of the centre in its plexi-glass tube. The view gets better and better as you rise high above the activity in the Centre's forecourt, before arriving at the top for the best view of all.

2 Top-Floor View

The view from the top of the Pompidou Centre is spectacular. The Eiffel Tower is visible, as is Montmartre in the north and the Tour Montparnasse to the south. On clear days views can stretch as far as La Défense *(see p151)*.

3 Buskers

Visitors and locals gather in the open space in front of the Centre, especially on sunny days, to enjoy the variety of street performers, ranging from enigmatic mime artistes to the extrovert dazzle of fire-eaters.

4 Stravinsky Fountain

his colourful fountain in lace Igor Stravinsky was esigned by Niki de Saint-halle and Jean Tinguely s part of the Pompidou entre development. nspired by composer travinsky's ballet *The irebird* (1910), the bird pins and sprays water!

9 Sorrow of the King

French artist Matisse (1869–1964) was one of the proponents of the Fauvist Movement, noted for its bold use of colour. This collage *(below)* was created in 1952.

10 Blues

Joan Miró (1893–1983) was born in Barcelona but moved to Paris in 1920. His three vast canvases known as *Bleus (Blues)* are hung together, demanding attention for their apparent simplicity.

5 Pipes

Part of the shock actor of the Pompidou Centre is that the utility pipes are outside the building. Not only that, hey are vividly coloured: bright green for water, yellow for electricity and blue for air-conditioning.

6 Bookshop

The ground-floor bookshop sells a range of postcards, posters of major works in the Modern Art Museum and books on artists associated with Paris.

7 Brancusi's Studio

The studio of revolutionary Romanian sculptor Constantin Brancusi (1876–1957) is to the north of the centre, displaying his abstract works.

8 Man with a Guitar

Within the Modern Art Museum, this 1914 work by artist Georges Braque (1882–1963) is one of the most striking of the Cubist Movement.

Centre Guide

The Pompidou Centre can be as confusing inside as it appears on the outside. At busy periods, separate queues are created for the different attractions, so be sure to join the right one. The entrance to the Modern Art Museum is on the fourth floor and to the cinema is on the first floor. Large signs usually indicate the whereabouts of temporary exhibitions.

TOP 10 The Panthéon

Today Paris's beautiful Panthéon building is a fitting final resting place for the city's great citizens. However, it was originally built as a church, on the instigation of Louis XV to celebrate his recovery from a serious bout of gout in 1744. Dedicated to Sainte Geneviève, the structure was finished in 1790 and was intended to look like the Pantheon in Rome, hence the name; in fact it more closely resembles St Paul's Cathedral in London. During the Revolution it was turned into a mausoleum for the city's great achievers, but Napoleon gave it back to the church in 1806. It was later desecularized, handed back to the church once more, before finally becoming a public building in 1885.

Panthéon façade

Flowers Café (5 rue Soufflot) has a good view of the Panthéon and a choice of light meals, snacks and drinks.

Ticket sales stop 45 minutes before closing time, so arrive on time.

- *Place du Panthéon, 75005*
- *Map N6*
- *01 44 32 18 00*
- *Open Apr–Sep 10am–6:30pm daily; Oct–Mar 10am–6pm daily*
- *Admission €7.00 (free under 12s)*
- *Disabled access to main floor only*

Top 10 Features

1. Dome
2. Dome Galleries
3. Crypt
4. Frescoes of Sainte Geneviève
5. Foucault's Pendulum
6. Monument to Diderot
7. Façade
8. Pediment Relief
9. Tomb of Voltaire
10. Tomb of Victor Hugo

1 Dome

Inspired by Sir Christopher Wren's design of St Paul's Cathedral in London, as well as by the Dôme Church at Les Invalides *(see p32)*, this iron-framed dome *(below left)* is made up of three layers. At the top a narrow opening only lets in a tiny amount of natural light, in keeping with the building's sombre purpose.

2 Dome Galleries

A staircase leads to the galleries immediately below the dome, affording spectacular 360-degree panoramic views of Paris. The pillars surrounding the galleries are both decorative and functional, providing essential support for the dome.

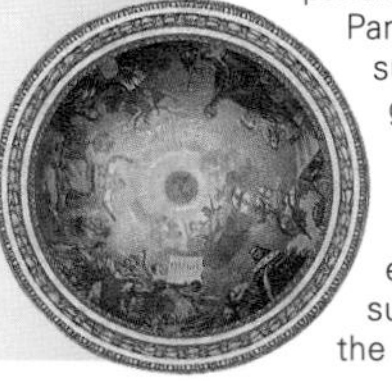

3 Crypt

The crypt is eerily impressive in its scale compared to most tiny, dark church crypts. Here lie the tombs and memorials to French citizens deemed worthy of burial here, including the prolific French writer Emile Zola *(see p47)*.

For more Paris burial sites **See p156**

4 Frescoes of Sainte Geneviève

Delicate murals by 19th-century artist Pierre Puvis de Chavannes, on the south wall of the nave, tell the story of Sainte Geneviève, the patron saint of Paris. In 451 she is believed to have saved the city from invasion by the barbaric Attila the Hun and his hordes due to the power of her prayers.

6 Monument to Diderot

French philosopher Denis Diderot (1713–84) is honoured by this grand 1925 monument by Alphonse Terroir.

7 Façade

The Panthéon's façade was inspired by Roman design. The 22 Corinthian columns support both the portico roof and *bas-reliefs*.

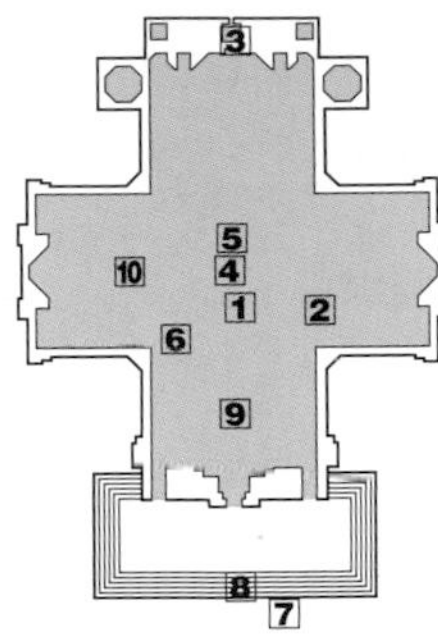

Panthéon Floorplan

9 Tomb of Voltaire

A statue of the great writer, wit and philosopher Voltaire (1694–1788) stands in front of his tomb.

10 Tomb of Victor Hugo

The body of the French author *(see p46)* was carried to the Panthéon in a pauper's hearse, at his own request.

5 Foucault's Pendulum

The landmark discovery of the earth's rotation was made from the Panthéon. In 1851 French physicist Jean Foucault (1819–68) suspended a weight from the dome. The weight swung back and forth, and as its position moved in relation to the floor below, so Foucault was able to prove his theory.

8 Pediment Relief

The *bas-relief* above the entrance *(below)* shows a female figure, representing France, handing out laurels to the great men of the nation – the same way that Greeks and Romans honoured their heroes.

Louis Braille

One of the most influential citizens to be buried in the Panthéon is Louis Braille. Born in France in 1809, Braille became blind at the age of three; at nine he attended the National Institute for the Young Blind in Paris and proved to be a gifted student. He continued at the Institute as a teacher and, in 1829, had the idea of adapting a coding system in use by the army, by turning words and letters into raised dots on card. Reading braille transformed the lives of blind people forever. Its inventor died in 1852.

TOP 10 Sainte-Chapelle

This Gothic masterpiece, built by Louis IX (1214–70) as a shrine for his holy relics and completed in 1248, is considered the most beautiful church in Paris, not least for its 15 stained-glass windows soaring 15 m (50 ft) to a star-covered vaulted roof. The church was damaged during the Revolution but was restored by Viollet-le-Duc from 1840 (see p21).

Sainte-Chapelle façade

For a little 1920s-style elegance, stop for coffee at the Brasserie des Deux Palais on the corner of Boulevard du Palais and rue de Lutèce.

A pair of binoculars comes in handy if you want to see the uppermost panels.

- *4 blvd du Palais, 75001*
- *Map N3*
- *01 53 40 60 80*
- *Open Apr–Sep: 9:30am–6pm; Oct–Mar: 10am–5pm; closed 1 Jan, 1 May, 1 & 11 Nov, 25 Dec*
- *Admission €6.10 (free 1st Sun of month Oct–May); €8.00 joint adm to Conciergerie* (see p69)
- *Restricted disabled access*

Top 10 Features

1. Upper Chapel Entrance
2. Rose Window
3. Window of Christ's Passion
4. Apostle Statues
5. Window of the Relics
6. The Spire
7. Main Portal
8. St Louis' Oratory
9. Seats of the Royal Family
10. Evening Concerts

1 Upper Chapel Entrance

As you emerge, via a spiral staircase, into this airy space *(right)*, the effect of light and colour is breathtaking. The 13th-century stained-glass windows, the oldest extant in Paris, separated by stone columns *(below)*, depict Biblical scenes from *Genesis* through to the Crucifixion. To "read" the windows, start in the lower left panel and follow each row left to right, from bottom to top.

2 Rose Window

The Flamboyant-style rose window, depicting St John's vision of the Apocalypse in 86 panels, was restored by Charles VIII in 1485. The green and yellow hues are at their brightest at sunset.

For more Paris churches **See pp40–41**

5 Window of the Relics

Another striking window *(below)*, this tells the story of St Helena and the True Cross and of St Louis bringing his many relics to Sainte-Chapelle.

6 The Spire

The open lattice-work and pencil-thin shape give the 75-m (245-ft) *flèche* (spire) a delicate appearance. Three earlier church spires burned down – this one was erected in 1853.

Louis IX's Relics

The devout Louis IX, later St Louis, was the only French king to be canonized. While on his first Crusade in 1239, he purchased the alleged Crown of Thorns from the Emperor of Constantinople. He subsequently acquired other relics, including pieces of the True Cross, nails from the Crucifixion and a few drops of Christ's blood, paying almost three times as much for them as he paid for the construction of Sainte-Chapelle itself. The beautiful chapel resembles a giant reliquary.

7 Main Portal

Like the Upper Chapel, the main portal has two tiers. Its pinnacles are decorated with a crown of thorns as a symbol of the relics within.

3 Window of Christ's Passion

Located above the apse, this stained-glass depiction of the Crucifixion is the chapel's most beautiful window.

4 Apostle Statues

Beautifully carved medieval statues of 12 apostles stand on pillars along the walls. Badly damaged in the Revolution, most have been restored: the bearded apostle *(right)*, fifth on the left, is the only original statue.

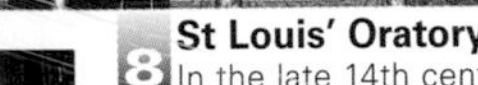

8 St Louis' Oratory

In the late 14th century Louis XI added an oratory where he could attend Mass unobserved, watching through a small grille in the door. The chapel originally adjoined the Conciergerie, the former royal palace on the Ile de la Cité *(see p69)*.

9 Seats of the Royal Family

During Mass, the royal family sat in niches located in the fourth bays on both sides of the chapel, away from the congregation.

10 Evening Concerts

Sainte-Chapelle has excellent acoustics. From March to November classical concerts are held here several evenings a week.

TOP 10 Hôtel des Invalides

The "invalides" for whom this imposing Hôtel was built were wounded soldiers of the late 17th century. Louis XIV had the building constructed between 1671–8, and there are still old soldiers housed here, although only a dozen or so compared to the 6,000 who first moved in. They share their home with the greatest French soldier of them all, Napoleon Bonaparte, whose body rests in a crypt directly below the golden dome of the Dôme Church. Other buildings accommodate military offices, the Musée de l'Armée and smaller military museums.

Musée de l'Armée façade

Café des Musées, between the Varenne metro station and the Musée Rodin *(see p111)* is a lovely spot for a drink.

To see Napoleon's Tomb, go to the entrance on avenue de Tourville to miss the museum queues.

- *129 rue de Grenelle, 75007*
- *Map D4*
- *01 44 42 38 77*
- *www.invalides.org*
- *Open Apr–Sep: 10am–6pm daily (Oct–Mar: until 5pm); closed 1 Jan, 1 May, 1 Nov, 25 Dec*
- *Admission €7.00 adults; €5.00 concessions; free under 18s*
- *Limited disabled access*

Top 10 Features

1. Napoleon's Tomb
2. Golden Dome
3. Musée de l'Armée
4. Dôme Church Ceiling
5. Hôtel des Invalides
6. Church Tombs
7. St-Louis-des-Invalides
8. Invalides Gardens
9. Musée de l'Ordre de la Libération
10. Musée des Plans-Reliefs

1 Napoleon's Tomb

Napoleon's body was brought here from St Helena in 1840, some 19 years after he died. He rests in splendid grandeur in a cocoon of six coffins *(left)*, almost situated "on the banks of the Seine" as was his personal wish.

2 Golden Dome

The second church at the Hôtel was begun in 1677 and took 27 years to build. Its magnificent dome stands 107 m (351 ft) high and glistens as much now as it did when Louis XIV, the Sun King, had it first gilded in 1715.

3 Musée de l'Armée

The Army Museum is one of the largest collections of militaria in the world. Enthusiasts will be absorbed for hours, but even the casual visitor will find fascinating pieces here, including collections of arms from ancient times and other exhibits from armies across the world *(see p114)*.

For the Invalides Quarter **See pp110–17**

4 Dôme Church Ceiling

The colourful, circular painting on the interior of the dome above the crypt is the *Glory of Paradise* painted in 1692 by the French artist, Charles de la Fosse. Near the centre is St Louis, who represents Louis XIV, presenting his sword to Christ.

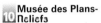

Hôtel des Invalides Floorplan

9 Musée de l'Ordre de la Libération

The Order of Liberation, France's highest military honour, was created by Général de Gaulle in 1940 to acknowledge contributions during World War II. The museum details the history of the honour and the wartime Free French movement.

5 Hôtel des Invalides

One of the loveliest sights in Paris *(above)*, the Classical façade of the Hôtel is four floors high and 196 m (645 ft) end to end. Features include the dormer windows with their variously shaped shield surrounds.

7 St-Louis-des-Invalides

Adjoining the Dôme Church is the Invalides complex's original church. It is worth seeing for its 17th-century organ, on which the first performance of Berlioz's *Requiem* was given.

10 Musée des Plans-Reliefs

Maps and models of French forts and fortified towns are displayed here and some of them are beautifully detailed, such as the oldest model on display, of Perpignan in 1686.

6 Church Tombs

Encircling the Dôme Church are the imposing tombs of great French military men, such as Marshal Foch and Marshal Vauban, who revolutionized military fortifications and siege tactics.

8 Invalides Gardens

The approach to the Hôtel is across public gardens and then through a gate into the Invalides Gardens themselves. Designed in 1704, their paths are lined by 17th-and 18th-century cannons.

Hôtel Guide

Approach the Hôtel from the Seine for the best view, going through the gates and then to the ticket office, which is on the right in the first building. You can look at the main courtyard for free but will need a ticket for the museums and to see Napoleon's Tomb. If time is short, concentrate on the Musée de l'Armée on the right, before walking through to the back of the buildings and reaching the entrance to the Dôme Church.

Left **Mona Lisa, Musée du Louvre** Centre **Musée Carnavalet** Right **Cannons, Musée de l'Armée**

Top 10 Museums

1 Musée du Louvre

French and Italian sculpture, Greek and Roman antiquities and paintings from the 12th to 19th centuries are just some of the highlights of the world's largest museum *(see pp8–11)*.

2 Musée Carnavalet

Housed in a grand Marais mansion, this museum presents Parisian decorative arts through the ages. The collection includes painting, sculpture and antique furniture, re-creating private residences of the 16th and 17th centuries. There is also a collection of mementoes from the Revolution. Classical music concerts are occasionally held here *(see p85)*.

3 Musée National de la Mode et du Textile

This museum is dedicated to Paris's most successful and most glamorous industry – fashion. The permanent collection features clothing from the 17th century up to the *haute couture* designers of today, and gowns that once belonged to royalty and celebrities are on show. The history and creation of various fabrics and textiles is also well presented through themed exhibitions that change every six months *(see p96)*.

4 Musée National du Moyen-Age

This splendid museum dedicated to the art of the Middle Ages is known by several names, including the Musée de Cluny after the beautiful mansion in which it is housed, and the Thermes de Cluny after the Roman baths adjoining the museum. Highlights include the famous "Lady and the Unicorn" tapestries, medieval stained glass and exquisite gold crowns and jewellery *(see p120)*.

Muséum National d'Histoire Naturelle garden

5 Muséum National d'Histoire Naturelle

Paris's Natural History Museum in the Jardin des Plantes contains a fascinating collection of animal skeletons, plant fossils, minerals and gemstones. Its highlight is the magnificent Grande Galerie de l'Evolution, which depicts the varying interaction between man and nature during the evolution of the planet *(see p129)*.

6 Musée de l'Homme

Head-shrinking, tattooing and mummification are some of mankind's more unusual rituals, explored in this ethnological and anthropological museum housed in the Palais de Chaillot. The collection of artifacts dates back to 3.5 million years BC, and ranges from Africa to South America, to Asia and the Pacific *(see p135)*.

7 Musée de l'Armée

France's proud military history is on display in this museum, housed in a wing of the Hôtel des Invalides. Exhibits include military art and artifacts from ancient times through to the 20th century, with a large modern exhibit devoted to World War II. Napoleon's campaign tent, his stuffed dog, and suits of armour and weapons from medieval times are among the many highlights *(see p114)*.

8 Musée Cognacq-Jay

The Hôtel Donon is a fine setting for this superb collection of 18th-century art, furniture, porcelain and other decorative arts, amassed by the wealthy founders of the Samaritaine department store. Paintings by Rembrandt, Gainsborough and other masters alone are worth the visit *(see p85)*.

Venus with Doves, Musée Cognacq-Jay

9 Musée de l'Erotisme

The Museum of Eroticism, appropriately located between the sex shows and cabarets of Pigalle, is a fascinating look at erotic art from around the world. Paintings, carvings, drawings, sculpture and other items illustrate how different cultures portray sex as either spiritual, satirical, humorous or titillating *(see p142)*.

10 Musée de Montmartre

Montmartre has long been home to the artists of Paris and several of them have lived in this old house, including Renoir, Dufy and Utrillo. Artifacts from the 19th century are on display, to help conjure up the era, along with posters, maps and documents on the house's history. The garden also gives good views of the surrounding district *(see p141)*.

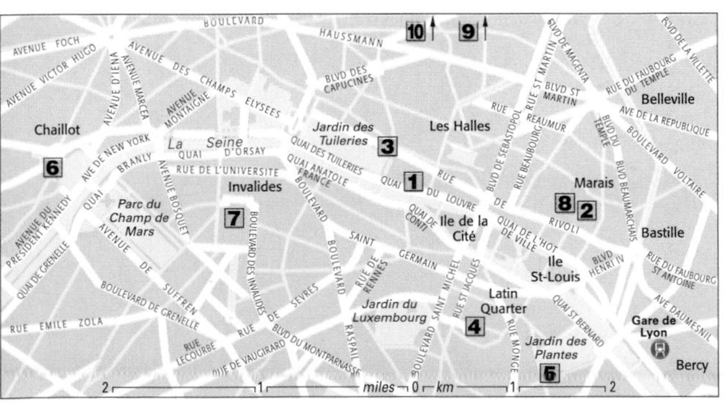

For Paris art galleries **See pp36–7**

Left **Bedroom at Arles (1889), Van Gogh, Musée d'Orsay** Right **Jeu de Paume**

Top 10 Art Galleries

1 Musée d'Orsay

See pp12–15.

2 Musée Picasso

A favourite of Parisians and visitors alike. The beautifully restored Hôtel Salé *(see p90)* in the Marais is a splendid setting for this extensive collection of paintings, sculptures, drawings and other works by Pablo Picasso (1881–1973), including works from his Cubist period. Large sculptures also adorn the garden and courtyard. Some of the artist's personal art collection of works by his contemporaries is also on display *(see p85)*.

3 Musée Rodin

On a sunny day, head straight for the gardens of the Musée Rodin, in the Hôtel des Invalides complex, where you can enjoy some of the French sculptor's most famous works, including *The Thinker* and *The Burghers of Calais*, while strolling among the shady trees and rose bushes. Then pay a visit inside the beautiful 18th-century mansion, the Hôtel Biron, where Auguste Rodin (1840–1917) lived and worked for nine years, until his death. An extensive collection of his works from throughout his career is on display *(see p111)*.

4 Musée National d'Art Moderne

The revolutionary Pompidou Centre is the perfect home for the city's outstanding Modern Art Museum. It features some 1,400 works on two levels, one focusing on the artists and movements of the first half of the 20th century, the other featuring art from the 1960s to the present day. Temporary exhibitions are held throughout the year *(see pp26–7)*. *Pl Georges Pompidou, 75004 • Map P2 • Open 11am–10pm, Wed–Mon • Admission charge*

5 Jeu de Paume

This gallery is one of the finest exhibition spaces in the city, being set within a 19th-century real tennis court *(jeu de paume)*. It is a showcase for outstanding photography, film and video. *1 pl de la Concorde, 75008 • Map D3 • Open noon– 9:30pm Tue, noon–7pm Wed–Fri, 10am– 7pm Sat–Sun • Admission charge*

Musée National d'Art Moderne

For more on Paris artists **See p144**

6 L'Orangerie

The prime exhibits here are eight of Monet's huge waterlily canvases *(see p13)* and the gallery, located in a corner of the Tuileries, has recently been renovated to provide an improved setting for their display. The Walter-Guillaume collection covers works by Renoir, Picasso, Modigliani and other modern masters from 1870–1930.

Jardin des Tuileries, 75001 • Map D3 • Admission charge

7 Espace Montmartre Salvador Dalí

This underground museum with its black walls, lighting effects and soundtrack features some of Dalí's lesser-known works, including bronzes, lithographs and book illustrations *(see p141)*.

Lip Sofa, Salvador Dalí

8 Musée Marmottan-Claude Monet

The Impressionist paintings of Claude Monet are the star attraction at this museum, featuring some 165 works donated by his son and perhaps the finest collection of his works in the world. They include a series of his late waterlily paintings. Other Impressionist and Realist painters are also represented, and there is a fine collection of illuminated medieval manuscripts *(see p153)*.

9 Musée Maillol

Works of the French artist Aristide Maillol, including his drawings, engravings, paintings and plastercasts, are the focal point of this museum which was created by his model, Dina Vierny. Works by Rodin and Picasso are also on display *(see p121)*.

10 Maison Européenne de la Photographie

If you're a photography fan, don't miss this splendid gallery in the Marais. Its exhibitions range from portraits to documentary work, retrospectives to contemporary photographers *(see p87)*.

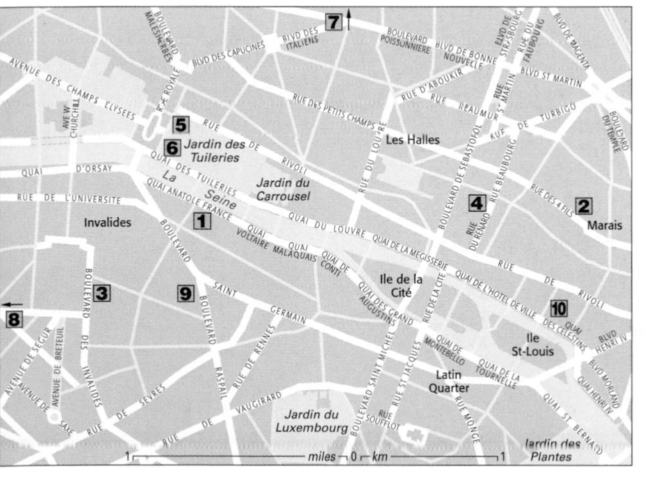

Left **Jardin du Luxembourg** Centre **Jardin des Plantes** Right **Bois de Boulogne**

Top 10 Parks and Gardens

1 Jardin du Luxembourg

Parisians love this centrally located park, set around the Palais du Luxembourg. The sweeping terrace is a great place for people-watching, while locals sunbathe around the Octagonal Lake or sail toy boats in the water. Statues are dotted throughout the grounds, and there is a café *(see p119)*.

2 Jardin des Tuileries

These formal gardens were laid out in the 17th century as part of the old Palais de Tuileries and stretch along the Seine between the Louvre and the Place de la Concorde. The walkways are lined with lime and chestnut trees, and there is a series of bronze figures by Aristide Maillol *(see p95)*.

3 Jardin des Plantes

Established as a medicinal herb garden for the king in 1626, these vast botanical gardens are a wonderfully tranquil spot. Paths are lined with statuary and mature trees, including the oldest in Paris, an *Acacia robinia* dating from 1636. There is also an alpine garden *(see p129)*.

4 Bois de Boulogne

At the weekends, Parisians head for this vast park on the western edge of the city, with a boating lake and paths for cycling, jogging and strolling. There are three formal gardens, lakes and waterfalls, and even two horse-racing tracks. A good spot for a break from the city bustle *(see p151)*.

5 Bois de Vincennes

Another great escape from the city, this park is to the east of Paris what the Bois de Boulogne is to the west. A former royal hunting ground, it was landscaped in the 1860s. Now it features ornamental lakes and waterfalls, a zoo, a funfair and horse-racing tracks *(see p151)*.

6 Parc Monceau

The most fashionable green space in Paris, full of well-heeled residents of the nearby mansions and apartments. The lush landscaping dates from the 18th century, and some architectural follies, such as the Classical colonnade, survive *(see p153)*.

Bois de Boulogne

7 Jardins du Palais Royal
These lovely gardens were once part of the Palais Royal, which now houses the State Council. They are surrounded by arcades which date from the late 18th century, and by an impressive modern pillar arrangement.
Pl du Palais Royal, 75001 • Map L1

8 Versailles
There are gardens galore at this famous royal palace, from the formal French gardens with their geometric paths and shrubberies, to the wandering paths through the rural-style English garden north of the Petit Trianon. In summer, you can row boats on the lovely cross-shaped Grand Canal *(see p151)*.

9 Parc Montsouris
Located south of Montparnasse, this is the second-largest park in central Paris and very popular with city residents. It was laid out in the English style atop an old granite quarry by landscape architect Adolphe Alphand between 1865 and 1878. Hemingway *(see p47)* and other writers and artists frequented the park in the mid-20th century. It has a jogging path, lake and a bandstand. *Blvd Jourdan, 75014 • Metro Cité Universitaire*

10 Parc des Buttes Chaumont
City-planner Baron Haussmann created this wonderful retreat northeast of the city centre in 1867, from what was formerly a rubbish dump. His architects built artificial cliffs, waterfalls, streams, and a lake complete with an island, which is crowned by a Roman-style temple. There's also boating available, a café and views of Sacré-Coeur *(see pp22–3)*. *Rue Manin, 75019 • Metro Buttes-Chaumont*

Top 10 Fountains

1 Agam Fountain
Jewish architect Yaacov Agam designed this fountain of water and lights. *La Défense • RER La Défense*

2 Four Seasons Fountain
Paris looks down on figures representing the Seine and Marne rivers, designed in 1739 by sculptor Edme Bouchardon. *Rue de Grenelle • Map C4*

3 Fontaine des Innocents
Carved by Jean Goujon in 1547, this is Paris's only Renaissance fountain. *Square des Innocents • Map N2*

4 Medici Fountain
This ornate 17th-century fountain with a pond was built for Marie de Médicis. *Jardin du Luxembourg • Map L6*

5 Molière Fountain
This 19th-century fountain honours the French playwright. *Rue de Richelieu • Map E3*

6 Observatory Fountain
Four bronze statues representing the continents hold aloft a globe. *Jardin du Luxembourg • Map L6*

7 Châtelet Fountain
The two sphinxes of this 1808 fountain commemorate Napoleon's victory in Egypt. *Pl du Châtelet • Map N2*

8 Fontaine de Stravinsky
Birds squirt water from this colourful fountain *(see p27)*.

9 Trocadéro Fountains
Spouting towards the Eiffel Tower, these fountains are illuminated at night *(see p17)*.

10 Versailles Fountains
The fountains at Versailles *(see p154)* flow to music on summer Sunday afternoons.

Left **Notre-Dame** Centre **Sacré-Coeur** Right **Sainte-Chapelle**

TOP 10 Places of Worship

1 Notre-Dame

See pp18–21.

2 Sacré-Coeur

See pp22–3.

3 Sainte-Chapelle

Although the chapel is no longer used for worship, the soaring stained-glass windows encourage reverence *(see pp30–31).*

4 Eglise du Dôme

The final resting place of Napoleon Bonaparte is the beautiful Dôme Church in the Hôtel des Invalides complex – an elaborate monument to French Classical style. Built as the chapel for the resident soldiers of the Invalides, its ornate high altar is in stark contrast to the solemn marble chapels surrounding the crypt, which hold the tombs of French military leaders. Its golden dome can be seen for miles around *(see pp32–3).*

Baptism of Christ, La Madeleine

5 Panthéon

Patterned after the Pantheon in Rome, this domed late 18th-century church only served as a house of worship for two years, before becoming a monument and burial place for the great and the good of the Revolution era. Later distinguished citizens are also buried here *(see pp28–9).*

6 St-Eustache

For centuries, this monumental Gothic edifice was the "market church" serving the traders of Les Halles. Taking more than 100 years to build, it was finally completed in 1637 and its cavernous interior displays the architectural style of the early Renaissance. Popular Sunday afternoon organ recitals and other classical concerts take place in this wonderfully atmospheric setting *(see p75).*

7 La Madeleine

Designed in the style of a Greek temple in 1764, this prominent church in Paris's financial district, on the edge of the Opéra Quarter, is one of the city's most distinctive sights, spectacularly surrounded by 52 Corinthian columns. The church was consecrated to Mary Magdalene in 1845. The bronze doors, which include *bas-reliefs* depicting the Ten Commandments, and the *Last Judgment* on the south pediment are exterior highlights, while the ornate marble and gold interior has many fine statues, including François Rude's *Baptism of Christ*. Organ recitals are often held in the church. *Pl de la Madeleine, 75008 • Map D3 • Open 7:30am– 7pm daily • Free*

8 Grande Synagogue de la Victoire

Built in the late 19th century, this elaborate synagogue is the second-largest in Europe. Its façade design represents the Tablets though, sadly, the building is not open to the public. Other smaller synagogues can be found in the Marais, which has a large Jewish community, including one at 10 rue Pavée, built in 1913 by Hector Guimard, the architect who designed the city's Art Nouveau metro stations. *44 rue de la Victoire, 75008 • Map E2*

9 Mosquée de Paris

The city's Grande Mosque was built during the 1920s as a tribute to North African Muslims who gave military support to France during World War I. It features beautiful Moorish architecture, executed by craftsmen brought over from North Africa, and a peaceful interior courtyard *(see p129)*.

10 St-Sulpice

Outstanding frescoes in the Chapel of the Angels by Eugène Delacroix are the highlight of this 17th-century church's otherwise sober interior. With more than 6,500 pipes, its organ, designed by Jean-François Chalgrin in 1776, is one of the largest in the world. The novelist Victor Hugo married Adèle Foucher here in 1822 *(see p119)*.

St-Sulpice façade

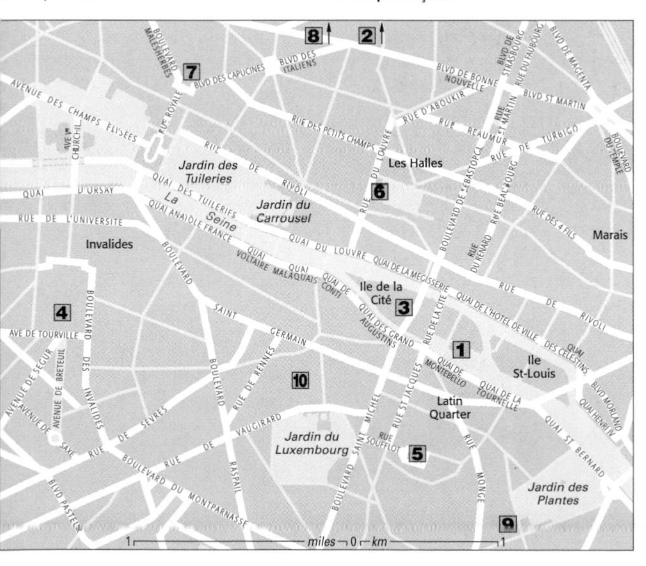

Left **Conciergerie** Right **Hôtel de Ville**

Historic Buildings

1 Hôtel des Invalides

See pp32–3.

2 Versailles

Louis XIV turned his father's old hunting lodge into the largest palace in Europe and moved his court here in 1678. It was the royal residence for more than a century until Louis XVI and his queen Marie-Antoinette fled during the Revolution *(see p151)*.

3 Conciergerie

Originally home to the caretaker and guards of the Palais de Justice, the Conciergerie was turned into a jail at the end of the 14th century. It took its place in history during the Revolution, when more than 4,000 citizens (including Marie-Antoinette) were held prisoner here, half of whom were guillotined. It remained a prison until 1914 *(see p69)*.

4 Palais de Justice

The enormous building that now houses the French law courts and judiciary dates back to Roman times and was the royal palace until the 14th century, when Charles V moved the court to the Marais. During the Revolution, thousands were sentenced to death in the Première Chambre Civile, allegedly the former bedroom of Louis IX *(see p70)*.

Palais de Justice

5 Hôtel Dieu

The Hôtel Dieu, now the hospital for central Paris, was built on the site of a foundling home in 1866–78; the original 12th-century building on the Ile de la Cité was demolished during the urban renewal schemes of the 19th century. A monument in the courtyard commemorates a courageous battle here in 1944 when Paris police held out against the German Nazis. *1 pl du Parvis Notre-Dame, 75001 • Map N4*

6 Palais de l'Elysée

This imposing palace has been the official residence of the President of the French Republic since 1873. It was built as a private mansion in 1718 and subsequently owned by Madame de Pompadour, mistress of Louis XV, who extended the English-style gardens to the Champs-Elysées. Napoleon signed his second abdication here in 1815 *(see p105)*.

7 Hôtel de Ville

Paris's town hall sports an elaborate façade, with ornate stonework, statues and a turreted roof. It is a 19th-century reconstruction of the original town hall, which was burned down in the Paris Commune of 1871 *(see* p45). Though the pedestrianized square in front is pleasant now, it was once the site of gruesome executions: Ravaillac, assassin of Henri IV, was quartered alive here in 1610. *4 pl de l'Hôtel de Ville, 75001 • Map P3 • 01 42 76 60 37 • Open for tours only (booking essential) • Free*

8 Palais-Royal

This former royal palace now houses State offices. Built by Cardinal Richelieu in 1632, it passed to the crown on his death 10 years later and was the childhood home of Louis XIV. The dukes of Orléans acquired it in the 18th century. *Pl du Palais Royal, 75005 • Map L1 • Closed to the public*

9 La Sorbonne

The city's great university had humble beginnings in 1253 as a college for 16 poor students to study theology, but France's first printing house was also established here in 1469. After suppression during the Revolution it became the University of Paris *(see p119)*.

10 Palais du Luxembourg

Marie de Médicis had architect Salomon de Brosse model this palace after her childhood home, the Pitti Palace in Florence. Shortly after its completion she was exiled by her son, Louis XIII. It was seized from the crown during the Revolution to become a prison. The building now houses the French Senate. *15 rue de Vaugirard, 75006 • Map L6 • 01 44 54 19 49 • Palais open 1st Sat of month for reserved tours, gardens open dawn-dusk • Admission charge*

Palais du Luxembourg

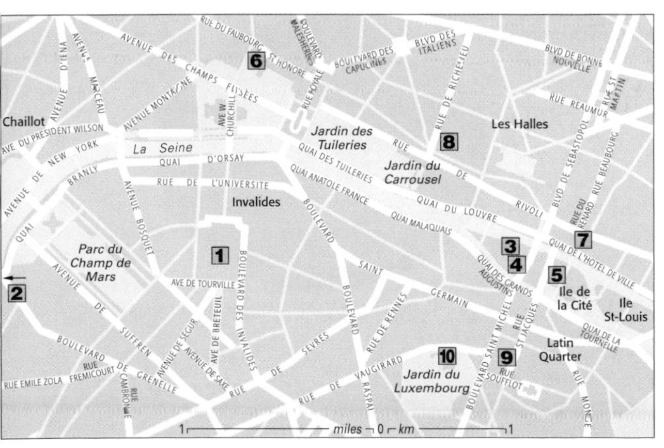

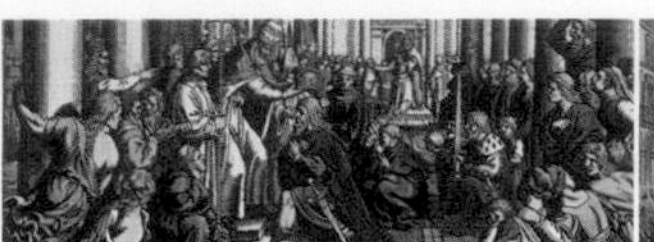

Left **Charlemagne crowned as Holy Roman Emperor** Right **Paris Commune burning of the city**

TOP 10 Historical Events in Paris

1 Arrival of the Parisii

Though the remains of Neolithic settlements have been found dating back to 4500 BC, the first inhabitants are considered to be a Celtic tribe called the Parisii, who settled on the Ile de la Cité in the 3rd century BC. Hunters and fishermen, they named the village Lutetia, meaning "boatyard on a river". The tribe minted their own gold coins and a pagan altar was found beneath Notre-Dame.

2 Roman Settlement

The Romans conquered the Parisii in 52 BC and destroyed their city. After rebuilding it as their administrative centre, they founded their own town on the Left Bank. The baths in the Hôtel de Cluny *(see p34)* and the amphitheatre in rue Monge are the only remains. In AD 360 the Roman prefect was declared emperor and Lutetia was renamed Paris, after its original inhabitants.

3 Founding of France

Roman rule weakened under Barbarian attacks. In 450 the prayers of a young nun, Geneviève, were credited with saving the city from invasion by Attila the Hun and she became patron saint of Paris. But in 476 the Franks captured the city. They converted it to Christianity and made Paris the capital of their new kingdom, France.

4 Charlemagne, Holy Roman Emperor

In 751 the Carolingian dynasty became rulers of France when Pepin the Short ascended the throne. His heir Charlemagne was crowned Holy Roman Emperor in 800 and moved the capital to Aix-La-Chapelle. Paris fell into decline until nobleman Hugues Capet became king in 987, moving the capital back to his home city.

5 Bourbon Dynasty

Henri III named his son-in-law, Henri of Navarre, as his heir, but when the king was assassinated in 1589, Catholics refused to accept a Protestant monarch. After a four-year war, Henri converted to Catholicism and entered Paris as the first Bourbon king. He, too, was assassinated in 1610, leaving his young son Louis XIII to usher in *Le Grand Siècle* (Grand Century), as the 17th century later came to be known.

Succession of Louis XIII

6 French Revolution

Following decades of excess by the monarchy and the gulf between rich and poor, Paris erupted with the storming of the Bastille prison in 1789 *(see box)*.

7 Napoleon's Coronation
As Paris rose from the ashes of the Revolution, a young general from Corsica, Napoleon Bonaparte, saved the city from a royalist revolt, then led military victories in Italy and Egypt. He crowned himself Emperor of France in Notre-Dame in 1804 *(see p20)*.

8 The Second Empire
In 1851, Napoleon's nephew, Louis-Napoleon, seized power as Emperor Napoleon III. He appointed Baron Haussmann to oversee massive building works that transformed Paris into the most glorious city in Europe. The wide boulevards, many public buildings, parks, sewer system and the first department stores date from 1852 to 1870.

9 The Paris Commune
Following France's defeat in the Franco-Prussian War in 1871 *(see p23)*, many citizens rejected the harsh terms of the surrender and a left-wing group revolted, setting up the Paris Commune. But, after 72 days, government troops marched on the city. In a week of street fighting (21–28 May), much of the city burned and thousands of rebellious citizens were killed.

10 Liberation of Paris
The Occupation of France by Germany during World War II were some of Paris's darkest days, but the city was also the centre for the French Resistance. Allied forces liberated Paris on 25 August 1944; just two days earlier, the German commander Von Choltitz had ignored Adolf Hitler's order to burn the city.

Top 10 Events in the French Revolution

1 14 July 1789
Storming of the Bastille prison, a symbol of repression, launches the Revolution.

2 4 August 1789
The abolition of feudalism, and the right of everyone to be a free citizen is declared.

3 26 August 1789
Formal declaration of the Rights of Man and the Citizen, which incorporated the ideals of equality and dignity, later incorporated into the 1791 Constitution.

4 October 1789
Citizens march on Versailles and the royal family returns to Paris as prisoners in the Tuileries Palace *(see p95)*.

5 20 June 1791
The royal family try to escape but are spotted in Varenne and return as captives.

6 10 August 1792
A mob storms the Tuileries and the royals are imprisoned in the Temple.

7 21 September 1792
The monarchy is formally abolished and the First Republic is proclaimed.

8 1792–4
"The Terror" reigns, under the radical Commune led by Robespierre, Danton and Marat. Thousands are executed by guillotine.

9 21 January 1793
Louis XVI is found guilty of treason and executed. His queen Marie-Antoinette follows him to the guillotine on 16 October.

10 28 July 1794
Robespierre is guillotined, ending the Terror, and the Revolution draws to a close.

Left **Plaque on Victor Hugo's house** Right **Film still from A Tale of Two Cities**

TOP 10 Historical Novels set in Paris

1 Les Misérables

The 1862 novel by Victor Hugo (1802–85) is an all-too-vivid portrayal of the poor and the dispossessed in early 19th-century Paris. At its centre is the tale of nobleman Jean Valjean, unfairly victimized by an unjust system. The younger character of Marius is based around Hugo's own experiences as an impoverished student.

2 The Hunchback of Notre-Dame

Better known by its English title, which inspired a film of the same name, Victor Hugo's Gothic novel was published in France in 1831 as *Notre-Dame de Paris*. Set in the Middle Ages, it tells the strange and moving story of a hunchback bell-ringer Quasimodo and his love for Esmeralda *(see p20)*.

3 A Tale of Two Cities

The finest chronicler of 19th-century London life, Charles Dickens (1812–70) broke with tradition to set his 1859 novel in Paris, against the background of the French Revolution *(see p45)*. His description of conditions in the Bastille prison makes for grim reading.

4 Le Père Goriot

Honoré de Balzac (1799–1850) chronicled Paris life masterfully in his 80-volume *La comédie humaine* series, and this 1853 novel is certainly among the finest. Balzac's house at 47 rue Raynouard in the 16th *arrondissement*, where he lived from 1840–47, is open to the public *(see p137)*.

5 Sentimental Education

Gustave Flaubert (1821–80) studied law in Paris but illness disrupted his chosen career and he devoted himself to literature. This work (*L'education sentimentale* in French), first published in 1870 in two volumes, stands alongside his greatest novel, *Madame Bovary* (1857), and marks the move from Romanticism to Realism in French literature.

6 Bel-Ami

Guy de Maupassant (1850–93) published this, one of his best novels, in 1885, criticizing the get-rich-quick Parisian business world of the *belle époque* (Beautiful Age). Maupassant is known as one of the world's greatest short-story writers, and he is buried in the cemetery at Montparnasse *(see p152)*.

Guy de Maupassant

7 A la Recherche du Temps Perdu

he master work of Marcel roust (1871–1922) was written 1 13 volumes, the first novel ppearing in 1913. Proust lived n boulevard Haussmann, and is epic tale is the fictionalized tory of his own life, and of Paris uring the *belle époque*. Proust ; buried in Père Lachaise ceme- ery in eastern Paris *(see p153)*.

8 Nana

Perhaps the greatest 'arisian chronicler of them all, :mile Zola (1840–1902) was orn, lived and died in the city, lthough he spent part of his 'outh in Aix-en-Provence in outhern France. *Nana* was pub- shed in 1880 and tells a shock- ng tale of sexual decadence, hrough the eyes of the central :haracter, a dancer and prostitute

9 L'Assommoir

Published in 1887, Zola's *'Assommoir* (The Drunkard) ;hows a side of Paris that many t the time would have preferred o ignore – the alcoholism of the vorking classes. It is one of the uthor's series of 20 linked ooks known as the *Rougon- Macquart* sequence, which lepict life in every quarter of society, through the eyes of two oranches of the same family.

10 Thérèse Raquin

Here Zola focuses on the secret passions that lurk behind a single Paris shopfront, opening up to reveal a tale of obsessive lust that ultimately leads to a brutal murder. It was published in 1867 and, only his second novel, shows the author's astonishing maturity and unflinching examination of all aspects of 19th-century life.

Top 10 Foreign Writers who Lived in Paris

1 Ernest Hemingway

The US author (1899–1961) wrote *A Moveable Feast* as an affectionate portrait of his time in Paris from 1921–1926.

2 F Scott Fitzgerald

Like Hemingway, US writer Fitzgerald (1896–1940) lived in Montparnasse and frequented the bar La Coupole *(see p125)*.

3 George Orwell

The English novelist (1903–50) tells of his shocking experiences living in poverty in *Down and Out in Paris and London* (1933)

4 Samuel Beckett

Born in Ireland in 1906, the playwright lived in Paris from 1928 until his death in 1989.

5 Anaïs Nin

US novelist Nin (1903–77) met her lover, fellow American Henry Miller, in Paris. Her *Diaries* tell of her time here.

6 Albert Camus

Algerian born Camus (1913–60) moved to Paris in 1935 and lived here until his death.

7 Henry Miller

Miller (1891–1980) showed the seedier side of Paris in his novel *Tropic of Cancer* (1934).

8 Diana Mitford

Controversial fascist sympathiser and authoress, Mitford (1910-2003) spent her dotage in Paris.

9 Edmund White

Prolific novelist White (b.1940) is the author of *The Flaneur, a Stroll Through the Paradoxes of Paris.*

10 Milan Kundera

Czech born Kundera (b.1929) moved to Paris in 1978 where he wrote *The Unbearable Lightness of Being.*

For literary haunts **See p125**

Left **Palais de Chaillot** Centre **Liberty Flame** Right **Pont Alexandre III**

Top 10 Riverfront Views

1 Eiffel Tower

Although the top of the Eiffel Tower can be seen above rooftops across the city, one of the best views of this Paris landmark is from the Seine. The Pont d'Iéna lies at the foot of the tower, bridging the river to link it to the Trocadéro Gardens. The tower, illuminated at night, is a highlight of a dinner cruise on the Seine *(see pp16–17)*.

Eiffel Tower

2 Palais de Chaillot

The curved arms of the Palais de Chaillot encircling the Trocadéro Gardens can be seen from the Seine. In the centre of the gardens the magnificent fountains spout from the top of a long pool lined with statues, while two huge water cannons spray their charges back towards the river and the Eiffel Tower on the opposite bank *(see p135)*.

3 Liberty Flame

A replica of the Statue of Liberty's torch in New York was erected in 1987 by the *International Herald Tribune* to mark their centenary and honour the freedom fighters of the French Resistance during World War II. It is located on the right bank of the Pont de l'Alma, the bridge over the tunnel where Diana, Princess of Wales, was killed in an automobile crash in 1997. The Liberty Flame has now become her unofficial memorial and is often draped with notes and flowers laid in her honour.
Map C3

4 Grand Palais and Petit Palais

Gracing either side of the Pont Alexandre III are these two splendid exhibition halls, built for the Universal Exhibition in 1900. The iron Art Nouveau skeleton of the Grand Palais is topped by an enormous glass roof, which is most impressive when illuminated at night. The Petit Palais is smaller but similar in style, with a dome and many Classical features *(see p103)*.

5 Pont Alexandre III

The most beautiful bridge in Paris is the Pont Alexandre III, a riot of Art Nouveau decoration including cherubs, wreaths,

For Paris boat trips **See p164**

lamps and other elaborate statuary. Built for the Universal Exhibition of 1900, it leads to the Grand Palais and Petit Palais. There are wonderful views of the Invalides complex and the Champs-Elysées from the bridge (see p104).

6 Dôme Church

An impressive view of the Eglise de Dôme in the Hôtel des Invalides complex can be had from the Pont Alexandre III. The golden dome beckons visitors down the long parkway lined with streetlamps and statues (see pp32–3).

7 Musée du Louvre

This grand museum stretches along the river from the Pont Royal to the Pont des Arts. The wing that can be seen from the Seine was largely built during the reigns of Henri IV and Louis XIII in the late 16th and early 17th centuries (see pp8–11).

8 Musée d'Orsay

The view of this modern art gallery from the Right Bank of the Seine is one of its finest angles, showing off the arched terminals and grand façade of this former railway station. Architect Victor Laloux designed it specifically to harmonize with the Louvre and Tuileries Quarter across the river (see pp12–15).

9 Conciergerie

This huge and imposing building, which served as a notorious prison during the Revolution, commands the western end of the Ile de la Cité. Within its walls are some of the few remaining medieval features on the island, including the torture chamber, clock and twin towers which rise above the quai de l'Horloge (see p69).

10 Notre-Dame

The great cathedral is never more majestic than when viewed from the Left Bank of the Seine. It rises on the eastern edge of the Ile de la Cité above the remains of the ancient tribes who first settled Paris in the 3rd century BC (see pp18–21).

Notre-Dame

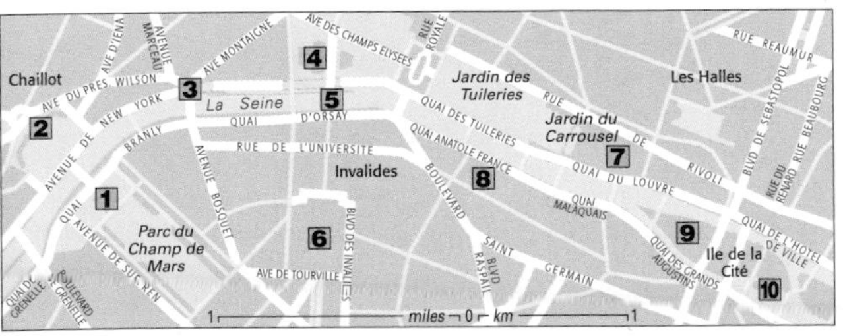

Left **The Passages** Right **Bois de Boulogne**

Top 10 Walks in Paris

1 Jardin des Tuileries

A stroll through the beautiful Tuileries Gardens is one of the must-dos of Paris. Before the Revolution this was a prime spot for the aristocracy to show off their latest fashions, and it remains a great place for people-watching *(see p95)*.

2 The Left Bank

A very Parisian walk, particularly on a Sunday, is along the Left Bank (Rive Gauche) of the Seine. The riverside quays of the Latin Quarter have been lined with second-hand bookstalls *(bouquinistes)* for centuries. The books are mostly in French, but you'll also find stalls selling prints and postcards *(see p122)*.

3 Montmartre

The steep streets of the Butte are a good place to get some exercise after indulging in the irresistible French cuisine. Although this famous artists' quarter is more touristy than Bohemian these days, its old charms can still be found in the winding back streets and small squares *(see pp140–43)*.

4 The Marais

With inspiring art galleries, delectable delis, and shop after shop filled with contemporary fashions and *objets d'art*, a walk in the Marais is great fun, even if you only window-shop. The beautiful mansions are a great backdrop for your stroll and there are plenty of cafés and bars for sustenance *(see pp84–7)*.

5 Jardin des Plantes

In this historic botanical garden you can escape the bustle of the city and lose yourself on the shady tree-lined avenues, amid colourful flowerbeds, or the hothouses and exotic gardens. Or simply relax on the lawns *(see p129)*.

6 Jardin du Luxembourg

Napoleon designated this the "garden of children", and whether or not you have little ones in tow you'll enjoy a walk through this favourite haunt of the Latin Quarter. After you've seen the octagonal pond and the Medicis Fountain, seek out the miniature Statue of Liberty and the statues of French queens *(see p119)*.

Montmartre

7 The Passages

These covered arcades were built at the end of the 18th century to shelter elegant shoppers from grimy streets and bad weather. Now lined with speciality and antiques shops, they are wonderfully

For more on getting around Paris **See p164**

atmospheric places to explore. Most are in the 2nd *arrondissement*, and connecting passages Verdeau, Jouffroy and Panoramas together form the longest in Paris. ✆ *Map H5*

8 Ile St-Louis
Although you could walk end to end in about 10 minutes, the Seine's smaller island demands a more leisurely stroll. You'll discover superb little art galleries, trendy boutiques, and a village-like atmosphere within this upmarket enclave *(see p60)*.

9 Bois de Boulogne
Come here at the weekend if you want to join the locals in the "great escape", and you'll have 865 ha (2,135 acres) from which to choose your path. The Bagatelle Gardens are a fine

Boulevard St-Germain

place for a walk in spring and summer, when a stunning array of roses and other flowers are in bloom *(see p152)*.

10 Boulevard St-Germain
There's no better way to enjoy the Latin Quarter than to do as the Parisians do – stroll the Boulevard St-Germain, preferably late on a Sunday morning. After your walk, honour the birthplace of café society with a coffee at either Les Deux Magots or Café de Flore, two of the city's most famous literary and intellectual haunts *(see p119)*.

Top 10 Outdoor Activities

1 Walking
Paris is a compact city so you can easily combine sightseeing with exercise.

2 Roller-blading
A fad which shows no sign of abating, skaters weave their way through traffic and pedestrians alike.

3 Cycling
Head for the Bois de Boulogne and Bois de Vincennes to escape the Paris traffic, or join a guided tour *(see p165)*.

4 Boating
Boating lakes in the Bois de Boulogne and Bois de Vincennes allow you to flex your rowing muscles.

5 Jogging
You can get your aerobic fix along the pathways of Paris's parks and gardens.

6 Tennis
You can play at any of the city's 170 courts. There is a small court fee.

7 Pétanque
This bowls-like game, where steel balls are tossed through the air, is said to be Paris's favourite sport.

8 Swimming
There are 34 public pools in Paris, but hours are restricted during school terms. Or try the pool at the Forum des Halles.

9 Football
France's football team has many young imitators in parks, gardens and streets.

10 Posing
A sport indulged in mainly by young men and women, it is best done at outdoor cafés to be sure of the biggest audience.

Left **Café de Flore** Centre **Harry's New York Bar** Right **Café Marly**

TOP 10 Cafés and Bars

1 Café de Flore

A hang-out for artists and intellectuals since the 1920s, its regulars have included Salvador Dali and Albert Camus. During World War II Jean-Paul Sartre and Simone de Beauvoir "more or less set up house in the Flore". Although its prices have skyrocketed, its Art Deco decor hasn't changed and it's still a favourite with French filmmakers and literati *(see p125)*.

2 Les Deux Magots

Rival to the neighbouring Flore as the rendezvous for the 20th-century intellectual élite. Hemingway, Oscar Wilde, Djuna Barnes, André Breton and Paul Verlaine were all regulars, and Picasso met his muse Dora Maar here in 1937. Similarly pricey, with outside tables facing the boulevard and the square *(see p125)*.

3 Harry's New York Bar

This legendary watering hole opened in 1911 and many an ex-pat found inspiration here, including F. Scott Fitzgerald, Ernest Hemingway and George Gershwin, who reportedly envisioned his *An American in Paris* orchestral work over a few drinks here. It still draws a lively American crowd, who come both for nostalgia and some of the best martini cocktails in town. *5 rue Daunou, 75001 • Map E2*

4 Café Marly

Superbly situated in the Richelieu wing of the Louvre *(see p9)*, the café offers simple but expertly prepared brasserie fare (steaks, salads, salmon tartare, sandwiches) as well as delicious cakes and pastries. The dining room has plush decor and velvet armchairs, but the best spot is under the arcade overlooking the glass pyramid and the cour Napoléon. *93 rue de Rivoli, 75001 • Map L2*

5 Café de la Paix

A grand Parisian café with prices to match, but it's worth a visit to enjoy the frescoed walls and sumptuous surroundings, designed by Charles Garnier, architect of the Opera House across the square *(see p95)*. This is another Paris landmark with a string of famous past patrons, and arguably the best *mille-feuille* cakes in town. *12 blvd des Capucines, 75008 • Map E3*

6 La Closerie des Lilas

The main restaurant here is expensive, but the bar is a good spot to soak up the atmosphere of this historic site where artists

Café de la Paix

For more places to eat in Paris **See pp64–5**

and writers from Baudelaire to Archibald MacLeish have drunk since 1808. Look for the famous names etched on the tables. The brasserie also has live piano music and attracts a chic crowd *(see p159)*.

days empty barrels are up-turned to make instant outdoor pavement tables, attracting an interesting local crowd. Cold snacks, such as pâté and cold meats, are also served all day *(see p93)*.

7 The China Club

This classy Bastille bar and restaurant has chic Chinese decor, as reflected in its name. The long ground-floor bar has romantically intimate tables and live jazz music is played at weekends. The upstairs bar is like an intimate drawing room. The cocktails are excellent, as is the Chinese food in the restaurant. Popular with Paris's young and trendy *(see p92)*.

The China Club

8 Le Baron Rouge

This tiny wine bar near the Aligre Market *(see p55)* is like taking a step back in time. Dozens of wines are available by the glass, or you can fill up your own bottle from the barrels bulging in the doorway. On fine

9 Le Café de l'Industrie

Unpretentious but stylish Bastille café with three large rooms, decorated with everything from spears, to old film star publicity stills. The simple food, such as onion soup, is good value. Popular local hang-out *(see p92)*.

10 Jacques Mélac Bar

A gregarious wine bar off the beaten track and full of character, with a rustic beamed ceiling hung with country hams and a vine growing around the walls. The moustached owner from Auvergne is an enthusiastic wine lover and aims to please with his reasonably priced cellar. Closed in August. *42 rue Léon-Frot, 75011 • Metro Charonne*

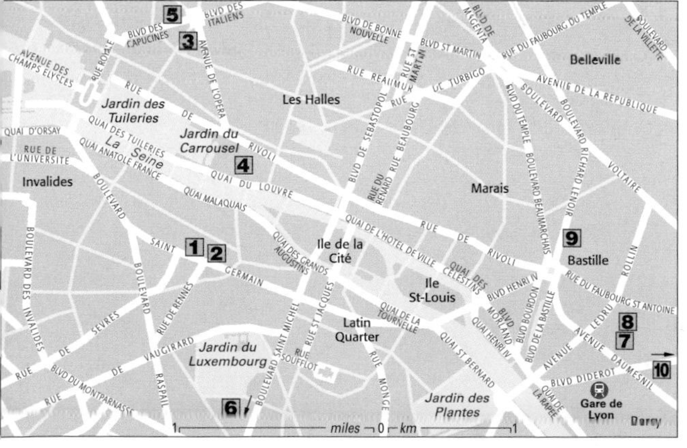

Left **Au Printemps** Right **Rue de Buci**

TOP 10 Shops and Markets

1 Flower and Bird Markets

Dating from 1808, the colourful Marché aux Fleurs (flower market) on the Ile de la Cité is the oldest and one of the largest flower markets in Paris. Its blooms brighten up the area between the stark walls of the Conciergerie and Hôtel Dieu from Monday to Saturday – everything from orchids to orange trees. On Sundays it is joined by the Marché aux Oiseaux (bird market) with equally colourful, caged species. *Pl Louis-Lépine, 75002 • Map P4*

2 Au Printemps

One of Paris's two top department stores, Printemps opened in 1864. Its goods range from designer clothing and accessories, to middle-of-the-range labels and funky fashions, home decor and furniture. The sixth-floor tea room is crowned with a lovely Art Nouveau stained-glass cupola. *64 blvd Haussmann, 75009 • Map E2*

3 Galeries Lafayette

Printemp's great rival store opened in 1894 and is a monument to Parisian style, topped by a glorious steel-and-glass dome. Along with designer clothes, there's a fabulous food hall. The seventh floor has great views. *40 blvd Haussmann, 75009 • Map E2*

4 Marché Richard-Lenoir

Every Thursday and Sunday morning, this market stretches along the tree-lined boulevard that separates the Marais from the Bastille. Sunday is the best day, when locals come to socialize as well as shop for foods such as fish, meat, bread and cheese. Some stalls sell North African and other international fare. *Blvd Richard-Lenoir, 75011 • Map H5*

Marché aux Fleurs (flower market)

5 Place de la Madeleine

This is a gourmand's delight. Some of the most delectable speciality food shops in Paris are dotted around the edges of this square, including the famous Fauchon supermarket and the smaller Hédiard. There's Maille for mustard, Kaspia for caviar, Marquise de Sévigné for chocolates and La Maison de la Truffe for truffles *(see p98)*.

6 Rue de Buci

The artist Picasso reputedly did his shopping at this daily morning market in the heart of

St-Germain. The huge fruit and vegetable stalls are of high quality but of greater interest are the food shops opening on to the street, which sell specialist and regional fare. You can also buy prepared Italian dishes and delicious pastries. *Map L4*

7 Rue Mouffetard

One of the oldest street markets in Paris winds downhill through the Latin Quarter every Tuesday to Sunday morning. Although this formerly cheap and Bohemian market has been discovered as a tourist spot, it retains its charm, the narrow street lined with colourful food stalls and speciality shops. There are also good restaurants in the quieter side streets. *Map F6*

8 Le Bon Marché

Paris's first department store was founded on the Left Bank in 1852, its structure partially designed by Gustave Eiffel *(see p17)*. Today it's even more hip than its competitors, with an in-store boutique featuring avant-garde fashions and music. It also has designer clothes, its own line of menswear and the enormous La Grande Epicerie food hall. *22 rue de Sèvres, 75007 • Map D5*

Marché aux Puces du St-Ouen

9 Aligre Market

Away from the tourist bustle, this Bastille market, dubbed the "Notre-Dame of markets", retains an authentic Parisian atmosphere. Every morning North African traders hawk inexpensive produce in the open-air market, and there's an adjacent flea market and a covered market selling top-quality fare. *Pl d'Aligre, 75012 • Map H5*

10 Marché aux Puces de St-Ouen

Every Saturday to Monday the largest antiques market in the world comes alive. There are actually several markets here: the oldest, Marché Vernaison, is the most charming; Marché Malik sells vintage clothing. Others offer furniture, jewellery and paintings. *Porte de Clignancourt, 75018 • Metro Porte de Clignancourt*

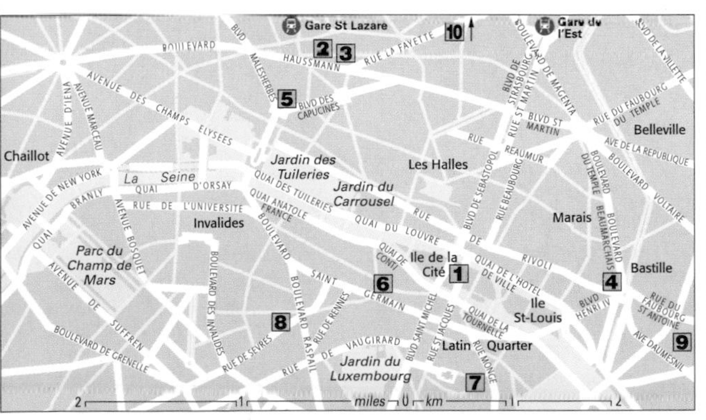

For more on shopping in Paris **See p169**

Left **Fête du Cinéma** Right **Tour de France**

Festivals and Events

1 The Paris Collections

The *haute couture* houses of Paris launch their Summer Collections in January and their Winter Collections in July, when the eyes of the world fashion trade focus on the city. Major events take place in the Carrousel du Louvre, giving an indication of their status. Visit the fashion houses in person at least one month in advance to see if there are tickets available.

2 Fête du Cinéma

Film buffs should be sure to verify the exact date of this annual event, held each June. For just one day, cinemagoers pay full price for the first film that they see, but can then see as many other films as they choose, for a few Euros each.

3 Paris Jazz Festival

Paris is home to jazz all year round *(see pp62–3)*, but every summer there is a major jazz festival in the city. Acts from all over the world come to play in the Parc Floral de Paris in the Bois de Vincennes *(see p151)*, but there are many lesser venues involved as well. *Jun–Sep*

4 Festival Estival

This classical music festival features concerts at the city's major music venues, as well as in museums and churches throughout Paris, making for some very atmospheric settings. A programme of events is available from the tourist office or any participating venue. *Mid-Jul–Sep*

5 Tour de France

Don't miss this summer highlight if you really want to understand the French passion for cycling. Towards the end of July each year, the world's greatest and most gruelling cycle race approaches Paris. The final stage is the Champs-Elysées, when thousands of fans pack the street to cheer the riders home and see who will win the coveted Yellow Jersey.

6 Festival d'Automne à Paris

This major festival promotes arts across the board in Paris, commissioning new works and encouraging all walks of life to see and enjoy performances of dance, music and drama. *Mid-Sep–Dec*

Paris Jazz Festival

7 Fêtes des Vendanges

Paris used to be one of the country's major wine producers, but these days only the vineyards at Montmartre remain *(see p142)*. These produce just under 500 litres (5 barrels) of wine each autumn, but great fun is had at the Fêtes des Vendanges when the wine is auctioned off for charity. There are parades, speeches and, of course, much drinking. *Oct: 1st Sat*

8 Prix de l'Arc de Triomphe

Europe's biggest horse race in terms of prize money takes place at the Hippodrome de Longchamp in the Bois de Boulogne *(see p152)*. Entry to the lawns is free, but a small admission charge is payable for the enclosure. *Oct: 1st Sun*

9 Beaujolais Nouveau Day

The arrival of the new vintage of Beaujolais Nouveau wine is celebrated throughout France, but especially in Paris. Bars, cafés, restaurants and wine shops all join in the fun, hosting lively tastings and other events. Look for signs saying "*Le Beaujolais Nouveau est arrivé*" (Beaujolais Nouveau has arrived). *Nov: 3rd Thu*

10 Mois de la Photo

Paris reveres the art of photography probably more than any other city in the world and every alternate November (in even-numbered years) it hosts the "Month of the Photo". Galleries, museums, shops, cultural centres and many other venues all give space to exhibitions, workshops and lectures on all aspects of the art. For anyone interested in photography, it is the most exciting time to visit Paris.

Top 10 Sports Events

1 Tour de France

This great cycle race reaches its climax in Paris.

2 Prix de l'Arc de Triomphe

This world-renowned horse race attracts the city's *crème de la crème.*

3 French Tennis Open

Forerunner to the Wimbledon Championships in London *Stade Roland Garros • end May–1st week Jun*

4 International Show-Jumping

Show-jumping fans and competitors descend on Paris for this annual event *Palais Omnisports de Paris-Bercy • 3rd week Mar*

5 Six Nations Rugby

The French team plays against England, Scotland, Ireland, Wales or Italy in this spring tournament. *Parc des Princes Stadium*

6 Paris Marathon

Runners start at the Champs-Elysées and end at avenue Foch. *Apr*

7 Football Cup Final

The biggest club event in French soccer. *Stade de France • 2nd week May*

8 Prix de Diane-Hermès

Parisian high society flocks to this up-market horse race *Chantilly • Jun: 2nd Sun*

9 International Pétanque Tournament

Players from all over the world compete in this bowls-like game. *Porte de Montreuil • 1st weekend Jul*

10 Garçons de Café race

Paris waiters run an 8-km (5-mile) circuit from place de l'Hôtel de Ville balancing a glass and bottle on a tray. *Jun*

Left **The Lido** Centre **Crazy Horse Saloon** Right **Théâtre de la Ville de Paris**

Top 10 Entertainment Venues

1 Opéra National de Paris Garnier

Not just a night out, but a whole experience, opera has now returned to its original Paris base after the theatre had a spell as a dance-only venue. The vast stage can hold a cast of 450, and the building itself is an example of excessive opulence, complete with grand staircase, mirrors and marble *(see p97)*.

2 Folies-Bergère

The epitome of Parisian cabaret, the Folies were, for a time, no more than a troupe of high-kicking, bare-breasted dancers. Today, the musical shows have largely returned to the nostalgic days when Maurice Chevalier and Josephine Baker *(see p63)* performed here. *32 rue Richer, 75009 • Map F2 • 08 92 68 16 50*

Folies-Bergère

3 The Lido

Home to the famous troupe of long-legged dancers, the Bluebell Girls, the fabulous special effects include aerial ballets and an on-stage skating rink. There are many who regard this dinner-cabaret as an essential Parisian experience. *116 bis ave des Champs-Elysées, 75008 • Map D3 • 01 40 76 56 10*

4 Moulin Rouge

The original home of the Can-Can, the theatre's dancers were immortalized on canvas by Toulouse-Lautrec during the *belle époque* and are on display in the Musée d'Orsay *(see p13)*. The show still has all the razzamatazz, feathers and sequins that it has been dazzling audiences with since 1889. The pre-show dinner is optional *(see p142)*.

5 Crazy Horse Saloon

More risqué than the other big-name cabaret shows, the Saloon has a reputation for putting on the most professional as well as the sexiest productions. Striptease features, along with glamorous dancing girls and other cabaret acts. The computer-controlled lighting effects are spectacular. *12 ave George V, 75008 • Map C3 • 01 47 23 85 56*

6 Au Lapin Agile

The "Agile Rabbit" got its name in 1880 when a painter called Gill came up with the trademark leaping rabbit: lapin à Gill became Lapin Agile. Utrillo once painted the cabaret too *(see p144)*. If your French is up to it you'll enjoy a mixture of songs, jokes and poetry in the heart of Montmartre *(see p142)*.

For more Paris cabarets and clubs **See p146**

7 Comédie Française

Paris's oldest theatre was founded in 1680 and is still the only one to have its own repertory of actors, staging both classical and modern drama (in French) from Molière to Tom Stoppard. The current building dates from the 18th century. Around the corner from the main box office, a special window opens 45 minutes before curtain-up, selling reduced price tickets for under-27s and concessions. *1 pl Colette, 75001 • Map L1 • 08 25 10 16 80*

8 Opéra National de Paris Bastille

Opened in 1992 as the largest opera house in the world, this modern building was heavily criticized, not least for its acoustics and poor facilities. Most problems have been ironed out, but plans for this to be the city's only opera venue have been changed. *Pl de la Bastille, 75012 • Map H5 • 08 92 89 90 90*

9 Théâtre du Châtelet

The city's largest concert hall and fourth-largest auditorium was built in 1862 and has recently been renovated. The repertoire covers classical music, ballet and opera, as well as popular Sunday morning chamber music concerts. *1 pl du Châtelet, 75004 • Map N2 • 01 40 28 28 40*

10 Théâtre de la Ville

Once known as the Sarah Bernhardt Theatre, in honour of the great Parisian actress who performed here and managed the theatre in the 19th century, today it puts on an eclectic range of modern dance and music shows, with some classical theatre too. *2 pl du Châtelet, 75004 • Map N2 • 01 42 74 22 77*

Top 10 Films set in Paris

1 Les Enfants du Paradis

The city's underworld is shown in this 1944 classic.

2 Everyone Says I Love You

Woody Allen's 1996 movie included many scenes shot around Notre-Dame and the Left Bank.

3 A Bout de Souffle

French New Wave director Jean-Luc Godard's 1959 film stars Jean-Paul Belmondo as a car thief on the run.

4 French Can-Can

The Jean Renoir classic (1955) tells the story of how the famous dance was created in Montmartre clubs.

5 Last Tango in Paris

Controversial, erotic 1972 film starring Marlon Brando.

6 The Trial

Orson Welles used the then empty Gare d'Orsay (now the Musée d'Orsay) to create a convincingly huge and anonymous office for his 1962 version of Kafka's novel.

7 Subway

The metro was the star in this 1985 Luc Besson film about a man who seeks refuge at night in its stations.

8 Les 400 Coups

Gritty Paris streets feature in this 1959 François Truffaut film about a boy on the run.

9 Amélie

Jean-Pierre Jeunet's 2000 sensation about a girl's quest for love features numerous scenes in Montmartre.

10 Prêt-à-Porter

Robert Altman takes a satirical look at the Paris fashion industry in his 1995 film.

Left **Grande Galerie de l'Evolution** Right **Jardin d'Acclimation**

Top 10 Children's Attractions

1 Disneyland Resort Paris

Formerly known as Euro-Disneyland, the French offspring of America's favourite theme park is a clone of its parent, and has now been joined by the Walt Disney Studios complex. Both have big queues, so arrive early. There are rides for children of all ages and most adults are equally enchanted *(see p151)*.

2 Parc de la Villette

One of the city's top children's attractions, with activities for all ages. The Cité des Sciences et de l'Industrie, a high-tech hands-on science museum, gets star billing, while the Cité des Enfants is a science and nature museum for younger children. Kids also love the Argonaute, a naval museum with a real submarine, the Géode with its IMAX screen and the Cité de la Musique, with musical activities for young people *(see p152)*.

Parc de la Villette

3 Eiffel Tower

A trip to the top is one of the most memorable activities for children in Paris *(see pp16–17)*.

4 Grande Galerie de l'Evolution

The most exciting and imaginatively designed display in the Natural History Museum is the Great Gallery of Evolution. Elephants, giraffes and other stuffed animals rise out of a re-created savannah, a huge whale skeleton hangs from the ceiling, while lighting, sound effects and interactive displays help tell the story of the development of life on earth. Nature workshops are held for children under 12 years old *(see p129)*.

5 Musée de la Curiosité et de la Magie

Kids are enchanted by this museum of magic, located in the atmospheric cellars of the former home of the Marquis de Sade. Magicians conjure up hourly shows involving optical illusions, card tricks and lots of audience participation. The exhibits include fun-house mirrors and memorabilia from master magicians such as escape artist Houdini (1874–1926). *11 rue St-Paul, 75004 • Map R4 • Open 2–7pm Wed, Sat, Sun • Admission charge*

6 Parc Zoologique de Paris

The Paris zoo is one of the largest in Europe. Here you can see a host of creatures in landscaped habitats. Children also love the miniature steam train that circles the zoo. ✆ *Bois de Vincennes, 94300 • Metro Porte Dorée • Open 9am–6pm Mon–Sat, 9am–6:30pm Sun (summer); 9am–5pm Mon–Sat, 9am–5:30pm Sun (winter) • Admission charge*

7 Jardin d'Acclimatation

An amusement park tucked away at the north end of the Bois de Boulogne *(see p152)*, with roller coasters, pony rides, puppet shows and two children's museums. On Wednesday and weekend afternoons, journey here on "le Petit Train", a steam train from Porte Maillot. ✆ *Bois de Boulogne, 75016 • Map A2 • Open 10am–7 pm daily (summer); 10am–6pm daily (winter) • Admission charge*

8 Grévin

This waxworks museum was founded in 1882 and retains an old-fashioned charm. Kids will get most enjoyment from seeing celebrities from the world of pop music and film, although there are also wonderful tableaux from French history. ✆ *10 blvd Montmartre, 75009 • Map F2 • Open 10am–6:30pm Mon–Fri, 10am–7pm Sat, Sun & public hols • Admission charge*

9 Cirque de Paris

A day out at the circus. In the morning kids can put on clown make-up, see the animals or try tightrope walking. After lunch, they watch the show. ✆ *115 blvd Charles-de-Gaulle, 92390 Villeneuve-la-Garenne • Map A2 • Open Oct–Jun: 10am–5pm Wed–Sun • Admission charge*

10 Jardin des Enfants aux Halles

This supervised playground for 7–15-year-olds is a real treat with its landscapes of tunnels and swings. ✆ *105 rue Rambuteau, 75001 • Map N1 • Open 9am–noon, 2–6pm Tue, Thu & Fri, 10am–6pm Wed & Sat, 1–6pm Sun • Admission charge*

Lift, Eiffel Tower

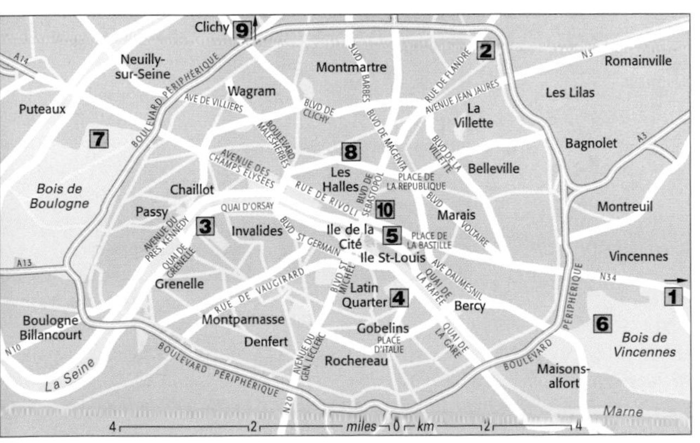

For family-friendly hotels **See p179**

Left **L'Arbuci** Centre **Au Duc des Lombards** Right **Le Bilboquet**

TOP 10 Jazz Clubs

1 L'Arbuci

A well-established favourite, in the heart of St-Germain *(see pp118–21)*, attracting a good mix of regular locals and curious tourists. Eat in the pleasant brasserie upstairs, then head to the basement for a music programme that relies heavily on old-fashioned Dixie-style jazz. *25 rue de Buci, 75006• Map L4*

2 Au Duc des Lombards

The Left Bank may be the traditional home of jazz clubs but this wood-panelled, velvet-seated club is firmly on the Right Bank, in the Les Halles district *(see pp74–7)*. The poster-covered walls illustrate some of the "greats" who have played here, and the club's policy is still to bring in the best overseas jazz artists to play alongside home-grown talent. *42 rue des Lombards, 75001 • Map N2*

3 Baiser Salé

Jazz, blues, Latin and African music are the mainstays at this tiny cellar club, which is low on space but high on volume. The Baiser was promoting World Music long before the phrase had been invented, and the eclectic approach has led to a relaxed and friendly atmosphere. It's cheaper than many clubs, too. *58 rue des Lombards, 75001 • Map N2*

4 Le Bilboquet

There's a great sense of history in this revered jazz club. It first opened its doors in 1947, since which time legends including Miles Davis and Billie Holiday have performed here. Today, however, it's mostly local talent that you will see on stage. As well as music, there's a relaxing bar and restaurant. *13 rue St-Benoît, 75006 • Map K4*

5 La Cave du Franc Pinot

Neither Left nor Right Bank, this fairly new club has added some buzz to the Ile St-Louis. It's jazz all the way, mostly swing but some modern jazz too, performed in a vaulted cellar. Bistro food is also available and there are lunchtime concerts on Sundays. *1 quai de Bourbon, 75004 • Map P4*

Le Slow Club

6 Jazz Club Lionel Hampton

The jazz club par excellence actually serves up a wider range of music than its name suggests. Check what's on as you might get blues, rock or even gospel music. There's a heavy emphasis

For more Paris entertainment **See pp58–9**

on visiting African-American musicians (Oscar Peterson has played here). A sophisticated experience. Ⓐ *Hôtel Le Méridien-Étoile, 81 blvd Gouvion-St-Cyr, 75017 • Map A2*

7 New Morning
An upstart by Paris standards, having opened in 1981. Its policy of embracing all kinds of music (jazz, blues, Latin, soul and the unclassifiable), not to mention inviting performers up from the floor, has led to a relaxed crowd of regulars. Ⓐ *7–9 rue des Petites-Ecuries, 75010• Map F2*

8 Le Petit Journal Montparnasse
The club that barely sleeps – the doors close at 2am, but open up again four hours later. You can just drink, or have a meal while listening to the live music, which is mainly big band jazz but on some nights takes in salsa, blues or rock. Ⓐ *13 rue du Commandant-Mouchotte, 75014 • Map D6*

9 Le Petit Journal St-Michel
Younger brother of the Montparnasse original, this club opened in 1971 and concentrates more on New Orleans-style swinging jazz. A fun atmosphere in this Latin Quarter cellar, together with a pleasant dining room in which to have a meal, just off the main stage area. Ⓐ *71 blvd St-Michel, 75005 • Map M5*

10 Le Slow Club
In the less touristy Les Halles stretch of the rue de Rivoli is this tiny cellar music club, with cheap admission. Unlike many Paris jazz clubs, which encourage seated appreciation, here you can dance the night away to the swinging rhythms. Ⓐ *130 rue de Rivoli, 75001 • Map M2*

Top 10 Musical Artistes in Paris

1 Edith Piaf
Discovered as a street singer in Paris, the diminutive Piaf (1915–63) became known as the "Little Sparrow".

2 Maurice Chevalier
The Parisian singer/actor (1888–1972) is, for many, *the* voice of France. In 1958 he won an Academy Award for his role in *Gigi*.

3 Django Reinhardt
Belgian gypsy guitarist Reinhardt (1910–53) first found fame in Paris in collaboration with Stephane Grappelli.

4 Lionel Hampton
US bandleader Hampton (*b.* 1909) regularly played in the Left Bank jazz clubs.

5 Sidney Bechet
US jazz virtuoso Bechet (1897–1959) settled in Paris in the 1940s and wrote his great tune "Les Oignons" in 1949.

6 Jacques Brel
Belgian singer/songwriter Brel (1929–78) moved to Paris in 1953, where audiences loved his melancholy songs.

7 Stephane Grappelli
Paris-born Grappelli (1908–97) studied classical violin, but later innovatively adapted the instrument to jazz.

8 Josephine Baker
The African-American dancer (1906–75) gained notoriety for dancing semi-nude at the Folies-Bergère.

9 Miles Davis
US trumpet-player Davis (1926–91) was a favourite in Paris for his "cool jazz" style.

10 Coleman Hawkins
US bebop saxophonist Hawkins (1904–69) played Paris many times in the 1930s.

Left **Guy Savoy** Centre **La Tour d'Argent** Right **Taillevent**

TOP 10 Places to Eat

1 Alain Ducasse
Arguably the best chef in Paris, Ducasse is now serving up his fabulous cooking in his stylish new restaurant in the Plaza Athénée hotel. Impeccable service, and signature dishes such as langoustines with caviar cannot be bettered *(see p109)*.

2 Guy Savoy
Artichoke and truffle soup is one of star chef Guy Savoy's signature dishes, in his chic and smart restaurant (jacket and ties required for male diners). One of the city's best dining experiences *(see p109)*. To sample Savoy's cooking at more affordable prices, also try the bistro-style Les Bookinistes in the St-Germain quarter *(see p127)*.

Brasserie Bofinger

3 La Tour d'Argent
Renowned for its wine list, which is considered to be the best in Paris, as well as for its lovely views of the Seine and Notre-Dame. Duck *à l'orange* is one of the specialities and the sauce is prepared before your eyes *(see p127)*.

4 Taillevent
Taillevent's atmospheric oak-panelled dining room is frequented by a mix of businessmen and romantic couples. *Crépinette d'andouillette* (sausage pancake) with foie gras is one memorable dish and there's an exceptional wine list. You need to book well ahead to dine here *(see p109)*.

5 L'Epi Dupin
Looking like any other Paris restaurant from the outside, inside the small room buzzes with noisy diners and tables must be booked ahead. Some of the best food in this price range, the menu is constantly changing but is always inventive. The home-baked bread is a delight, as is the dessert menu for those with a sweet tooth *(see p127)*.

6 Brasserie Bofinger
Paris's oldest brasserie, dating from 1864, is worth a visit if only for the original wood and glass decor and leather banquette seating. The menu offers staple bistro dishes such as oysters and pepper steak, briskly but politely served *(see p93)*.

7 C'Amelot

The bargain five-course ıenu is fixed, except for your hoice of dessert, so whatever ıe chef buys, you eat. Don't be ut off – the food is always uperb and the candlelit atmoshere warmly relaxing. ⊘ *50 rue ımelot, 75011 • Map H4 • 01 43 55 54 4 • €€*

8 Le Scheffer

One bistro looks much like nother, but inside this one in he Chaillot Quarter is a different tory. The food is superb, the ervice friendly, the atmosphere un, the prices reasonable. For all of these reasons, it's wise to ook ahead. Try the ed mullet Provençal, f available *(see p139).*

9 Le Baron Rouge

A place for atmosphere rather han gourmet ooking, but the food s still good and eliable in this basic vine bar, which is ılways full of noisy ocals. Numerous vines are available by he glass or bottle, accompanied by cold meats, pâté, and other simple traditional meals *(see p93).*

10 Chartier

The food is simple and filling (pepper steak, tarragon chicken and fish are traditional examples) but the real reason to come here is for the authentic period atmosphere. This early 20th-century workers' canteen has retained its original, tightly packed tables set amid wood panelling and gilded mirrors. It's always busy so come early to get a table. No reservations are taken, but the inevitable queues usually move quickly *(see p99).*

Chartier

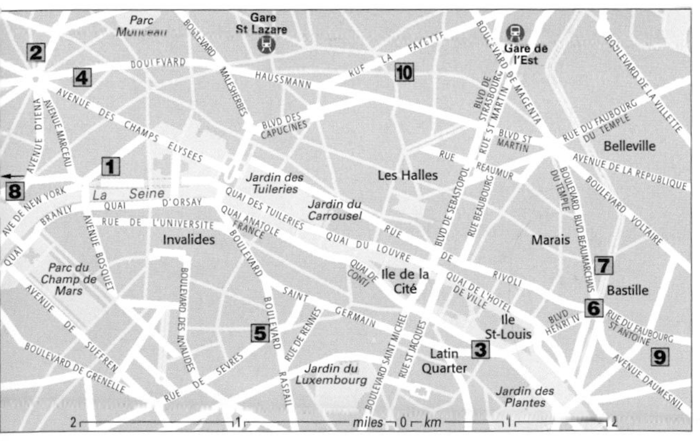

For a price guide to Paris restaurants **See p73**

AROUND TOWN

Left **Notre-Dame** Right **Salle des Gens d'Armes, Conciergerie**

Ile de la Cité and Ile St-Louis

PARIS WAS BORN ON THE ILE DE LA CITÉ. *The first settlers came to this island on the Seine in 300 BC* (see p44) *and it has remained a focus of church and state power through the centuries, with the great cathedral of Notre-Dame and the law courts of the Palais de Justice commanding the island. This tiny land mass also has the honour of being the geographical heart of the country – all French distances are measured from Point Zéro, just outside Notre-Dame. While the Ile de la Cité seems overrun with tourists, the smaller Ile St-Louis, connected to its neighbour by a bridge, has a village-like feel and has been an exclusive residential enclave since the 17th century. Its main street is lined with shops, galleries and restaurants and is a wonderful place for a stroll.*

TOP 10 Sights

1. Notre-Dame
2. Sainte-Chapelle
3. Conciergerie
4. Marché aux Fleurs
5. Crypte Archéologique
6. Pont Neuf
7. Palais de Justice
8. Place Dauphine
9. St Louis-en-l'Ile
10. Square du Vert-Galant

Angel detail, Sainte-Chapelle

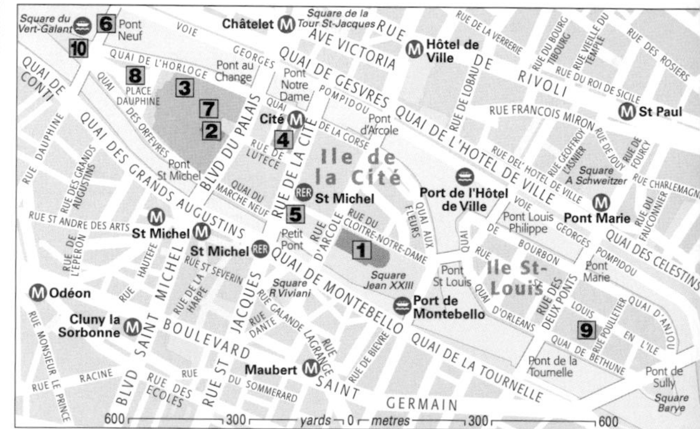

1 Notre-Dame

See pp18–21.

2 Sainte-Chapelle

See pp30–31.

3 Conciergerie

This imposing Gothic palace, uilt by Philippe le Bel (the Fair) 1301–15, has a rich history. arts of it were turned into a rison, controlled by the oncierge, or keeper of the ng's mansion, hence the name. availlac, assassin of Henri IV, vas tortured here, but it was uring the Revolution that the rison became a place of terror, vhen thousands were held here waiting execution at the uillotine. Today you can see the alle des Gardes and the nagnificent vaulted Salle des ens d'Armes (Hall of the Men-at rms), the medieval kitchens orture chamber, the Bonbec ower, and the prison. The cell vhere Marie-Antoinette was held nd the history of other famous evolution prisoners is on isplay. Outside, look for the quare Tour de l'Horloge, erected 1370, which houses the city's rst public clock, still ticking way. *2 blvd du alais, 75001 • Map N3 Open Apr–Sep: 9:30am 6pm daily; Oct–Mar: 0am–5pm daily • dmission charge*

Sainte-Chapelle

4 Marché aux Fleurs

)ne of the last emaining flower narkets in the city entre, the beautiful Marché aux Fleurs is lso the oldest, ating from the early 9th century. It is eld year-round, Monday to Saturday, in place Louis-Lépine, filling the north side of the Ile de la Cité with dazzling blooms from 8am to 7pm. There is also a bird market here on Sundays *(see p54).* *Map N3*

5 Crypte Archéologique

Fascinating remnants of early Paris dating back to Gallo-Roman times were discovered in 1965 during an excavation of the square in front of Notre-Dame in order to build an underground car park. The archaeological crypt displays parts of 3rd-century Roman walls, rooms heated by hypocaust, as well as remains of medieval streets and foundations. The scale models showing the evolution of the city from its origins as a Celtic settlement are particularly interesting. *Place du Parvis-Notre-Dame, 75001 • Map P4 • Open 10am–6pm Tue–Sun • Admission charge*

Crypte Archéologique

The Guillotine

Dr Joseph Guillotine invented his "humanitarian" beheading machine at his home near the Odéon and it was first used in April 1792. During the Revolution some 2,600 prisoners were executed on the places du Carrousel, de la Concorde, de la Bastille and de la Nation, after awaiting their fate in the Conciergerie prison.

6 Pont Neuf

An incongruous name (New Bridge) for the oldest surviving bridge in Paris. Following its completion in 1607, Henri IV christened it by charging across on his steed; the bronze equestrian statue of the king was melted down during the Revolution but replaced in 1818. The city's first pedestrian bridge was unique for its time in that it had no houses built upon it. The bridge has 12 arches and a span of 275 m (912 ft) extending both sides of the island. *Map M3*

7 Palais de Justice

Stretching across the west end of the Ile de la Cité from north to south, the Palais de Justice, along with the Conciergerie, was once part of the Palais de la Cité, seat of Roman rule and the home of th French kings until 1358. It took its present name during the Revolution and the buildings no contain the city's law courts. Yo can watch the courts in session from Monday to Friday and wander through the public areas with their many ornate features The Cour du Mai (May Courtyar is the area through which prisor ers passed during the Revolutio on their way to execution. *4 blvd du Palais, 75001 • Map M3 • Open 8am–6:30pm Mon–Fri, 9:30am– 6:30pm Sat • Free*

8 Place Dauphine

In 1607 Henri IV transforme this former royal garden into a triangular square and named it after his son, the Dauphin and future King Louis XIII. Surroundir the square were uniformly built houses of brick and white stone No. 14 is one of the few that retains its original features. One side was destroyed to make wa for the expansion of the Palais de Justice. Today this quiet, charming spot is a good place t watch locals play *pétanque (see p51)*. *Map M3*

Pont Neuf and Square du Vert-Galant

ɔulptured relief, Palais de Justice

9 St-Louis-en-l'Ile

This lovely Baroque church ɒ Ile St-Louis was designed ɘtween 1664 and 1726 by the ɔyal architect Louis Le Vau. The ×terior features an iron clock 1741) at the entrance and an ɔn spire, while the interior, ɕhly decorated with gilding and ıarble, has a statue of St Louis olding his Crusader's sword.

19 bis rue St-Louis-en-l'Ile, 75004 Map Q5 • Open 9am–noon, 2–7pm, ue–Sun

10 Square du Vert-Galant

The tranquil western tip of ıe Ile de la Cité, with its ɘrdant chestnut trees, lies ɪeneath the Pont Neuf – take the teps behind Henri IV's statue. his king had a notoriously morous nature and the name of ɪis peaceful square recalls his ickname, meaning "old flirt". rom here there is a wonderful iew of the Louvre *(see pp8–11)* nd the Right Bank. It is also the eparture point for cruises on ɪe Seine on Les Vedettes du 'ont-Neuf *(see p165)*. *Map M3*

A Day on the Islands

Morning

Arrive at **Notre-Dame** *(see pp18–21)* by 8am to beat the crowds and appreciate its magnificence, then head for the fragrant Marché aux Fleurs. As well as flowers, you can buy all kinds of garden accessories and seeds. Return to Notre-Dame if you want to ascend the towers, which open at 10am. Take a coffee break at **Le Flore en l'Ile** *(see p73)*, with its views of the cathedral.

The fascinating Crypte Archéologique is worth a half-hour visit, then spend the late morning at **Sainte-Chapelle** *(see pp30–31)*, when the sun beams through the stained-glass windows.

There are plenty of places for lunch, but on a sunny day try **La Rose de France** *(see p73)* with its terrace seating.

Afternoon

Spend a leisurely afternoon strolling the narrow streets of the Ile St-Louis, which are filled with characterful shops and galleries *(see p72)*.

Wind up with an afternoon treat by visiting **Berthillon**, considered the best ice cream purveyor in Paris *(31 rue St-Louis-en-l'Ile • Open 10am–8pm Wed–Sun, closed Aug)*. With more than 70 flavours on offer, from plain vanilla to whisky, and including virtually any fruit you can think of, the hardest part will be choosing, although there is plenty of time to make your choice as there will inevitably be a queue, especially in summer.

Left **L'Epicerie** Centre **Librairie Ulysse** Right **Boulangerie Rioux**

TOP 10 Shopping

1 L'Épicerie

This tiny shop packs in a great array of gourmet delights, from orange sauce to speciality vinegars and mustards, to chocolate "snails", all prettily packaged. *51 rue St-Louis-en-l'Ile, 75004 • Map Q5*

2 Lafitte

Preserved and packaged poultry products such as foie gras and goose confit are the speciality here, but there is a range of other items. A good place for gifts for foodie friends. *8 rue Jean-du-Bellay, 75004 • Map Q5*

3 Librairie Ulysse

Today Paris, tomorrow the world. This eccentric travel bookshop will take you there with thousands of titles in French and English – including many on Paris itself. *26 rue St-Louis-en-l'Ile, 75004 • Map Q5*

4 Calixte

The place to stock up for a picnic or the day's treats: superb croissants for the morning, pâtés and terrines and irresistible desserts for lunch. *64 rue St-Louis-en-l'Ile, 75004 • Map Q5*

5 Blasphème

A stylish shop that sells French-designed jewellery along with all manner of other tastefully made items including pens, photograph frames and a range of stationery. *37 rue St-Louis-en-l'Ile, 75004 • Map Q5*

6 Alain Carion

A wealth of meteorites, fossils and minerals. Some specimens are put to good use in imaginative jewellery. *92 rue St-Louis-en-l'Ile, 75004 • Map Q5*

7 Pylones Boutique

Wild about rubber? That's the magic material for the whimsical jewellery and accessories sold here, along with baby bibs and novelty gifts. *57 rue St-Louis-en-l'Ile, 75004 • Map Q5*

8 Boulangerie Rioux

You won't be able to resist the bread baking in the wood-burning oven from this old-fashioned bakery. *35 rue des Deux-Ponts, 75004 • Map Q5*

9 Bamyan

A wonderful collection of ethnic goods including carvings, furniture, jewellery and other craft items from all over the world. *24 rue St-Louis-en-l'Ile, 75004 • Map Q5*

10 La Ferme Saint Aubin

Cheese in all shapes and sizes from all over France. An aromatic delight. *76 rue St-Louis-en-l'Ile, 75004 • Map Q5*

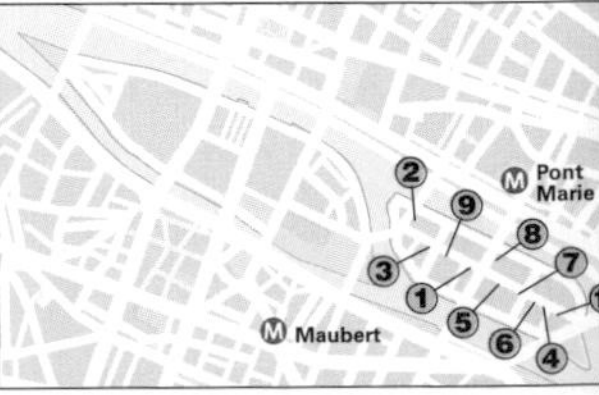

For more on shopping in Paris **See p169**

Left **La Rose de France** Right **Taverne Henry IV**

Price Categories

For a three-course meal for one with half a bottle of wine (or equivalent meal), taxes and extra charges		
	€	under €30
	€€	€30–€40
	€€€	€40–€50
	€€€€	€50–€60
	€€€€€	over €60

10 Places to Eat

1 Isami

One of the best Japanese restaurants in the city, but tiny so book ahead. Good choice of sushi. *4 quai d'Orléans, 75004 • Map P5 • 01 40 46 06 97 • Closed Sun L, Mon, Aug • No disabled access • €€€*

2 Au Gourmet de Isle

Bargain bistro in a 17th-century building. *Andouillettes* (offal sausages) are a house speciality, but there are plenty of other options. Bustling at lunch-time, candlelit in the evening. *42 rue St Louis en l'Ile, 75004 • Map Q5 • 01 43 26 79 27 • No disabled access • €€€*

3 L'Orangerie

Perfect spot for a romantic dinner with candles, flowers and relaxing music. The food is good too, with dishes such as leg of lamb. *28 rue St-Louis-en-l'Ile, 75004 • Map Q5 • 01 46 33 93 98 • Closed Aug • No disabled access • €€€€€*

4 Le Vieux Bistro

This ancient bistro, full of locals, serves staple dishes such as *boeuf bourguignon* and lemon tart. *14 rue du Cloître-Notre-Dame, 75004 • Map P4 • 01 43 54 18 95 • No disabled access • €€€*

5 Brasserie de l'Ile St-Louis

Wooden tables and a rustic look complement hearty Alsace fare, such as tripe in Riesling wine. *55 quai de Bourbon, 75004 • Map P4 • 01 43 54 02 59 • Closed Wed, Thu L, Aug • No disabled access • €€€*

6 La Rose de France

Lovely terrace and a cosy dining room. Lamb with Provençale herbs is one speciality. *24 pl Dauphine, 75001 • Map M3 • 01 43 54 10 12 • Closed Sat, Sun, Aug • €€*

7 Taverne Henry IV

A fine wine list accompanies simple plates of pâté or cheese. *13 pl du Pont-Neuf, 75001 • Map M3 • 01 43 54 27 90 • Closed Sun • €€*

8 Le Franc Pinot

Combine staple French food, such as steak-*frites*, with funky live jazz in these medieval cellars. *1 quai de Bourbon, 75004 • Map G5 • 01 46 33 60 64 • Closed Sun, Mon • €€€€*

9 Le Flore en l'Ile

Go for the views as well as the food in this tearoom, open from breakfast until 2am. *42 quai d'Orléans, 75004 • Map P5 • 01 43 29 88 27 • No disabled access • €*

10 Brasserie Les Deux Palais

Ornate mirrored walls and gold decor complement a simple but quality menu including omelettes and salads. *3 blvd du Palais, 75004 • Map N4 • 01 43 54 20 86 • No disabled access • €*

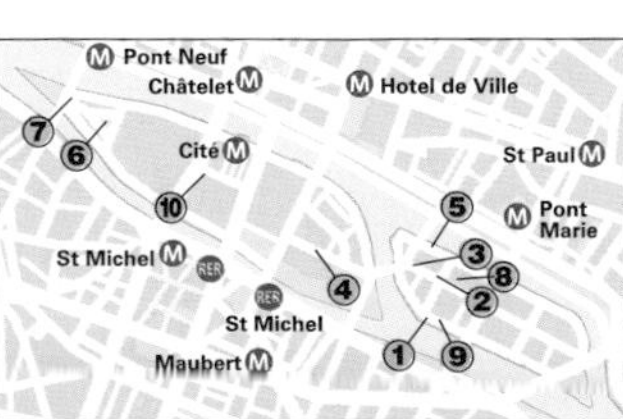

Note: *Unless otherwise stated, all restaurants accept credit cards and serve vegetarian meals*

Left **Stravinsky fountains** Centre **Fashion in Les Halles** Right **Forum des Halles**

Beaubourg and Les Halles

THE SMALL BUT LIVELY BEAUBOURG QUARTER, *brimming with art galleries and cafés, has become a major tourist attraction since the construction of the Centre Georges Pompidou. This inside-out hulk of modern architecture has become the focus of the area and receives more annual visitors than either the Musée du Louvre or the Eiffel Tower. Les Halles was the marketplace of Paris for 800 years, its glass-covered pavilions packed with butchers, fishmongers and fruit and vegetable stalls; novelist Emile Zola called it "the belly of Paris". In 1969, the market was demolished and moved to the suburbs to alleviate traffic congestion. Sadly, the soulless underground shopping mall, Forum des Halles, replaced it, but there are still a few old-time bistros and specialist food shops that survive to recall its former character.*

La Défense du Temps

TOP 10 Sights

1. Centre Georges Pompidou
2. Forum des Halles
3. St-Eustache
4. Bourse du Commerce
5. La Défense du Temps
6. Fontaine des Innocents
7. Eglise St-Merry
8. St-Germain l'Auxerrois
9. Musée de la Poupée
10. Tour St-Jacques

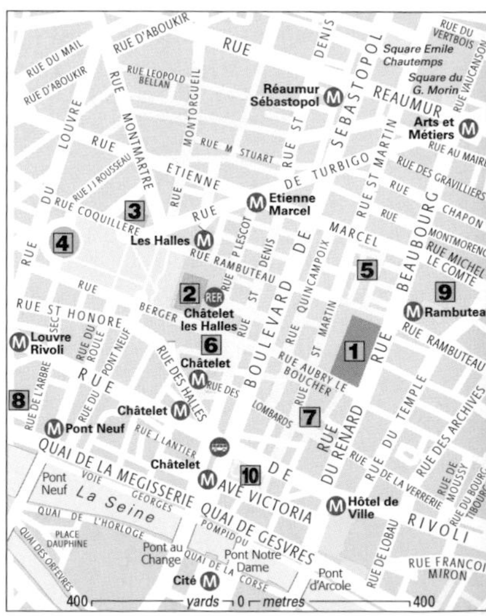

1 Centre Georges Pompidou

See pp26–7.

2 Forum des Halles

Ten years after the original arket was demolished, the -called "largest urban hole in urope" was filled with this con-oversial shopping complex. This rgely underground maze caters the young, with music shops nd boutiques selling trendy ashions. Outside, buskers, tudents and tourists mill about e steps and gardens. Separate etal and glass buildings house he Pavillion des Arts and the Aaison de la Poésie, cultural entres for art and poetry espectively. Today, however, it's nore of a sore spot than a otspot and French architect David Mangin has been brought to revamp the area. *Map N2*

3 St-Eustache

With its majestic arches and illars, St-Eustache is one of the nost beautiful churches in Paris. Although Gothic in design, it ook 105 years to build (1532–1637) and its interior decoration eflects the Renaissance style that blossomed during this time. The church was modelled on Notre-Dame *(see pp18–21)*, with double side aisles and a ring of side chapels. The stained-glass windows made from sketches by Philippe de Champaigne (1631) and the ornate tomb of politician Jean-Baptiste Colbert (1619–83) are highlights. Don't miss the naive sculpture in Chapelle St-Joseph which recalls Les Halles' market days. *2 impasse St-Eustache, 75001 • Map M1 • Open 9:30am–6:45pm daily • Free*

4 Bourse du Commerce

The circular building which houses the Commercial Exchange was erected as a grain market in 1767 and remodelled in the 19th century. It was first covered with a wooden dome, then by subsequent structures of iron and copper. Under today's glass dome, activity in the coffee and sugar commodities market is covered at a leisurely pace compared to the way other world financial centres operate. *2 rue de Viarmes, 75001 • Map M1 • Open 9am–6pm Mon–Fri (identification papers are required to visit)*

St-Eustache

Georges Pompidou

Georges Pompidou (1911–74) had the unenviable task of following General de Gaulle as President of France, from 1969 until his death. During his tenure he initiated many architectural developments in Paris, including the controversial but ultimately successful Pompidou Centre, and the less popular scheme to demolish the Les Halles market.

5 Le Défenseur du Temps

The "Defender of Time", Paris's modern public clock, stands appropriately in the Quartier de l'Horloge (Clock Quarter) shopping area. This fantasy mechanical sculpture of brass and steel by Jacques Monastier is 4 m (13 ft) high and weighs one tonne. When the clock strikes the hour, the warrior fends off a savage bird, crab or dragon (representing air, water and earth) with his sword, with accompanying sound effects. At noon, 6pm and 10pm he vanquishes all three, to the crowd's delight. *Rue Bernard-de-Clairvaux, 75003 • Map P2*

6 Fontaine des Innocents

The Square des Innocents is a Les Halles crossroads and a hang-out for street performers and students. It was built atop a cemetery in the 18th century, and two million remains were transferred to the Catacombs at Denfert-Rochereau. The splendid Renaissance fountain, the last of its era built in the city, was designed by Pierre Lescot and carved by sculptor Jean Goujon in 1547. It originally stood against a wall on rue St-Denis, and was later moved to the new square, when the fourth side was added *(see p39)*. *Rues St-Denis & Berger, 75001 • Map N2*

7 Eglise St-Merry

Formerly the parish church of the Lombard moneylenders, St-Merry was built between 1520 and 1612, and reflects the Flamboyant Gothic style. Its name is a corruption of St-Médéric, who was buried on thi site in the early 8th century. The bell in the church's northwest turret, thought to be the oldest in Paris, dates from 1331 and hung in a chapel which once stood on the site. Other high-lights include the decorative west front, the 17th-century organ loft, beautiful stained glas and carved wood panelling. *78 rue St-Martin, 75004 • Map P2 • Open 3–6:45pm daily • Free*

8 St-Germain l'Auxerrois

When the Valois kings moved to the Louvre palace in the 14th century *(see p8)*, this became the church of the royal

St-Germain l'Auxerrois

amily. On 24 August 1572, the olling of its bell was used as the ignal for the St Bartholomew's Day Massacre, when thousands f Huguenots who had come to Paris for the wedding of Henri of Navarre to Marguerite of Valois were murdered *(see p20)*. The church features a range of architectural styles, from its flamboyant Gothic façade to its Renaissance choir. Try and visit on Sunday afternoon when there are organ recitals. *2 pl du Louvre, 75001 • Map M2 • Open 8am–8pm daily • Free*

9 Musée de la Poupée

This delightful doll museum has a superb collection of 300 rare French dolls, including unglazed hand-painted porcelain dolls which were manufactured between 1850 and 1950. Many are imaginatively displayed in tableaux which portray various scenes, such as dolls having tea or playing with nursery toys. The museum is run by a father and son team, Guido and Samy Odin, who also handle doll repair. *Impasse Berthaud, 75003 • Map P2 • Open 10am–6pm Tue–Sun • Closed public hols • Admission charge*

10 Tour St-Jacques

The late Gothic tower, dating from 1523, is all that remains of the church of St-Jacques-la-Boucherie, once the largest medieval church in Paris and a starting point for pilgrims on their journey to Santiago de Compostela in Spain. In the 17th century the physicist Blaise Pascal used the tower for barometrical experiments. The church was pulled down after the Revolution. Today the tower is used as a meteorological observatory. *Pl du Châtelet, 75004 • Map N3 • Closed to public*

A Day in Les Halles

Morning

Tackle the **Centre Georges Pompidou** *(see pp26–7)* early, as the expansive modern art museum is worth a leisurely visit, and some of the excellent temporary exhibits may catch your eye. If you need refreshment after all that art, it has to be **Georges,** the brasserie at the top of the centre with good views and a choice of drinks, snacks or main meals.

On leaving the centre turn left to see the adjacent Stravinsky Fountain, then walk to the far end to visit the **Eglise St-Merry**.

Providing you have booked ahead, lunch at the 1912 bistro **Benoit** *(see p81)*, whose lunchtime menu is far cheaper than in the evening. If you're out by 3pm watch the clock on the **Défenseur du Temps** strike.

Afternoon

Pass the **Fontaine des Innocents** as you head for Les Halles, but first go into the church of **St-Eustache** *(see p75)* which was the place of worship of the market workers at the old Les Halles. You could then spend the rest of the afternoon shopping at the vast, if somewhat unprepossessing **Forum des Halles** *(see p75)*.

Stop for a drink at A La Tour de Montlhéry, more commonly known as **Chez Denise** *(see p81)*. It's packed at mealtimes, but by late afternoon you might be lucky enough to get a seat and be ready to try their famous Gâteau Marguerite with strawberries and cream.

Left **Le Cochon à l'Oreille** Right **St-Eustache Sculpture.**

TOP 10 Memories of Les Halles

1 Le Cochon à l'Oreille

Dating back to the early 20th century, this ornate working men's café/bar decorated with wall murals is where you'll see the last remaining market traders sipping their dawn drinks. *15 rue Montmartre, 75001 • Map F3*

2 Au Pied de Cochon

This 24-hour brasserie still serves dishes which used to appeal to the earthy tastes of market workers, including pigs' trotters *(see p81)*.

3 St-Eustache Sculpture

The naive sculpture by Raymond Mason in the church's Chapelle St-Joseph is a tribute to the beloved market. Its colourful figures depict *The Departure of Fruit and Vegetables from the Heart of Paris, 28 February 1969.*

4 Rue Montorgueil

The colourful market (Tuesday to Sunday) along this cobbled street is a reminder of the old Les Halles and is frequented by many Paris chefs. *Map N1*

5 Stöhrer

One of the loveliest old-fashioned patisseries in the city, founded in 1730 by a pastry chef who had worked for Louis XV. *51 rue Montorgueil, 75002 • Map N1*

6 Bistrot d'Eustache

A visit here is like stepping back into the jazz spots of Paris in the 1930–40s. It offers good, reasonably priced brasserie fare and live jazz on Thursdays. *37 rue Berger, 75001 • Map N2*

7 Papeterie Moderne

The old-fashioned enamel plaques and street signs sold here make an original Paris souvenir. *12 rue de la Ferronerie, 75001 • Map N2*

8 Dehillerin

Since 1820, everyone from army cooks to gourmet chefs has come to this shop for copper pots, cast-iron pans and cooking utensils. *18 rue Coquillière, 75001 • Map M1*

9 Duthilleul et Minart

For more than 100 years this shop has sold French work clothes and uniforms such as chef's hats and watchmaker's smocks. Good for unique gifts. *14 rue de Turbigo, 75001 • Map P1*

10 A La Cloche des Halles

This wine bar literally rings with history. The "cloche" is the bronze bell whose peal once signalled the beginning and end of the market day *(see p81)*.

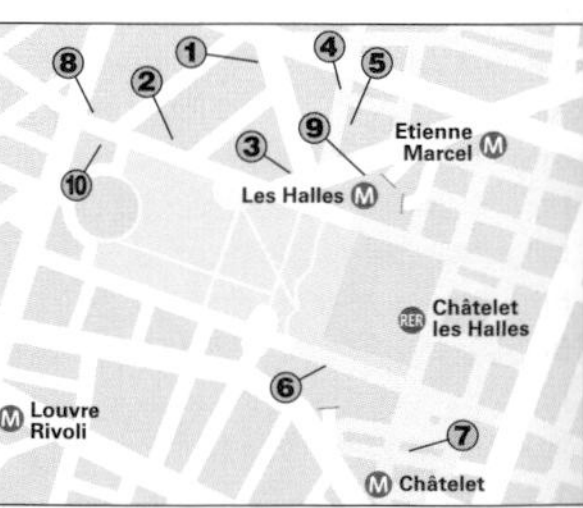

Left **Typical Paris beer bar** Centre **Le Tambour** Right **Au Trappiste**

Top 10 Beer Bars

1 Le Sous-Bock

A good place for *moules* (mussels), with 400 types of beer to wash them down with. There are also 200 whiskies. *49 rue St-Honoré, 75001 • Map M2*

2 Le Petit Opportun

Archetypal Paris jazz bar with drinks upstairs and live jazz in the tiny basement at night. *15 rue des Lavandières-Ste-Opportune, 75001 • Map N2*

3 Flann O'Brien's

Paris was home to this Irish pub before there were Irish pubs in every city. With live Irish bands and draught Guinness, it's as close to the real thing as it gets. *6 rue Bailleul, 75001 • Map M2*

4 Carpe Diem

While you're at it, you could also be seizing a pint or three at this cosy pub that's kept the warmth of its previous incarnation as an Irish pub. *21 rue des Halles, 75001 • Map N2*

5 The Frog and Rosbif

For homesick English or Anglophiles, this is the place to find real ale and pub grub like bangers and mash, play snooker, to read English newspapers and watch live football and rugby matches on the bar's satellite TV. *116 rue St-Denis, 75002 • Map F3*

6 Le Tambour

The interior decor here is junkyard chic – old glass screens, recycled signs – and the crowd is a lively mix of students and businessmen. *41 rue Montmartre, 75002 • Map F3*

7 Au Trappiste

Among the many beers on tap you can sample Jenlain, a French brew and Blanche Riva, a Belgian beer. Food is also served. *4 rue St-Denis, 75001 • Map F3*

8 Guinness Tavern

Fourteen beers are on tap in this Irish bar with live music every night and a bigger Irish concert once a month. The party really kicks in after 10pm. *31 bis rue des Lombards, 75004 • Map N2*

9 Café Oz

A range of Australian beers and wines combined with archetypal Outback decor makes this rowdy bar popular with antipodean ex-patriates and French patrons alike. *18 rue St-Denis, 75001 • Map F3*

10 Le Fumoir

Fashionable offshoot of The China Club *(see p53)*, this spacious bar with chic decor and an even smarter clientele rarely closes its doors. *6 rue de l'Amiral-de-Coligny, 75001 • Map M1*

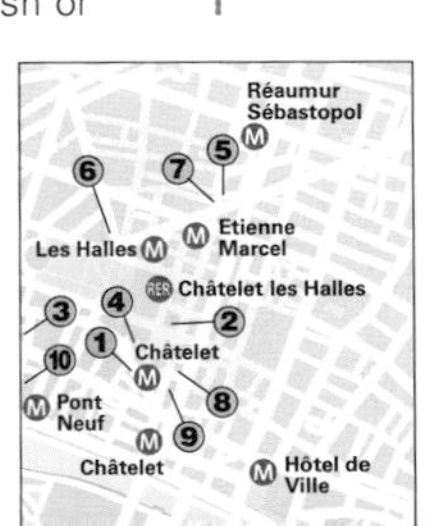

For more cafés and bars See pp52–3

Left **Forum des Halles** Right **Les Halles bookshop**

Top 10 Historical Events in Les Halles

1 Roman Era
A marketplace was first established on the Right Bank of the Seine in a place then called Les Champeaux.

2 10th Century
A larger market for meat, fruit and vegetables was at this time known to exist in the part of Paris which is now Les Halles.

3 1183
The market is enlarged by King Philippe Auguste, who built shelters for the market traders near St-Eustache church *(see p75)*. This date is generally accepted as the founding of Les Halles as the city's market.

4 1850s
Twelve huge iron structures are built to house the market. Napoleon III declares that Les Halles is essential to Paris life.

5 1965
Work begins on a modern wholesale market south of Paris, at Rungis.

6 1969
The market is closed and moved to Rungis, partly to ease the traffic congestion that was by now too much for the centre of the city.

7 1971
The old buildings are demolished and digging begins, to create for a time what is known as the *trou des Halles* (the hole of Les Halles).

8 Mid-1970s
As well as the shopping development, gardens are created and nearby buildings can be seen properly for the first time, including the church of St-Eustache.

9 1977
The Forum des Halles opens and ensures that the area remains as busy as ever, although the goods for sale (high fashion, CDs, fast food) have changed considerably since the market's early days.

10 1986
Second phase of the Forum des Halles opens, creating the biggest collection of shops under one roof in Paris, though many will always lament the passing of the original market.

St-Eustache

For more on shopping in Paris **See p169**

Above **Au Pied de Cochon**

Price Categories

For a three-course meal for one with half a bottle of wine (or equivalent meal), taxes and extra charges

€	under €30
€€	€30–€40
€€€	€40–€50
€€€€	€50–€60
€€€€€	over €60

TOP 10 Places to Eat

1 Gérard Besson

The *haute cuisine* menu here may break the bank but it's worth it, especially the candied fennel with vanilla ice cream. *5 rue du Coq-Héron, 75001 • Map M1 • 01 42 33 14 74 • Closed Mon L, Sat L, Sun D • €€€€€*

2 Au Pied de Cochon

Long-time Les Halles favourite. If your taste is not for offal, there are options such as oysters and steak. Open 24 hours a day. *6 rue Coquillière, 75001 • Map M1 • 01 40 13 77 00 • €€€€*

3 Benoit

Try the lunchtime menu to cut costs at what is, justifiably, the most expensive bistro in Paris. *20 rue St-Martin, 75004 • Map P1 • 01 42 72 25 76 • Closed Aug • No disabled access • €€€€€*

4 L'Ambassade d'Auvergne

Auvergne cooking, with lots of pork and cabbage dishes. Good for solo diners too, as they operate a shared-table policy. *22 rue du Grenier-St-Lazare, 75003 • Map P1 • 01 42 72 31 22 • Closed mid-Jul–mid-Aug • No disabled access • €€*

5 Tour de Montlhéry, Chez Denise

This bistro is an institution in Les Halles, which gets busier as the night wears on. Noted for its huge portions of meat, such as grilled steak. *5 rue des Prouvaires, 75001 • Map N2 • 01 42 36 21 82 • Closed Sat–Sun, mid-Jul–mid-Aug • €€€*

6 Le Grizzli

Charcuterie and pâtés are some of the simple dishes here *7 rue St-Martin, 75004 • Map P1 • 01 48 87 77 56 • Closed Sun • No disabled access • €€*

7 Café Beaubourg

The terrace here overlooks the Pompidou Centre. Flash-fried steak is a house special. *43 rue St-Merri, 75004 • Map P2 • 01 48 87 63 96 • No disabled access • €*

8 La Cloche des Halles

Simple bar-bistro where you can dine on plates of cheese and cold meats. *28 rue Coquillière, 75001 • Map M1 • 01 42 36 93 89 • Closed Sun, 2 weeks in Aug • No credit cards • €*

9 L'Escargot Montorgueil

All variations of *escargots* (snails) here in a grand 1830s setting. *38 rue Montorgueil, 75001 • Map N1 • 01 42 36 83 51 • Closed 2 weeks in Aug • €€€€*

10 Joe Allen Restaurant

A great brunch, and for lunch and dinner a mixed French/ US menu is served. *30 rue Pierre-Lescot, 75001 • Map N2 • 01 42 36 70 13 • Closed Aug • €€*

Note: Unless otherwise stated, all restaurants accept credit cards and serve vegetarian meals

Left **Place des Vosges street sign** Centre **Place de la Bastille** Right **Maison de Victor Hugo**

Marais and the Bastille

FOR MANY, THE MARAIS IS THE MOST ENJOYABLE *quarter of Paris, with its mansions, museums and medieval lanes, but the district was little more than a muddy swamp until Henri IV built the place Royale (now place des Vosges) in 1605. Following its notoriety as the birthplace of the Revolution, the Bastille sank into oblivion, until artists and designers arrived in the 1990s. Its streets are now home to the city's liveliest nightspots.*

Sights

1. Musée Picasso
2. Musée Cognacq-Jay
3. Place des Vosges
4. Musée Carnavalet
5. Place de la Bastille
6. Marché d'Aligre
7. The Passages
8. Rue de Lappe
9. Maison Européenne de la Photographie
10. Maison de Victor Hugo

Bastille passage

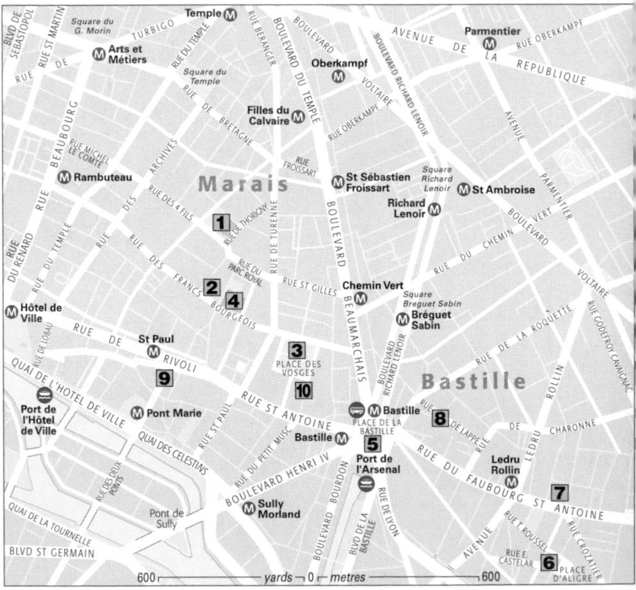

Preceding pages **Notre-Dame seen from the Seine**

1 Musée Picasso

When the Spanish-born rtist Pablo Picasso died in 1973, is family donated thousands of is works to the French state in eu of estate taxes. Thus Paris njoys the largest collection of icassos in the world. Housed in he Hôtel Aubert de Fontenay *(see 90)*, the museum displays the ange of his artistic development, om his Blue and Pink Periods o Cubism, and reveals his profi- iency in an astonishing range of echniques and materials *(see 36)*. *5 rue de Thorigny, 75003 • Map 2 • Open 9:30am–6pm (5:30pm winter) Ved–Mon • Admission charge (free first un of month)*

2 Musée Cognacq-Jay

This small but excellent nuseum portrays the ophisticated French lifestyle in he so-called Age of Enlighten- nent, which centred around Paris. The 18th century art and urniture on display were once he private collection of Ernest Cognacq and his wife, Louise Jay, founders of the Samaritaine department store. It is superbly displayed in the Hôtel Donon, an elegant late 16th-century building with an 18th-century façade *(see p35)*. *8 rue Elzévir, 75003 • Map Q3 • Open 10am–6pm Tue–Sun*

3 Place des Vosges

Paris's oldest square also has the honour of being one of the most beautiful in the world. Once the site of jousting tourna- ments, the square was commis- sioned by Henri IV. Its 36 houses with red-gold brick and stone façades, slate roofs and dormer windows were laid out with striking symmetry in 1612. Although they were originally built for silk workers, the likes of Cardinal Richelieu (1585–1642) and the playwright Molière (1622–73) quickly moved in and it remains an upper-class residen- tial address. But everyone can enjoy a stroll around the area and the art galleries under the arcades. *Map R3*

4 Musée Carnavalet

Devoted to the history of Paris, this museum sprawls through two mansions, the 16th- century Carnavalet and 17th- century Le Peletier. The former was the home of Madame de Sévigné, the famous letter-writer, from 1677–96 and a gallery here portrays her life. The extensive museum contains everything from period rooms filled with art and portraits to Revolutionary artifacts and memorabilia of 18th-century philosophers Rousseau and Voltaire *(see p34)*. *23 rue de Sévigné, 75003 • Map R3 • Open 10am–6pm Tue–Sun*

5 Place de la Bastille

Today this notorious square is surrounded by a busy traffic circle, which is not the best spot for contemplating its grim history. Originally the Bastille

Musée Cognacq-Jay

The Jewish Quarter

The Jewish Quarter, centred around rues des Rosiers and des Écouffes, was established in the 13th century and has attracted immigrants since the Revolution. Many Jews fled here to escape persecution in Eastern Europe, but were arrested during the Nazi Occupation. Since World War II, Sephardic Jews from North Africa have found new homes here.

was a fortress built by Charles V to defend the eastern edge of the city, but it soon became a jail for political prisoners. Angry citizens, rising up against the excesses of the monarchy, stormed the Bastille on 14 July 1789 *(see p45)*, setting off the French Revolution, and destroyed this hated symbol of oppression. In its place is the bronze Colonne de Juillet (July Column), 52 m (171 ft) high and crowned by the Angel of Liberty, which commemorates those who died in the revolutions of 1830 and 1848. Looming behind it is the Opéra Bastille, the largest opera house in the world, which opened on the bicentennial of the Revolution in 1989. *Map H5*

6 Marché d'Aligre

Set around an old guardhouse and clock-tower, the wonderful Aligre market is a melting pot of Paris-ians from all walks of life. It dates back to 1643 and was once as important as the more famous Les Halles *(see p75)*. In the gourmet covered market you'll see everything from rows of pheasants to a whole wild boar hanging from the stalls. North African traders give the outdoor produce market an ethnic flare. The flea market dates back to the days when nuns distributed second-hand clothing to the poor *(see p55)*.
pl d'Aligre • Map H5 • Open am daily

7 The Passages

The Bastille has been a quarter of working-class artisans and craft guilds since the 17th century and many furniture makers are still located in these small alleyways, called *passages*. The rue du Faubourg-St-Antoine is lined with shops displaying a striking array of both traditional period furniture and modern designs, but don't neglect to visit the narrow *passages*, such as the Passage de la Main D'Or, running off this and other streets

Rue de Lappe

the Bastille. Many artists and craftspeople have their ateliers (workshops) in these atmospheric alleys, which are great fun to explore. ⊗ Map H5

8 Rue de Lappe

Once famous for its 1930s dance halls *(bals musettes)*, rue de Lappe is still the Bastille's after-dark hotspot. This short, narrow street is filled with bars, pubs, restaurants and cafés, and positively throbs with music. Crowds of hip night-owls trawl the cobblestones looking for action, and spill into the adjoining rue de la Roquette and rue de Charonne where there are even more trendy bars and restaurants. ⊗ *Map H5*

9 Maison Européenne de la Photographie

This excellent gallery showcasing contemporary European photography opened in 1996 in an early 18th-century mansion, Hôtel Hénault de Cantorbe. The restoration is a mix of historic features and modern spaces that show off its permanent collection and changing exhibitions, including multimedia works. ⊗ *5–7 rue de Fourcy, 75004 • Map Q3 • Open 11am–8pm Wed–Sun • Admission charge (free Wed after 5pm & for under 8s)*

10 Maison de Victor Hugo

French author Victor Hugo (1802–85) lived on the second floor of the Hôtel de Rohan-Guéménée, the largest house on the place des Vosges, from 1832 to 1848. He wrote most of *Les Misérables* here *(see p46)* and many other works. In 1903 the house became a museum of his life, with portraits and memorabilia. ⊗ *6 pl des Vosges, 75004 • Map R4 • Open 10am–6pm Tue–Sun • Admission charge (free 10am–1pm Sun)*

A Day in the Marais

Morning

Begin the morning at the **Musée Picasso** *(see p85)*, to beat the crowds and allow enough time to view the huge collection. There is also an excellent gift shop. Afterwards, walk to the place des Vosges, and do a circuit of the arcades. Stand in the centre near the fountains to take in the whole square.

Have a coffee at Ma Bourgogne *(19 pl des Vosges • 01 42 78 44 64)*, right on the square. Afterwards, tour the **Maison de Victor Hugo**, on the south-east corner to the **Musée Picasso** *(see p87)*. Take the rue de Birague which leads to rue Faubourg-St-Antoine. Turn left and walk to place de la Bastille.

A good lunch choice is **Bofinger** *(see p93)*, with its ornate decor and true Parisian feel.

Afternoon

The **Place de la Bastille** *(see p85)* is something of a traffic nightmare, but take time to admire the statue in the centre and contemplate the events that happened here when this was the site of the city's dreaded prison. Walk around the square and along rue Faubourg-St-Antoine, a now fashionable shopping street. Turn off down some of the passageways to see the furniture-makers and craft workshops that have a long history in the area.

From here it's not far to **Le Baron Rouge** wine bar *(see p93)*, for a restorative glass of wine, coffee and cake or a light early evening meal.

Left **Isabel Marant** Right **Issey Miyake Europe**

TOP 10 Shops

1 Izraël
Also called the "World of Spices" (and it does have every spice you could wish for) this is a treasure trove of the world's best food and drink. Tiny but packed with meat, cheese, wine, rum, dates, honey, mustard… it has to be seen. *30 rue François-Miron, 75004 • Map P3*

2 BHV
The Bazar de l'Hôtel de Ville is an upmarket all-round shopper's paradise at which you can track down everything from DIY products to stylish underwear. *52–64 rue de Rivoli, 75004 • Map F4*

3 Issey Miyake Europe
Superstar Japanese designer sells his limited edition clothing in a chic shop that blends in well with the buildings on the square. *3 pl des Vosges, 75004 • Map R3*

4 Sacha Finkelsztajn
Try the freshly made cheesecake called *vatrouchka*, or other cakes and pastries. *27 rue des Rosiers, 75004 • Map Q3*

5 Florence Finkelsztajn
The sister shop to the above offers a similar range, with freshly baked rye bread plus a deli. *24 rue des Ecouffes, 75004 • Map Q3*

6 Délices
One of the best bakers in the Marais, almost worth having a picnic just as an excuse to try the croissants, baguettes and the cake-like walnut bread. *32 rue Vieille-du-Temple, 75004 • Map P3*

7 Isabel Marant
A designer better known to Parisians than overseas, her work is hip but elegant. *16 rue de Charonne, 75011 • Map H5*

8 Aladine
Fabulous displays of old kitchenware, boxes, jars, ashtrays… anything with a colourful old advertisement on it from the 1960s back to whatever the owner can get her hands on. *12 rue Trousseau, 75011 • Map H5*

9 Au Levain du Marais
Exceptional baker producing traditional breads and pastries, and more unusual flavours such as a raisin rye bread. *32 rue de Turenne, 75003 • Map R3*

10 Emery & Cie
Stylish, coloured ceramics, tiles, lamps and other goods, run by an interior decorator. *29 rue du Faubourg-St-Antoine, 75011 • Map H5*

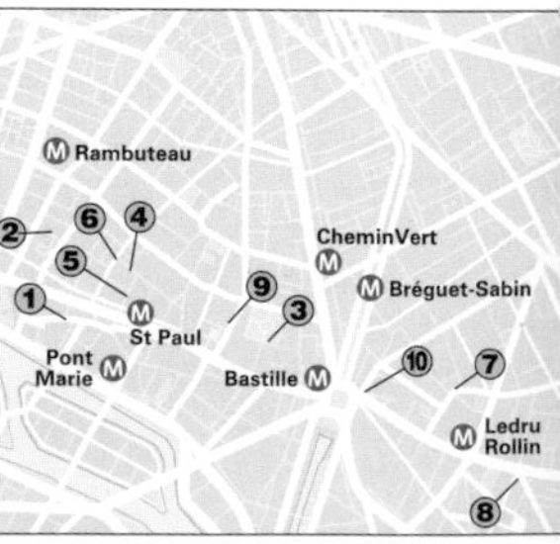

For more on shopping in Paris **See p169**

ft **André Bissonet** Centre **La Petite Fabrique** Right **Librairie l'Arbre à Lettres**

10 Specialist Shops

1 The Red Wheelbarrow Bookstore

n English-language bookshop here you can pick up that anslated French classic you ay have been inspired to read. *13 rue Charles-V, 75004 • Map R4*

2 André Bissonet

A delightful hidden treasure ; this shop/workshop where the wner lovingly restores antique usical instruments such as umpets, harps and violins. *6 ue du Pas-de-la-Mule, 75003 • Map H5*

3 La Chaiserie du Faubourg

Bastille has always been the rea for furniture makers, and his chair repair shop keeps the adition alive. *26 rue de Charonne, 5011 • Map H5*

4 Chez Teil

Specializing in products from he Auvergne, mostly foodstuffs uch as Auvergne sausages. *6 ue de Lappe, 75011 • Map H5*

5 The Filofax Centre

The name says it all, for the biquitous binder that palmtop rganizers have not ousted completely. Also stationery, pens nd associated items. *32 rue des Francs-Bourgeois, 75013 • Map R3*

6 L'Art du Bureau

If your desk is your altar, ou'll find everything you could ossibly need here, and it's all in he most modern designs. In act, this shop is worth visiting for the design aspects alone. *47 rue des Francs-Bourgeois, 75004 • Map R3*

7 Librairie l'Arbre à Lettres

Beautiful bookshop, though the content is on the serious side, concentrating on art, philosophy and politics. *56 rue du Faubourg-St-Antoine, 75012 • Map H6*

8 A l'Olivier

For 150 years this shop has specialized in all kinds of oil, from the finest olive oil to massage oil. *23 rue de Rivoli, 75004 • Map H5*

9 Papeterie Saint Sabin

Parisian stationery shops are a class apart, and here you will find stylish notebooks, pens, pads and other tasteful items. *16 rue St-Sabin, 75011 • Map H4*

10 A la Petite Fabrique

This shop doesn't just sell chocolate, you can watch it being made. More than 40 flavours and novelty chocolates in all shapes. *12 rue St-Sabin, 75011 • Map H4*

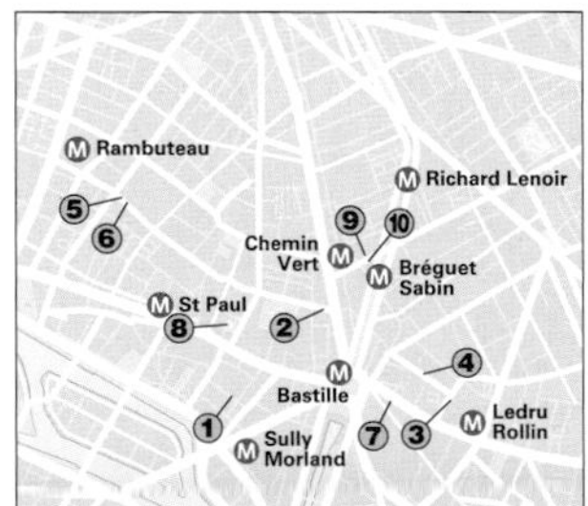

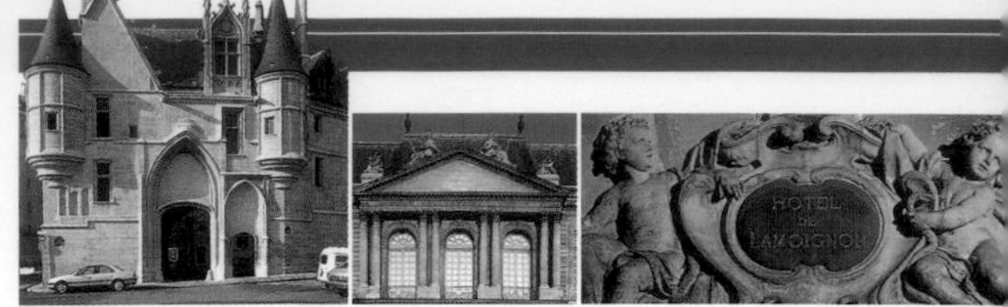

Left **Hôtel de Sens** Centre **Hôtel de Soubise** Right **Hôtel de Lamoignon**

Top 10 Mansions

1 Hôtel de Coulanges

This mansion boasts beautiful early 18th-century architecture, although the right wing dates from the early 1600s. *35 rue des Francs-Bourgeois, 75004 • Map Q2 • Open only for concerts*

2 Hôtel Aubert de Fontenay

Built in 1656–9 for Aubert de Fontenay, a salt-tax collector, this mansion was restored in 1986 to provide a home for the Musée Picasso *(see p85)*.

3 Hôtel Guénégaud

Designed by the architect François Mansart in the mid-17th century, this splendid mansion now houses a Hunting Museum. *60 rue des Archives, 75003 • Map P3 • Open 11am–6pm Tue–Sun • Admission charge*

4 Hôtel de Beauvais

The young Mozart performed at this 17th-century mansion. Notice the balcony decorated with goats' heads. *68 rue François-Miron, 75004 • Map P3 • Closed to the public*

5 Hôtel de Sully

This 17th-century mansion was home to the Duc de Sully, chief minister to Henri IV. From the courtyard admire its Renaissance façade. *62 rue St-Antoine, 75004 • Map R4 • Closed to the public*

6 Hôtel de Sens

One of Paris's few medieval mansions. Henri IV's wife Marguerite de Valois *(see p20)* lived here after their divorce. Now a fine arts library. *1 rue Figuier, 75004 • Map Q4 • Closed to the public*

7 Hôtel de St-Aignan

The plain exterior hides an enormous mansion within. It is now the Museum of Jewish Art and History. *71 rue du Temple, 75003 • Map P2 • Open 11am– 6pm Mon–Fri, Sun • Admission charge*

8 Hôtel de Soubise

Along with the adjacent Hôtel de Rohan, this 17th-century mansion houses the national archives. *60 rue des Francs-Bourgeois, 75003 • Map Q2 • Open 2–5:30pm Wed–Mon*

9 Hôtel de Lamoignon

Built in 1584 for the daughter of Henri II. Note the Greek-style pediment. *24 rue Pavée, 75004 • Map Q3 • Closed to the public*

10 Hôtel de Marle

This beautiful 16th-century mansion houses the Swedish Cultural Centre. *11 rue Payenne, 75003 • Map G4 • Open 10am–1pm & 2–6pm Tue–Fri • Admission charge*

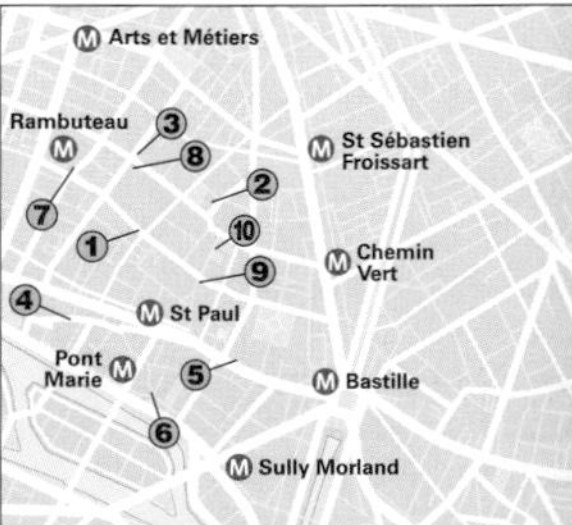

For more historic buildings in Paris **See pp42–3**

eft **Galerie Patrick Seguin** Centre **Galerie Lavignes-Bastille** Right **Galerie Durand-Dessert**

10 Galleries

1 Galerie Marian Goodman

Housed in a 17th-century mansion, this gallery is a slice of New York in a Parisian setting. Artists on show include Jeff Wall and video-maker Steve McQueen. *79 rue du Temple, 75003 • Map 2P Open 11am–7pm Tue–Sat*

2 Galerie Akié Aricchi

Eclectic exhibitions covering photography, sculpture and paint, often with an Asian influence. *26 rue Keller, 75011 • Map H5 • Open 2–7pm Tue–Sat*

3 Galerie Gutharc-Ballin

Alain Gutharc devotes his space to the work of young artists, whether they be working in paint, photography, sculpture or mixed media. *47 rue de Lappe, 75011 • Map H5 • Open 2–7pm Tue–Fri, 11am–1pm & 2–7pm Sat*

4 Galerie Jorge Alyskewycz

Large space devoted mainly to sculpture and kinetic works, but some art and photography are on show too. *14 rue des Taillandiers, 75011 • Map H4 • Open 2–7pm Tue–Sat*

5 Galerie Seguin

Challenging gallery which shows avant-garde work alongside more conventional offerings. *34 rue de Charonne, 75011 • Map H5 • Open 10am–7pm Mon–Sat*

6 Galerie Patrick Seguin

This off-shoot gallery features stylish furniture from the 1930–50s. *5 rue des Taillandiers, 75011 • Map H4 • Open 10am–7pm Mon–Sat*

7 Galerie Lavignes-Bastille

Modern posters, books and prints for sale as well as originals. *27 rue de Charonne, 75011 • Map H5 • Open 2–7pm Tue–Sat*

8 Galerie Liliane et Michel Durand-Dessert

Housed in a former factory, the gallery concentrates on contemporary art. *28 rue de Lappe, 75011 • Map H5 • Open 11am–7pm Tue–Sat*

9 Galerie Yvon Lambert

Changing exhibitions cover sculpture, photography and art, from conventional to challenging. *108 rue Vieille du Temple, 75003 • Map Q1 • Open 10am–1pm, 2:30–7pm Tue–Fri, 10am–7pm Sat*

10 Gallery Nikki Diana Marquardt

A gallery of politically motivated artworks executed in all types of art media. *9 pl des Vosges, 75004 • Map H3 • Open 2–5pm Tue–Fri, noon–6pm Sat*

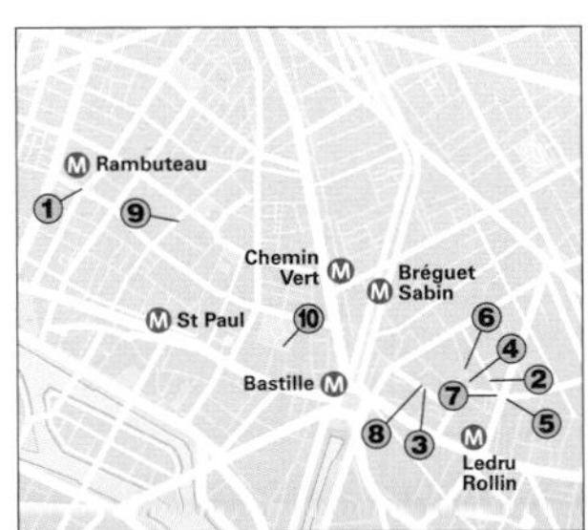

Left **The China Club** Right **La Fabrique**

Top 10 Fashionable Hang-outs

1 The China Club

A long-established favourite, with its bar, live music at weekends, expensive cocktails and all done out in Chinese decor *(see p53)*. *50 rue de Charenton, 75012 • Map H5*

2 Le Balajo

Balajo has been going since 1936, serving up different styles of dancing on different days. They range from Saturday night disco to Sunday afternoon tea dances. *9 rue de Lappe, 75011 • Map H5*

3 Barrio Latino

Vast club on three floors with a generally louche Latin atmosphere. *46–8 rue du Faubourg-St-Antoine, 75012 • Map H5*

4 La Fabrique

A bar, a nightclub with top DJs, and a restaurant. The club thumps out anything loud, and the bar serves trendy bottled beers. *53 rue du Faubourg-St-Antoine, 75011 • Map H5*

5 Café Iguana

Tex-Mex bar-restaurant that straddles two floors and is open almost non-stop. Serves beer, cocktails and some basic dishes. *15 rue de la Roquette, 75011 • Map H4*

6 Café de l'Industrie

This fashionable and sizeable café has three rooms where the walls are lined with paintings and old-fashioned artifacts. The food is cheap but pretty good, and the later it gets the better the buzz *(see p53)*. *16 rue St-Sabin, 75011 • Map H4*

7 L'Armagnac

A place doesn't have to be avant-garde to be fashionable: L'Armagnac is simply one of the best places in Paris to eat, drink play pool or just hang out. *104 rue de Charonne, 75011 • Map H5*

8 Le Fanfaron

This is a must for lovers of rare film music, the Rolling Stones and Iggy Pop, with hip tunes and the cheapest beer in Bastille. *6 rue de la Main d'Or, 75011 • Map H5*

9 Le Square Trousseau

This bistro was one of the first media watering holes when the Bastille became chic a few years ago. *1 rue Antoine-Vollon, 75012 • Map H5*

10 SanZSanS

Video screens show what's happening in this trendy, modern bar. *49 rue du Faubourg-St-Antoine, 75011 • Map H5*

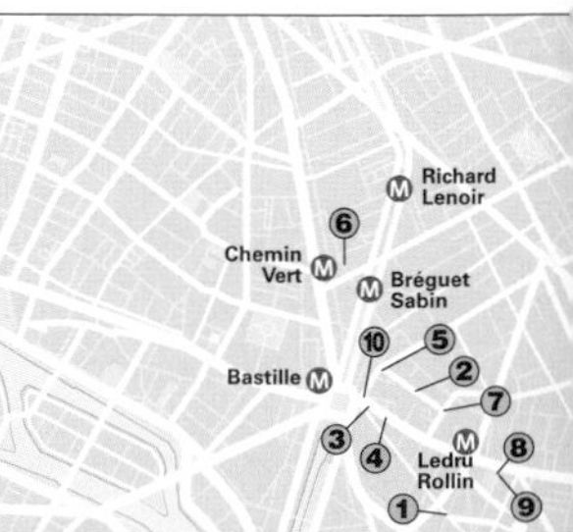

For more bars in Paris **See pp52–3**

Price Categories

For a three-course meal for one with half a bottle of wine (or equivalent meal), taxes and extra charges

€	under €30
€€	€30–€40
€€€	€40–€50
€€€€	€50–€60
€€€€€	over €60

eft **Bofinger**

10 Places to Eat

1 L'Ambroisie
The finest service matching he finest of food, traditionally ooked. Renowned wine list, and he chocolate tart is out of this vorld. *9 pl des Vosges, 75004 • Map 3 • 01 42 78 51 45 • €€€€€*

2 Gli Angeli
One of Paris's best Italian estaurants. Their *carpaccio* is ighly rated, as is the *tiramisù.* *5 rue St-Gilles, 75003 • Map R3 • 01 2 71 05 80 • No disabled access • €*

3 La Guirlande de Julie
Owned by Claude Terrail of he Tour d'Argent *(see p127)*, this lelightful restaurant offers *haute cuisine* at affordable prices. *25 l des Vosges, 75003 • Map R3 • 01 48 37 94 07 • €*

4 La Galoche d'Aurillac
Food from the Auvergne in uge quantities in this busy and riendly place. Stuffed cabbage is he delicious speciality. *41 rue de Lappe, 75011 • Map H5 • 01 47 00 77 15 • Closed Sun–Mon, 21 Jul–4 Sep • €€€*

5 Bistrot les Sans-Culottes
This bustling bistro serves a range of dishes from steaks to more ambitious fare. Outdoor seating in summer. *27 rue de Lappe, 75011 • Map H5 • 01 48 05 42 92 • Closed Wed, Mon L, Tue L, Thu L, Fri L • €*

6 Bofinger
Paris's oldest brasserie (1864) offers staple dishes such as oysters and peppered steak. Several fixed-price menus. *5-7 rue de la Bastille, 75004 • Map H5 • 01 42 72 87 82 • No disabled access • €€*

7 Le Baron Rouge
A true Parisian atmosphere and simple food, such as cold meats and cheese. *1 rue Théophile-Roussel, 75012 • Map H5 • 01 43 43 14 32 • Closed Mon • €*

8 Chez Paul
This old bistro has a fairly simple menu but it is always delicious. Book ahead. *13 rue de Charonne, 75011 • Map H5 • 01 47 00 34 57 • No disabled access • €€€*

9 Havanita
A loud Cuban bar-restaurant with dishes such as Cuban chicken salad. *11 rue de Lappe, 75011 • Map H5 • 01 43 55 96 42 • €€*

10 Jo Goldenberg
This Jewish deli-restaurant serves dishes such as chicken soup, chopped liver and potato *latkes*. *7 rue des Rosiers, 75004 • Map Q3 • 01 48 87 20 16 • No disabled access • €*

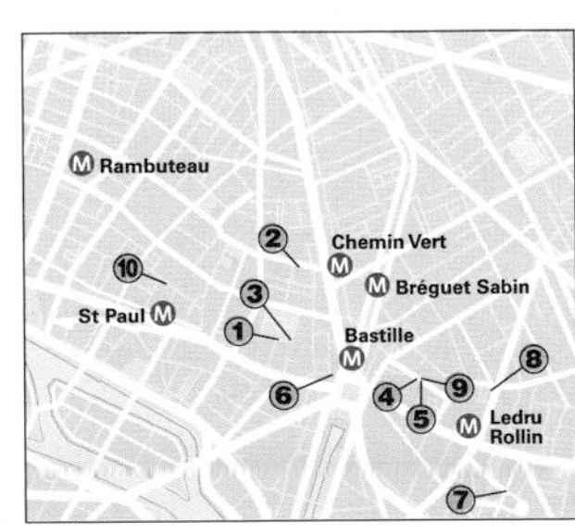

Note: *Unless otherwise stated, all restaurants accept credit cards and serve vegetarian meals*

Left **Louvre façade** Centre **Café Marly, Louvre** Left **Musée Nationale de la Mode et du Textile**

Tuileries and Opéra Quarters

THESE TWO QUARTERS *were once the province of the rich and the royal. Adjoining the Tuileries Gardens is the largest museum in the world, the Louvre, while the grand opera house gives the second quarter its name. The Place de la Concorde is one of the most historic sites in the city.*

Sights

1. Musée du Louvre
2. Rue de Rivoli
3. Place de la Concorde
4. Jardin des Tuileries
5. Musée des Arts Décoratifs
6. Musée de la Mode et du Textile
7. Palais-Royal
8. Place Vendôme
9. Opéra de Paris Garnier
10. Place de la Madeleine

Opéra de Paris Garnier

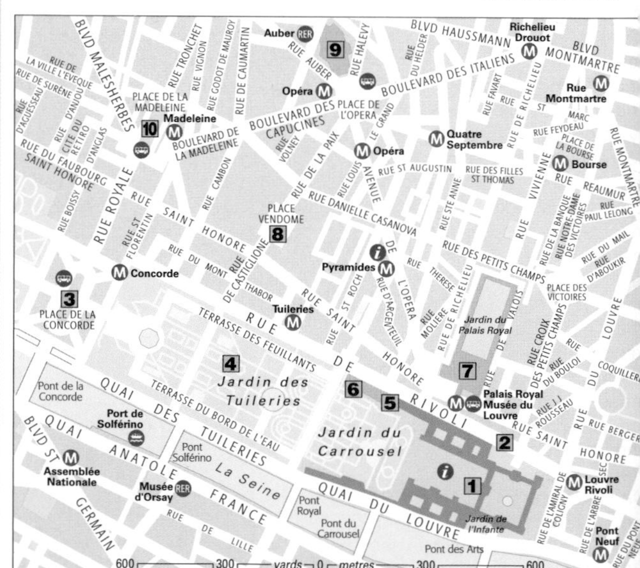

1 Musée du Louvre

See pp8–10.

2 Rue de Rivoli

Commissioned by Napoleon ıd named after his victory over ıe Austrians at Rivoli in 1797, ıis grand street links the Louvre ith the Champs-Elysées *(see 103)*. It was intended as a ackdrop for victory marches but as not finished until the 1850s, ıng after the emperor's death. long one side, railings replaced ıe old Tuileries walls, opening ɔ the view, while opposite, eo-Classical apartments sit top the long arcades. These are ow filled with a mix of shops, elling luxury goods or tourist ouvenirs. ⓢ *Map M2*

3 Place de la Concorde

This historic octagonal quare, covering more than 8 ha 20 acres), is bounded by the uileries Gardens on one side nd marks the starting point of ıe Champs-Elysées on the other. : was built between 1755–75 to esigns by architect Jacques-nge Gabriel as the grand set-ng for a statue of Louis XV, but y 1792 it had become the place e la Révolution and its central ıonument was the guillotine. ouis XVI, Marie-Antoinette and ıore than 1,000 others were xecuted here *(see p70)*. In 795, in the spirit of reconcilia-ion, it received its present name. he central obelisk, 23 m (75 ft) all and covered in hieroglyphics, s from a 3,300-year-old Luxor emple, and was a gift from Egypt, rected in 1833. Two fountains nd eight statues representing rench cities were also added.)n the north side of the square re the mansions Hôtel de la Marine and Hôtel Crillon, also by abriel. ⓢ *Map D3*

Arcades on rue de Rivoli

4 Jardin des Tuileries

These gardens *(see p38)* were first laid out as part of the old Tuileries Palace, adjacent to the Louvre, which was built for Catherine de Médici in 1564 but burned down in the Paris Commune of 1871. André Le Nôtre redesigned them into formal French gardens in 1664, and they were opened to the public. At the Louvre end is the Arc de Triomphe du Carrousel, erected by Napoleon in 1808. Here is also the entrance to the underground shopping centre, the Carrousel du Louvre. Nearby, sensuous nude sculptures by Aristide Maillol (1861–1944) adorn the ornamental pools and walkways. At the far end is the hexagonal pool, the Jeu de Paume gallery *(see p36)* and the Musée de l'Orangerie, which is currently closed for restoration. ⓢ *Map J2*

5 Musée des Arts Décoratifs

This extensive collection covers the decorative arts from the Middle Ages through to the 20th century. With more than 100 rooms, the many highlights include the Medieval and Renaissance rooms, the Art Nouveau and Art Deco rooms, and a wonderful doll collection. ⓢ *107 rue de Rivoli, 75001 • Map M2 • Closed for renovations until late 2006 • Admission charge*

Storming of the Tuileries

Looking at the Tuileries Gardens now, where children play and lovers stroll, it is hard to imagine the scenes that took place here on 20 June 1792. The palace and gardens were invaded by French citizens seeking to overthrow the monarchy. This was finally achieved on 10 August, when the Tuileries Palace was sacked and Louis XVI overthrown.

6 Musée de la Mode et du Textile

Paris is a world leader in fashion and this wonderful museum, set alongside the Musée des Arts Décoratifs in the Louvre's Pavillon de Marsan, features beautiful costumes and accessories dating from the 17th century to present-day *haute couture* designs. There are also several interesting collections on the history of textile design through the ages *(see p34)*. *107 rue de Rivoli, 75001 • Map M2 • Open 11am–6pm Tue–Fri, 10am–6pm Sat–Sun • Admission charge*

7 Palais-Royal

In the late 18th century thi[s] former royal palace and garden underwent extensive changes under the dukes of Orléans. Th[e] architect, Victor Louis, was commissioned to build 60 uniformly styled houses around three sides of the square and the adjacent theatre, which no[w] houses the Comédie Française, France's national theatre *(see p59)*. Today the arcades house specialist shops, galleries and restaurants, and the courtyard i[s] filled with striking modern works of art *(see p43)*. *Pl du Palais Roya[l] 75001 • Map L1 • Public access to gardens and arcades only*

8 Place Vendôme

Jules Hardouin-Mansart, th[e] architect of Versailles *(see p151* designed the façades of this elegant royal square for Louis XIV in 1698. The square was intended to house foreign embassies but bankers soon moved in and built lavish dwellings. It remains home to

Palais Royal courtyard

ɔéra de Paris Garnier façade

ɪwellers and financiers today. ɪe world-famous Ritz hotel was ɜtablished here at the turn of ɪe 20th century *(see p172)*. The ɜntral column, topped by a ɫatue of Napoleon, is a replica f the one destroyed by the ommune in 1871. ✎ *Map E3*

9 Opéra National de Paris Garnier

ɪesigned by Charles Garnier for ɪapoleon III, Paris' opulent opera ɔuse resembles a giant wedding ɜke. Begun in 1862, it took 13 ears to complete and comprises range of styles from Classical ɔ Baroque, incorporating stone ɪiezes and columns, statues, ɪulticoloured marbles and a reen, copper cupola. The ornate ɪterior has a Grand Staircase, ɪosaic domed ceiling over the ɪrand Foyer and an auditorium ɪith a ceiling by Marc Chagall. here's even an underground ɪke beneath the building – the ɪspiration for Gaston Leroux's *ʼhantom of the Opera (see p58)*. ✎ *Pl de l'Opéra, 75009 • Map E2 • Open 0am–5pm daily • Admission charge*

10 Place de la Madeleine

Surrounded by 52 Corinthian olumns, the huge Classical-tyle La Madeleine church *(see ɪ40)* commands this elegant quare. On the east side a olourful flower market is held uesday to Saturday. The square ɜ surrounded by some of the ɪost up-market *épiceries* (food tores) and speciality shops in he city *(see p98)*. ✎ *Map D3*

A Day in the Tuileries

Morning

Visiting the **Louvre** *(see pp8–11)* takes planning, and you should get there at least 15 minutes before opening time. Spend the whole morning in the museum, and pick up a map as you enter so that you can be sure to see the main highlights. Do bear in mind that two shorter visits are much easier than one. Have a morning coffee in the Café Marly in the museum.

From the Louvre, either visit the Carrousel du Louvre's underground shops or walk along **rue de Rivoli** towards **place de la Concorde** *(see p95)*. This end of the street is now filled with souvenir shops but avoid the overpriced cafés and turn right to rue Mondavi for a good lunch at Lescure, a little rustic bistro *(7 rue de Mondovi • 01 42 60 18 91)*.

Afternoon

After being indoors all morning at the Louvre, get some fresh air in the **Jardin des Tuileries** *(see p95)* then walk down to **place de la Madeleine** to spend the afternoon browsing and shopping in its many excellent food stores. This will definitely work up an appetite, so take tea in the restaurant of one of the best shops, **Hédiard** *(see p98)*.

If you are on a budget however, reverse this itinerary, as admission to the Louvre is much cheaper after 3pm, even on Wednesday when late-night opening means you could still spend more than six hours exploring the collection.

Left **Fauchon biscuits** Right **La Maison du Miel honey**

Top 10 Food Shops

1 Hédiard
Founded in 1854, this world food emporium features a cornucopia of fruits and vegetables, exotic spices and oils and a host of other gourmet delights. *21 pl de la Madeleine, 75008 • Map D3*

2 Fauchon
The king of Parisian *épiceries* (grocers). The mouth-watering window displays are works of art and tempt you inside for pastries, exotic fruits and some 20,000 other items. *26 & 28–30 pl de la Madeleine, 75008 • Map D3*

3 Au Verger de la Madeleine
Vintage wines are the speciality at this store. The owner will help you find a wine to match the year of any special occasion. *4 blvd Malesherbes, 75008 • Map D3*

4 Caviar Kaspia
The peak of indulgence. Caviars from around the world, plus smoked eels, salmon and other fishy fare. *17 pl de la Madeleine, 75008 • Map D3*

5 La Maison de la Truffe
France's finest black truffles are sold here during the winter truffle season, and you can get preserved truffles and other delicacies the rest of the year. *19 pl de la Madeleine, 75008 • Map D3*

6 La Maison du Miel
The "house of honey", family-owned since 1908, is the place to try speciality honeys, to spread on your toast or your body in the form of soaps and oils. *24 rue Vignon, 75009 • Map D3*

7 Boutique Maille
The retail outlet for one of France's finest mustard-makers. Try flavoured mustards such as Cognac or champagne. There are also lovely ceramic condiment jars. *6 pl de la Madeleine, 75008 • Map D3*

8 Marquise de Sévigné
A superb chocolate shop and salon, where you can have a tea, coffee or hot chocolate at the bar and sample the sweets too. *32 pl de la Madeleine, 75008 • Map D3*

9 Betjamen and Barton
This tea shop offers some 200 varieties from all over the world, as well as wacky teapots. *23 blvd Malesherbes, 75008 • Map D3*

10 Jabugo Iberico & Co
You'll be glazed with delight at this, Paris' head-quarters of ham (and it's Spanish ham, too). *21 rue Royale, 75008 • Map D3*

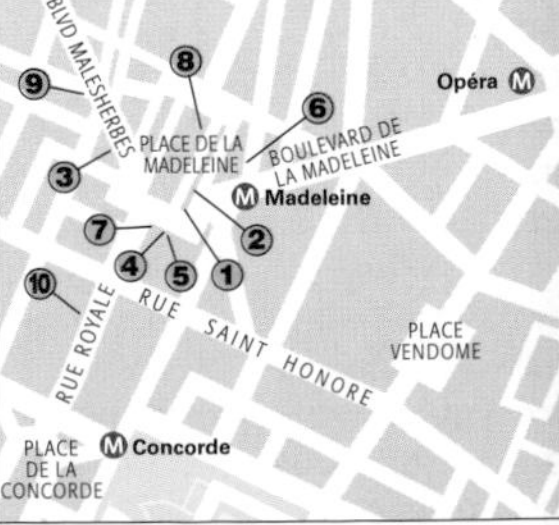

For more on shopping in Paris **See p169**

Left **Lucas Carton** Right **Chartier**

Price Categories

For a three-course meal for one with half a bottle of wine (or equivalent meal), taxes and extra charges	
€	under €30
€€	€30–€40
€€€	€40–€50
€€€€	€50–€60
€€€€€	over €60

Top 10 Places to Eat

1 Le Carré des Feuillants
Top chef Alain Dutournier prepares subtle dishes such as guinea-foul supreme. *14 rue de Castiglione, 75001 • Map E3 • 01 42 86 82 82 • Closed Sat, Sun, Aug • No disabled access • €€€€€*

2 L'Espadon
Everything you would expect from a Michelin-starred restaurant: great service, decor and cooking. *Hôtel Ritz, 15 pl Vendôme, 75001 • Map E3 • 01 43 16 30 80 • €€€€€*

3 Le Grand Véfour
This beautiful 18th-century restaurant with two Michelin stars is hard to beat. *17 rue de Beaujolais, 75001 • Map E3 • 01 42 96 56 27 • Closed Fri D, Sat–Sun, Aug • No disabled access • €€€€€*

4 Lucas Carton
Belle époque decor and three Michelin stars. Foie gras wrapped in cabbage is one speciality. *9 pl de la Madeleine, 75008 • Map D3 • 01 42 65 22 90 • Closed Mon L, Sat, Sun • No disabled access • €€€€€*

5 Mimosat
This pretty restaurant fully deserves its popularity: the emphasis is on keeping you happy and well fed. *44 rue d'Argout, 75002 • Map E3 • 01 40 28 15 75 • €*

6 Angl' Opera
Chef Gilles Choukroun's iconoclastic approach comes off a treat here in dishes such as fois-gras crème brulée. *39 avenue de l'Opéra, 75002 • Map E3 • 01 42 61 86 25 • Closed Sat, Sun, public hols • €€€*

7 Il Cortile
Italian specialities, such as veal with sage and strawberry soup, are served on a lovely patio in summer. *Hotel de Castille, 37 rue Cambon, 75001 • Map E3 • 01 44 58 45 67 • Closed Sat–Sun, Aug • €€€€*

8 Les Bacchantes
More than 40 wines by the glass and good food. *21 rue Caumartin, 75009 • Map E3 • 01 42 65 25 35 • Closed Sun, one week in Aug • No disabled access • €€*

9 La Fermette du Sud-Ouest
Hearty cooking, with pâtés, and sausages, all homemade. *31 rue Coquillière, 75001 • Map E3 • 01 42 36 73 55 • Closed Sun • No disabled access • €€*

10 Chartier
Waiters race back and forth serving simple soups, meat and fish dishes. No bookings *(see p65)*. *7 rue du Faubourg-Montmartre, 75009 • Map E3 • 01 47 70 86 29 • €*

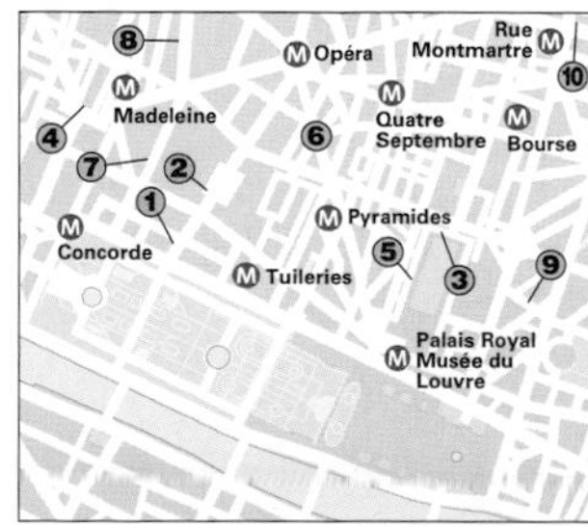

Note: Unless otherwise stated, all restaurants accept credit cards and serve vegetarian meals

BON
Bon
Bon
Bon

Left **Arc de Triomphe** Right **Palais de L'Elysée**

Champs-Elysées Quarter

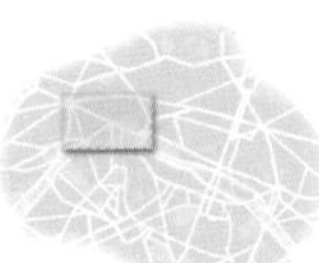

THE CHAMPS-ELYSEES IS UNDOUBTEDLY *the most famous street in Paris and the quarter which lies around it is brimming with wealth and power. It is home to the president of France, great* haute couture *fashion houses, embassies and consulates, and the five-star hotels and fine restaurants frequented by the French and foreign élite. The Champs-Elysées itself runs from the place de la Concorde to the place Charles de Gaulle, which is known as L'Etoile (the star) because of the 12 busy avenues that radiate out from it. It is the most stately stretch of the so-called Triumphal Way, built by Napoleon, where Parisians celebrate national events with parades or mourn at the funeral cortèges of the great and good.*

TOP 10 Sights

1. Arc de Triomphe
2. Avenue des Champs-Elysées
3. Grand Palais
4. Petit Palais
5. Pont Alexandre III
6. Palais de la Découverte
7. Rue du Faubourg-St-Honoré
8. Avenue Montaigne
9. Palais de l'Elysée
10. Musée Jacquemart-André

Home of La Marseillaise

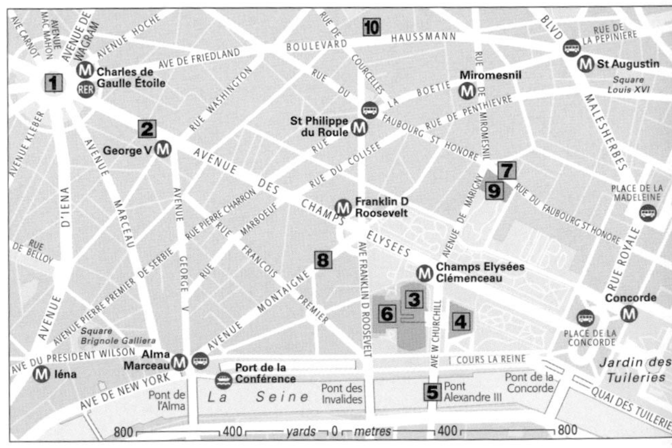

1 Arc de Triomphe

See pp24–5.

2 Avenue des Champs-Elysées

›ne of the most famous venues in the world came into eing when the royal gardener ndré Le Nôtre planted an arbour f trees beyond the border of ne Jardin des Tuileries in 1667 *see p95).* First called the Grand 'ours (Great Way), it was later enamed the Champs-Elysées Elysian Fields). In the mid-19th entury the avenue acquired edestrian paths, fountains, gas ghts and cafés, and became the ashionable place for socializing nd entertainment. Since the uneral of Napoleon in 1840, this vide thoroughfare has also been ne route for state processions, ictory parades and other city vents. The Rond Point des 'hamps-Elysées is the prettiest art, with chestnut trees and ower beds, but the upper end, ear the Arc de Triomphe, has adly lost its glamour with the nflux of fast-food chains and ourist services. Yet a walk along ne avenue is still an obligatory art of any visit to Paris. ✎ *Map C3*

3 Grand Palais

This immense *belle époque* exhibition hall was built for the Universal Exhibition in 1900. Its splendid glass roof, visible from all over Paris, is a landmark of the Champs-Elysées. The façade, the work of three architects, is an eclectic mix of Art Nouveau ironwork, Classical stone columns and a mosaic frieze, with bronze horses and chariots at the four corners of the roof. The Galleries du Grand Palais host temporary art exhibitions. ✎ *3 ave du Général-Eisenhower, 75008 • Map D3 • 01 44 13 17 30 • All areas except Palais de la Découverte (see p104) and temporary exhibitions area closed for renovation until 2006 • Admission charge*

4 Petit Palais

The "little palace" echoes its neighbour in style. Set around a semi-circular courtyard, with Ionic columns and a dome, the building now houses the Musée des Beaux-Arts de la Ville de Paris. This includes medieval and Renaissance art, 18th-century furniture and a collection of 19th-century paintings. ✎ *Ave Winston-Churchill, 75008 • Map D3 • Closed for renovation until 2006*

Avenue des Champs-Elysées

La Marseillaise

The stirring French national anthem was written in 1792 by a French army engineer named Claude Joseph Rouget de Lisle. He lived for a time in this district, at 15 rue du Faubourg-St-Honoré. The rousing song got its name from the troops from Marseille who were prominent in the storming of the Tuileries during the Revolution *(see p45)*.

5 Pont Alexandre III

Built for the 1900 Universal Exhibition to carry visitors over the Seine to the Grand and Petit Palais, this bridge is a superb example of the steel architecture and ornate Art Nouveau style popular at the time. Named after Alexander III of Russia, who laid the foundation stone, its decoration displays both Russian and French heraldry. The bridge creates a splendid thoroughfare from the Champs-Elysées to the Invalides *(see p48)*. *Map D3*

6 Palais de la Découverte

Set in a wing of the Grand Palais, this museum showcasing scientific discovery was created by a physicist for the World's Fa[ir] of 1937. The exhibits focus on invention and innovation in various scientific areas, from biology to chemistry, to astronomy and physics, including good interactive exhibits and demonstrations. The planetarium gives realistic views of space using fibre optics, while the Planète Terre (Planet Earth) rooms examine global warming and the sun. *Ave Franklin-D-Roosevelt, 75008 • Map D3 • Open 9:30am–6pm Tue–Sat, 10am–7pm Sun • Admission charge*

Pont Alexandre III

7 Rue du Faubourg-St-Honoré

Running roughly parallel to the Champs-Elysées, the Paris equivalent of Fifth Avenue, Bond Street or Rodeo Drive is this high street of international glamour. From Christian La Croix and Versace to Gucci and Hermès, the shopfronts read like a *Who's Who* of fashion. Even if the prices may be out of reach, window-shopping is fun. There are also elegant antiques and art galleries, such as La Cour aux Antiquaires at No. 54. *Map D3*

8 Avenue Montaigne

In the 19th century the Avenue Montaigne was a night-life hotspot. Parisians danced the night away at the Mabille Dance Hall until it closed in 1870 and Adolphe Sax made music with his newly invented saxophone in the Winter Garden. Today this chic avenue is a rival to the rue Faubourg-St-Honoré as the home to more *haute couture* houses such as Christian Dior and Valentino. There are also luxury hotels, top restaurants, popular cafés and two theatres, the Comédie des Champs-Elysées and the Théâtre des Champs-Elysées. *Map C3*

ue du Faubourg-St-Honoré

9 **Palais de l'Elysée**

Built in 1718, after the :evolution this elegant palace /as turned into a dance hall, then, ı the 19th century, became the esidence of Napoleon's sister :aroline Murat, followed by his /ife Empress Josephine. His ephew, Napoleon III, also lived ere while plotting his 1851 oup. Since 1873 it has been ome to the president of France. or this reason, it is worth noting ıat the palace guards don't like eople getting too close to the uilding, especially when there re VIPs inside *(see p42)*. *55 rue u Faubourg-St-Honoré, 75008 • Map D3 Closed to the public*

10 **Musée Jacquemart-André**

This fine display of art and urniture, once belonging to avid rt collectors Edouard André and is wife Nélie Jacquemart, is oused in a beautiful late 19th-entury mansion. It is best known or its Italian Renaissance art, ıcluding frescoes by Tiepolo and 'aolo Uccello's *St George and the)ragon* (c.1435). The reception ooms feature the art of the 18th-entury "Ecole française", with aintings by François Boucher nd Jean-Honoré Fragonard. 'lemish masters are in the brary. *158 blvd Haussmann, 75008 Map C2 • Open 10am–6pm Tue–Sun, 0am–9:30pm Mon • Admission charge*

A Day of Shopping

Morning

The **Champs-Elysées** *(see p103)* is an area for leisurely strolls. Begin by window-shopping along one side of the **avenue Montaigne**, where Prada, Nina Ricci, Dior and many more have their flagship stores – the area oozes money. Have a break in the Bar des Théâtres, where fashion names and the theatre crowd from the Comédie des Champs-Élysées across the street sometimes hang out *(6 ave Montaigne • 01 47 23 34 63)*.

Return up the other side of avenue Montaigne to the Champs-Elysées, for the stroll to the Arc de Triomphe. This is where the "real world" shops, at more affordable prices. Break for lunch at **Spoon, Food and Wine**, but get there early to get a table *(see p109)*.

Afternoon

Continuing up the Champs-Elysées, look past the car showrooms and fast food outlets to note the many interesting buildings which house them. Stay on the left-hand side to visit the main Paris tourist information centre *(see p163)*.

Take the underpass to the **Arc de Triomphe** *(see pp24–5)* and climb to the top for the views. Walk or take the metro to the **rue du Faubourg-St-Honoré**, where more designer shops can be found.

Take afternoon tea in Le Café Bleu, in the Lanvin boutique *(15 rue du Faubourg-St-Honoré • 01 44 71 32 32)*.

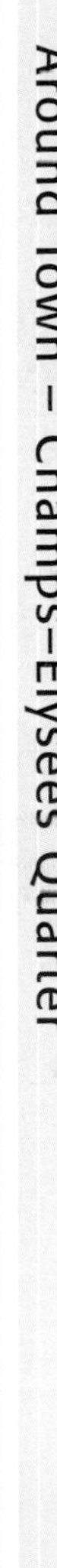

Left **Avenue de Marigny** Centre **Avenue Franklin-D.-Roosevelt** Right **25 Avenue Montaigne**

Top 10 International Connections

1 Avenue de Marigny

American author John Steinbeck lived here for five months in 1954 and described Parisians as "the luckiest people in the world". ✆ *Map C3*

2 8 Rue Artois

Here, in September 2001, the legendary Belgian mobster François Vanverbergh – godfather of the French Connection gang – fell victim to a drive-by assassin as he took his afternoon mineral water. ✆ *Map C2*

3 37 Avenue Montaigne

Having wowed Paris with her comeback performances, iconic German actress and singer Marlene Dietrich spent her reclusive final years in a luxury apartment here. ✆ *Map C3*

4 Pont de l'Alma

Diana, Princess of Wales, was killed in a tragic accident in the underpass here in 1997. Her unofficial monument nearby attracts thousands of visitors each year *(see p48)*. ✆ *Map C3*

5 31 Avenue George V, Hôtel George V

A roll-call of rockers – from the Rolling Stones and Jim Morrison to J-Lo and Ricky Martin – have made this their regular Paris home-from-home. ✆ *Map C3*

6 Hôtel d'Elysée-Palace

Mata Hari, the Dutch spy and exotic dancer, set up her lair in Room 113 before finally being arrested outside 25 Avenue Montaigne. ✆ *Map C3*

7 37 Avenue George V

Franklin D. Roosevelt and his new bride visited his aunt's apartment here in 1905. He was later commemorated in the name of a nearby avenue. ✆ *Map C3*

8 49 Avenue des Champs-Elysées

Author Charles Dickens may well have had "the best of times and the worst of times" when he resided here from 1855–6. Ten years earlier he had also lived at 38 Rue de Courcelles. ✆ *Map C3*

9 114 Avenue des Champs-Elysées

Brazilian aviation pioneer Alberto Santos-Dumont planned many of his amazing aeronautical feats – notably that of circling the Eiffel Tower in an airship in 1901 – from this address. ✆ *Map C2*

10 102 Boulevard Haussmann

Hypochondriac author Marcel Proust lived in a soundproofed room here, turning memories into a masterwork. ✆ *Map D2*

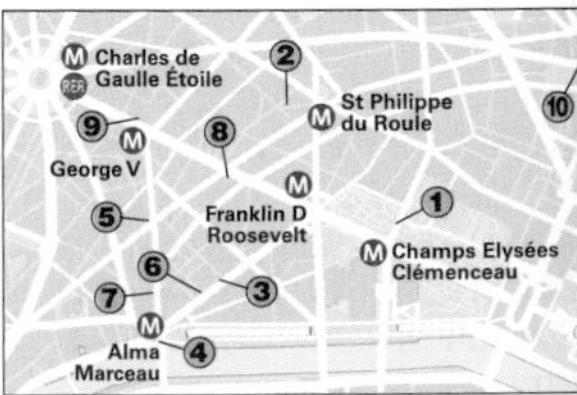

Left **Student riots, 1968** Right **Bastille Day celebrations**

Top 10 Events on the Champs-Elysées

1 1616
Paris's grand avenue was first laid out when Marie de Médici, wife of Henri IV, had a carriage route, the Cours-la-Reine (Queen's Way), constructed through the marshland along the Seine.

2 1667
Landscape gardener Le Nôtre lengthened the Jardin des Tuileries to meet the Cours-la-Reine, and opened up the view with a double row of chestnut trees, creating the Grand Cours.

3 1709
The avenue was re-named the Champs-Elysées (Elysian Fields). In Greek mythology, the Elysian Fields were the "place of ideal happiness", the abode of the blessed after death.

4 1724
The Duke of Antin, overseer of the royal gardens, extended the avenue to the heights of Chaillot, the present site of the Arc de Triomphe *(see pp24–5)*.

5 1772
The Marquis of Marigny extended the avenue again, this time all the way to the Neuilly bridge over the Seine, the stretch of street now called avenue Charles-de-Gaulle.

6 1774
Architect Jacques-Germain Soufflot lowered the hill of the Champs-Elysées by 5 m (16 ft) to reduce the steep gradient, therefore making an easier and safer passage for residents' horses and carriages.

7 1789
On 14 July every year Parisians celebrate Bastille Day to commemorate the start of the French Revolution *(see p45)*. There are marching bands, military processions and Air Force jets fly overhead. In late July, "les Champs" is also the final stretch for the Tour de France bicycle race *(see pp56)*.

8 26 August 1944
Parisians celebrated the liberation of the city from the German Nazi Occupation of World War II with triumphant processions and festivities.

9 30 May 1968
The infamous student demonstrations of May 1968, when riotous students protested against state authority, spilled over to massive gatherings. The demonstration here, at one of the city's main focal points, captured world news.

10 12 November 1970
The death of President Charles de Gaulle was an immense event in France, as he had been the single most dominant French political figure for 30 years. He was honoured by a silent march along the Champs-Elysées.

Left **Christian Dior bag** Centre **Chanel** Right **Boutique Prada**

Top 10 Designer Shops

1 Christian Dior

The grey and white decor, with silk bows on chairs, makes a chic backdrop for fashions from lingerie to evening wear. *30 ave Montaigne, 75008 • Map C3*

2 Chanel

Chanel classics, from the braided tweed jackets to two-toned shoes as well as Lagerfeld's more daring designs, are displayed in this branch of the main rue Cambon store. *42 ave Montaigne, 75008 • Map C3*

3 Nina Ricci Mode

After treating yourself to the gorgeous lingerie or jewellery, go round the corner on rue François 1er to The Ricci Club for menswear or the discount shop where last year's fashions are sold. *39 ave Montaigne, 75008 • Map C3*

4 Emanuel Ungaro

This shop carries the less expensive U line as well as Ungaro's main collection. *2 ave Montaigne, 75008 • Map C3*

5 Boutique Prada

The signature bags, shoes and leather goods are displayed on the ground floor, while the fashions are upstairs. *10 ave Montaigne, 75008 • Map C3*

6 Joseph

The largest of the four Joseph stores in Paris, selling knitwear, evening wear and accessories. *14 ave Montaigne, 75008 • Map C3*

7 Jil Sander

Minimal and modern store, just like the clothes. Sander's trouser suits, cashmere dresses and overcoats in neutral colours are displayed on four floors. *52 ave Montaigne, 75008 • Map C3*

8 Calvin Klein

The American designer's simple, classic women's wear and accessories are sold on the ground floor. Upstairs is the home collection in restful, neutral colours. *42 ave Montaigne, 75008 • Map C3*

9 Valentino

The Milanese designer's range of sophisticated clothes for the society set and casual fashions for the younger Miss Valentino label are displayed in this elegant marble bou-tique. *17–19 ave Montaigne, 75008 • Map C3*

10 MaxMara

The chic Italian womenswear label promotes a sleek, well-groomed look with beautiful fabrics. Suits, coats, evening wear and the trendier Sportmax line are sold here. *31 ave Montaigne, 75008 • Map C3*

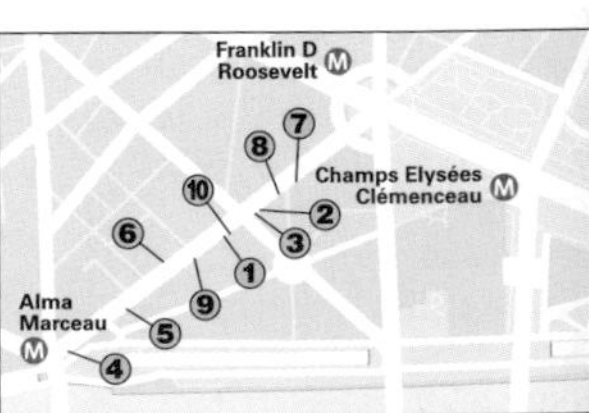

For more on shopping in Paris **See p169**

Price Categories

For a three-course meal for one with half a bottle of wine (or equivalent meal), taxes and extra charges	
€	under €30
€€	€30–€40
€€€	€40–€50
€€€€	€50–€60
€€€€€	over €60

Above **Au Plaza Athénée**

10 Places to Eat

1 Alain Ducasse au Plaza Athénée

Superchef Alain Ducasse's flagship restaurant. Langoustines with caviar is just one mouth-watering bite *(see p64)*. ✆ *Hôtel Plaza Athénée, 25 ave Montaigne, 75008 • Map C3 • 01 53 67 65 00 • Closed Mon–Wed L, Sat– Sun • €€€€€*

2 Guy Savoy

Another star chef, Guy Savoy is experimental with his food. Sea bass grilled in sweet spices is an example *(see p64)*. ✆ *18 rue Troyon, 75017 • Map C3 • 01 43 80 40 61 • Closed Sat L, Sun–Mon • €€€€€*

3 Les Ambassadeurs

Jacket and tie are required here. *Filet mignon* of suckling pig is one speciality. ✆ *Hôtel de Crillon, 10 pl de la Concorde, 75008 • Map D3 • 01 44 71 16 16 • €€€€€*

4 Spoon, Food and Wine

Alain Ducasse's affordable offshoot. Choose your main dish and a sauce to go with it. ✆ *14 rue de Marignan, 75008 • Map C3 • 01 40 76 34 44 • Closed Sat–Sun, Aug • €€€€€*

5 Taillevent

One of the city's best dining experiences. Langoustine parcels with shellfish pastry is a signature dish *(see p64)*. ✆ *15 rue Lamennais, 75008 • Map C3 • 01 44 95 15 01 • Closed Sat–Sun, Aug • €€€€€*

6 Gagnaire

Chef Pierre Gagnaire is legendary for blending flavours, such as lamb cutlets with truffles. ✆ *6 rue Balzac, 75008 • Map C3 • 01 58 36 12 50 • Closed Sat–Sun, mid-Jul–mid-Aug • No disabled access • €€€€€*

7 Ledoyen

Jacket and tie here. Do try scallops marinated in citrus fruits with caviar. ✆ *1 ave Dutuit, 75008 • Map C3 • 01 53 05 10 01 • Closed Sat–Sun, Mon L, Aug • No disabled access • €€€€€*

8 Le Boeuf sur le Toit

Fabulous Art Deco setting, and *andouillettes* (sausages) are one speciality. ✆ *34 rue du Colisée, 75008 • Map C3 • 01 53 93 65 55 • No disabled access • €€€*

9 Le Fouquet's

Until recently refusing entry to women, this established restaurant specializes in French classics. ✆ *99 ave des Champs-Élysées, 75008 • Map C3 • 01 47 23 70 60 • No disabled access • €€€€€*

10 Ladurée

A tea room loved by locals and visitors alike. Regulars swoon over the hot chocolate and the delicious patisseries. ✆ *75 ave des Champs-Élysées, 75008 • Map C3 • 01 40 75 08 75 • €*

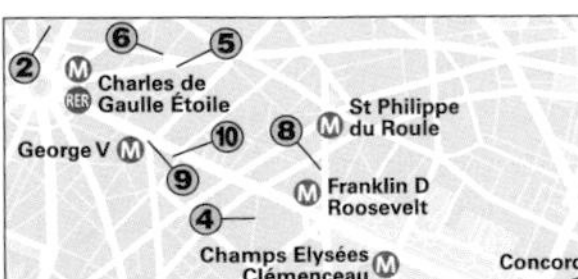

Note: *Unless otherwise stated, all restaurants accept credit cards and serve vegetarian meals*

Left **Dôme church** Centre **Eiffel Tower** Right **Champs-de-Mars**

Invalides and Eiffel Tower Quarters

TWO OF PARIS'S MOST BEAUTIFUL LANDMARKS, *the golden-domed Hôtel des Invalides and the world-famous Eiffel Tower, are found in these quarters. Large parts of the area were created in the 19th century, when there was still room to construct wide avenues and grassy esplanades leading to the monumental buildings. To the east of the Invalides are numerous stately mansions now converted into embassies, and the French parliament.*

TOP 10 Sights

1. Hôtel des Invalides
2. Eiffel Tower
3. Les Egouts
4. Musée de l'Armée
5. Musée Rodin
6. Champ-de-Mars
7. Rue Cler
8. Ecole Militaire
9. UNESCO
10. Assemblée Nationale

The Thinker, Musée Rodin

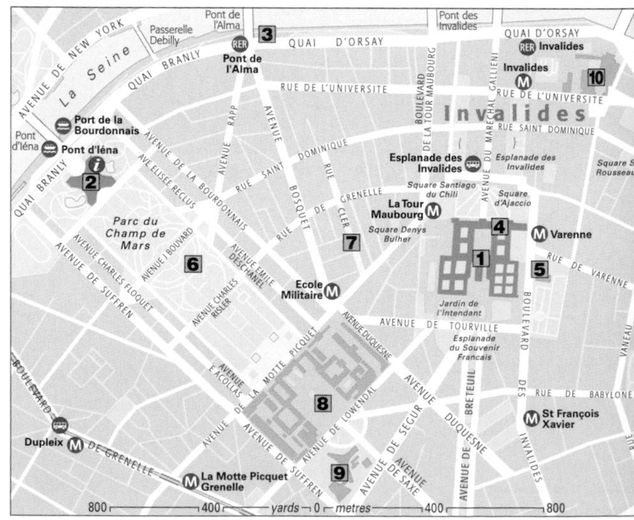

1 Hôtel des Invalides

See pp32–3.

2 Eiffel Tower

See pp16–17.

3 Les Egouts

In a city of glamour and grandeur, the sewers *(egouts)* of Paris are an incongruously popular attraction. They date from the Second Empire (1851–70), when Baron Haussmann was transforming the city *(see p45)*, and the sewers which helped to sanitize and ventilate Paris are considered one of his finest achievements. Most of the work was done by an engineer named Belgrand. The 2,100-km (1,300-mile) network covers the area from Les Halles to La Villette – if laid end-to-end the sewers would stretch from Paris to Istanbul. An hour-long tour includes a walk through some of the tunnels, where you'll see water pipes, telephone lines and various cables, while the museum tells the story of the city's water and sewers, from their beginnings to the present day. There is an audio-visual show and a room devoted to sanitation techniques of the future. *Face au 93, quai d'Orsay, 75007 • Map C4 • Open May–Sep: 11am–5pm Sat–Wed; Oct–Apr: 11am–4pm Sat–Wed • Admission charge*

General Foch, Musée de l'Armée

4 Musée de l'Armée

The Army Museum contains one of the largest and most comprehensive collections of arms, armour and displays on military history in the world. There are weapons ranging from prehistoric times to the end of World War II, representing countries around the world. Housed in the Hôtel des Invalides, the vast galleries occupy the old refectories in two wings on either side of the courtyard. Many rooms on the east side contain Napoleonic memorabilia. On the west side, the Oriental gallery features arms from Asia and the Middle East *(see p114)*. *Hôtel des Invalides, 75007 • Map C4 • Open 10am–6pm daily (until 5pm in winter) • Closed 1st Mon of month, public hols • Admission charge*

5 Musée Rodin

An impressive collection of works by the sculptor and artist Auguste Rodin (1840–1917) is housed in a splendid 18th-century mansion, the Hôtel Biron *(see p116)*, where he spent the last nine years of his life. The rooms display his works roughly chronologically, including his sketches and watercolours. Masterpieces such as *The Kiss* and *Eve* are displayed in the airy rotundas. One room is devoted to works by his talented model and muse, Camille Claudel, and Rodin's personal collection of paintings by Van Gogh, Monet and other masters hang on the walls. The museum's other highlight is the gardens, the

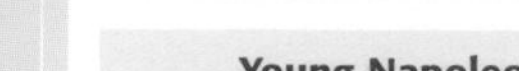

Young Napoleon

The most famous alumnus of the Ecole Militaire was Napoleon Bonaparte, who was admitted as a cadet, aged 15, in 1784 and deemed "fit to be an excellent sailor". He graduated as a lieutenant in the artillery, and his passing-out report stated that "he could go far if the circumstances are right". The rest, as they say, is history.

third-largest private gardens in Paris, where famous works such as *The Thinker* and *The Gates of Hell* stand among the lime trees and rose bushes. *77 rue de Varenne, 75007 • Map C4 • Open 9:30am–5:45pm Tue–Sun (until 4:45pm in winter) • Admission charge*

6 Champ-de-Mars

These long formal gardens, stretching between the Eiffel Tower and the Ecole Militaire, were laid out in 1765–7 as a parade ground for the military school, but the "Field of Mars" was opened to the public in 1780. Three years later crowds gathered for the launch of the first hydrogen-filled balloon. On 14 July 1790, a sullen Louis XVI watched as 300,000 citizens celebrated the first anniversary of the storming of the Bastille, an event which is commemorated here annually *(see p86)*. Five world exhibitions were held here between 1867 and 1937; the 1889 event gave Paris the Eiffel Tower. *Map C4*

7 Rue Cler

The cobblestone pedestrianized road that stretches south of rue de Grenelle to avenue de La Motte-Picquet is the most exclusive street market in Paris. Here greengrocers, fishmongers butchers, and wine merchants sell top-quality produce to the well-heeled residents of the area every Tuesday to Saturday. Tear yourself away from the mouth-watering displays of cheese and pastries, however, to feast your eyes on the Art Nouveau buildings at Nos. 33 and 151. *Map C4*

8 Ecole Militaire

At the urging of his mistress Madame Pompadour, Louis XV approved the building of the Royal Military Academy in 1751. Although its purpose was to educate the sons of impoverished officers, a grand edifice was designed by Jacques-Ange

UNESCO headquarters

Gabriel, architect of the place de la Concorde *(see p95)* and the Petit Trianon at Versailles, and completed in 1773. The central pavilion with its quadrangular dome and Corinthian pillars is a splendid example of the French Classical style. *1 pl Joffre, 75007 • Map C5 • Open to the public by special permission only (apply in writing)*

9 UNESCO

The headquarters of the United Nations Educational, Scientific and Cultural Organization (UNESCO) were built in 1958 by an international team of architects from France (Zehrfuss), Italy (Nervi) and the United States (Breuer). Their Y-shaped building of concrete and glass may be unremarkable, but inside the showcase of 20th-century art by renowned international artists is well worth a visit. There is a huge mural by Picasso, ceramics by Joan Miró, and a 2nd-century mosaic from El Djem in Tunisia. Outside is a giant mobile by Alexander Calder and a peaceful Japanese garden. *7 pl de Fontenoy, 75007 • Map C5 • Open 9am–6pm Mon–Fri • Free*

10 Assemblée Nationale

Built for the daughter of Louis XIV in 1722, the Palais Bourbon has housed the lower house of the French parliament since 1827. The Council of the Five Hundred met here during the Revolution, and it was the headquarters of the German Occupation during World War II. Napoleon added the Classical riverfront façade in 1806 to complement La Madeleine *(see p97)* across the river. *33 Quai d'Orsay, 75007 • Map D4 • Open for tours only (identity papers compulsory) 10am, 2pm, 3pm Sat, except public hols and when parliament is in session • Free*

A Day Around the Invalides Quarter

Morning

Try to get to the **Eiffel Tower** *(see pp16–17)* early, to beat the worst of the queues, and take the lift to the top to admire the spectacular panorama. After descending, take tea at the Pâtisserie de la Tour Eiffel *(21 ave de la Bourdonnais)*, whose terrace has a great view.

Walk towards the Seine and turn right before crossing the river. A stroll along the riverbank is always pleasant if the weather is kind *(see pp48–9)*, and before long you will reach the Place de la Résistance. Cross the road, staying on the south side of the river, where a ticket booth masks one of the city's great secrets, **Les Egouts** *(see p111)*. Don't worry about taking a torch or wearing special footwear – the area visited is well-lit and dry underfoot.

If the sewers don't put you off your food, lunch at the excellent fish restaurant, **Le Divellec** *(see p117)*.

Afternoon

After lunch, walk to the **Hôtel des Invalides** *(see pp32–3)* to see Napoleon's Tomb and the beautiful domed church, and then visit the almost adjacent **Musée Rodin** *(see p111)* and stroll in its gardens.

On leaving the museum turn right along rue de Varenne, until it meets rue du Bac. Here, at No. 109, is Le Bac à Glaces, a combined tearoom and ice cream parlour – perfect for a refreshing rest.

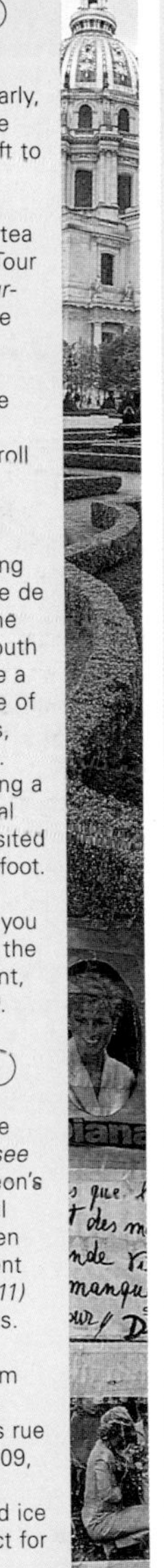

Left **The Abdication of Napoleon (1814), François Pigeot** Right **Suit of armour**

TOP 10 Musée de l'Armée Exhibits

1 Napoleon's Room

This careful reconstruction in the Salle de la Restoration shows the room where the emperor died in 1821. Other Napoleonic items and paintings are on display.

2 Napoleonic Mementoes

In the Salle Boulogne, on the second floor, are a number of items which belonged to Napoleon. The most interesting is the emperor's coat, displayed with his hat, sword and medals.

3 Portrait of Napoleon

Napoleon's coronation in Notre-Dame in 1804 is commemorated in this portrait by the French artist Jean Ingres (1780–1867), then only at the start of his career.

4 Napoleon's Flag of Farewell

The highlight of the collection of banners is the flag Napoleon flew at Fontainebleau in 1814, in acknowledgement of his abdication.

5 The World Wars

Two rooms on the second floor are devoted to World War I and World War II. Documents, uniforms, maps, photographs and other memorabilia bring the conflicts of both wars to life, often to disturbing effect.

6 The Banners

A fine collection of banners, from 1619 to 1945, is on display in the Salle Turenne.

7 The Armour

A powerful and impressive collection of more than 40 complete suits of armour, as well as horse armour.

8 Galerie des Plans Reliefs

On the fourth floor is a collection of relief models of French towns which show the development of fortifications from the 17th century onwards.

9 Salle Préhistorique

A fascinating collection of ancient weaponry, from primitive clubs up to the 9th-century reign of Charlemagne.

10 Salle Orientale

This collection of arms and armour reflects the military styles of different nations.

Verdun (1917), Felix Vallotton, Two World Wars

For the Musée de l'Armée **See p111**

t View from the Eiffel Tower Right **Pont Alexandre III and Hôtel des Invalides**

10 Views

1 Top of the Eiffel Tower
There is nowhere in Paris to atch the view from the top of e tower, so hope for good eather. With the Seine spark- g below and lush greenery, it the highlight of any visit *(see* *p16–17)*. *Map B4*

2 Pont d'Iéna
There is no bad approach to e Eiffel Tower, but the best is om the Trocadéro direction, alking straight to the tower cross the Pont d'Iéna. *Map B4*

3 Base of the Eiffel Tower
Everybody wants to race to e top, but don't neglect the ew from the ground. Looking rectly up at the magnificent tructure makes one appreciate e feat of engineering all the ore *(see pp16–17)*. *Map B4*

4 Eiffel Tower at Night
Such was the success of aris's breathtaking Millennium reworks display, centred on the ower, that the city authorities ontinued the idea with an hourly ghting display that makes the vhole edifice twinkle. *Map B4*

5 Saxe-Breteuil Market
This old street market in venue de Saxe is a little off the sual tourist track, but the view of the Eiffel Tower above the fruit nd vegetable stalls is totally Parisian and will especially ppeal to photographers. *Map D5 • Tue & Thu am*

6 Pont Alexandre III
The view of the Hôtel des Invalides, seen from the banks of the Seine, is stunning *(see p48)*. *Map D4*

7 Musée Rodin Gardens
The view of the golden Dôme church, through the branches of the trees that line these gardens, is awe-inspiring. *Map D5*

8 Napoleon's Tomb
You cannot help but be impressed as you enter the Dôme Church and stand gazing down at the massive tomb which holds the body of the diminutive emperor *(see pp32–3)*. *Map D4*

9 Pont de la Concorde
The Egyptian obelisk at the centre of place de la Concorde *(see p95)* is at its most impressive from the bridge. *Map D4*

10 Hôtel des Invalides
Walk into the centre of the courtyard to fully appreciate this magnificent set of buildings *(see pp32–3)*. *Map D4*

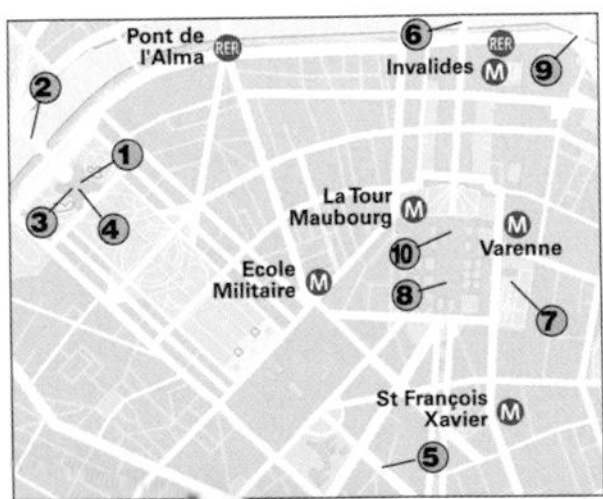

Left **Hôtel de Biron** Right **Hôtel de Villeroy**

Top 10 Mansions

1 Hôtel Biron

Built in 1730, this elegant mansion was home to the duc de Biron. From 1904 it was transformed into state-owned artists' studios and among its residents was Auguste Rodin (1840–1917), who agreed to donate his works to the nation in return for his flat and studio space. After the sculptor's death the house became the Musée Rodin *(see p111)*.

2 Hôtel de Villeroy

Built in 1724 for Charlotte Desmarnes, an actress at the Comédie-Française, it is now the Ministry of Agriculture. *78–80 rue de Varenne, 75007 • Map D4*

3 Hôtel Matignon

One of the most beautiful mansions in the area, built in 1721, is now the official residence of the French prime minister. *57 rue de Varenne, 75007 • Map D4*

4 Hôtel de Boisgelin

Built in 1732 by Jean Sylvain Cartaud, this mansion has housed the Italian Embassy since 1938. *47 rue de Varenne, 75007 • Map D4*

5 Hôtel de Gallifet

This attractive mansion was built in 1739 with Classical styling. It is now the Italian Institute. *50 rue de Varenne, 75007 • Map D4*

6 Hôtel d'Estrées

Three floors of pilasters feature on this 1713 mansion. Formerly the Russian embassy, Czar Nicolas II lived here in 189 It is now a government building *79 rue de Grenelle, 75007 • Map B5*

7 Hôtel d'Avaray

Dating from 1728, this man sion belonged to the Avaray fami for nearly 200 years. It became the Dutch Embassy in 1920. *8 rue de Grenelle, 75007 • Map B5*

8 Hôtel de Brienne

This mansion houses the Ministry of Defence, so no photo are allowed. Napoleon's mother lived here from 1806–17. *14–16 rue St Dominique, 75007 • Map D4*

9 Hôtel de Noirmoutiers

Built in 1722, this was once the army staff headquarters and World War I commander Marsha Foch died here in 1929. It now houses ministerial offices. *138-140 rue de Grenelle, 75007 • Map B5*

10 Hôtel de Monaco de Sagan

Now the Polish Embassy, this 1784 mansion has fountains framing the entrance. It served as the British Embassy until 1825. *57 rue St-Dominique, 75007 • Map D4*

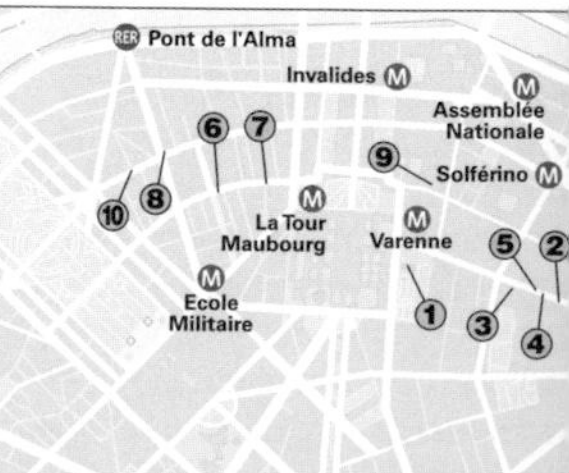

For more historic buildings in Paris **See pp42–3**

ove **Vin Sur Vin**

Price Categories

For a three-course meal for one with half a bottle of wine (or equivalent meal), taxes and extra charges		
	€	under €30
	€€	€30–€40
	€€€	€40–€50
	€€€€	€50–€60
	€€€€€	over €60

10 Places to Eat

1 Le Jules Verne

Book a window table for the onderful views. The menus roam c world – try sea bass *tagine*. *2nd Level, Eiffel Tower, Champ-de-ırs, 75007 • Map B4 • 01 45 55 61 44 No disabled access • €€€€€*

2 Le Divellec

One of the best fish restau-nts in town, including oysters, lmon and sea bass. *107 rue de Iniversité, 75007 • Map C4 • 01 45 51 96 • Closed Sat–Sun, Aug • €€€€€*

3 L'Arpège

Among the best restaurants the city. Chef Alain Passard oduces exquisite food such as 12-flavoured tomato dessert. *84 rue de Varenne, 75007 • Map D4 01 45 51 47 33 • Closed Sun–Mon • No sabled access • €€€€€*

4 Le Violin d'Ingres

Chef Christian Constant is nother shining star. Sea bass in mond pastry appeals. *135 rue -Dominique, 75007 • Map C4 • 01 45 5 15 05 • Closed Sun–Mon • €€€€€*

5 Vin Sur Vin

Owner Patrice Vidal knows is wine. Club-like atmosphere; ooking essential. *20 rue de Iontessuy, 75007 • Map C4 • 01 47 05 4 20 • Closed Sat L, Sun–Mon L • €€€€*

6 Altitude 95

Cost ranges widely between ınch and dinner in this family-iendly restaurant. Good views: y to reserve a window table. *1st Level, Eiffel Tower, Champ de Mars, 75007 • Map B4 • 01 45 55 20 04 • No disabled access • €€€*

7 Chez Remi

Classic bistro with dishes such as *escargots* (snails). *79 rue St-Dominique, 75007 • Map C4 • 01 47 05 49 75 • Closed Sun • No disabled access • €€*

8 Au Petit Tonneau

Steak with Roquefort, veal poached in port and tarte Tatin in this great bistro. *20 rue Surcouf, 75007 • Map C4 • 01 47 05 09 01 • €€*

9 L'Auberge du Champ de Mars

Inexpensive choice near the Eiffel Tower, with a cosy feel. Dishes are simple but reliable. *18 rue de l'Exposition, 75007 • Map B4 • 01 45 51 78 08 • Closed Sat L, Sun–Mon L, Aug • No disabled access • €€*

10 Café Max

Lively atmosphere and hearty food in this quirky bistro. *7 ave de la Motte-Picquet, 75007 • Map C4 • 01 47 05 57 66 • Closed Sun, Mon L • No credit cards • €*

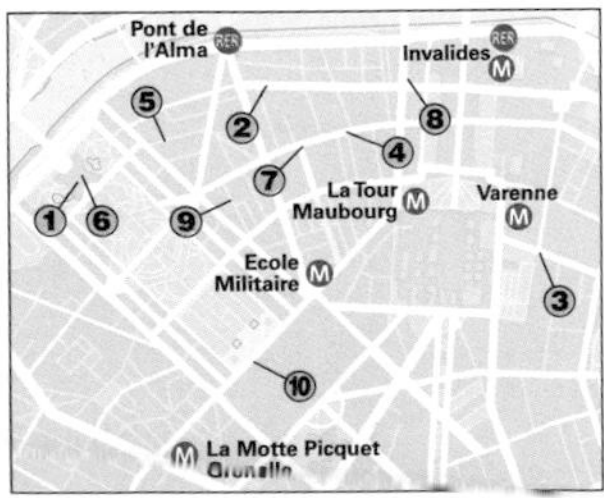

Note: *Unless otherwise stated, all restaurants accept credit cards and serve vegetarian meals*

Left **Musée d'Orsay** Centre **Panthéon** Right **St-Sulpice**

St-Germain, Latin and Luxembourg Quarters

THIS AREA OF THE LEFT BANK IS *possibly the most stimulating in Paris. St-Germain-des-Prés, centred around the city's oldest church, is a synony[m] for Paris's café society, made famous by the writers and intellectuals who held court here in the first half of the 20th century. Although it's more touristy today, a stroll around the back streets reveals lovely old houses plastered with plaques noting famous residents. The Latin Quarter takes its name from the Latin spoken by students of the Sorbonne until the Revolution. The scholastic centre of Paris for more than 700 years, it continues to buzz with student bookshops, cafés and jazz clubs. It was also the site of a Roman settlement and remains from that era can be seen in the Musée du Moyen-Age. The area's western boundary is the bustling boulevard Saint-Michel and to the south is the tranquil greenery of the Luxembourg Quarter.*

Jardin du Luxembour[g]

Top 10 Sights

1. Musée d'Orsay
2. Panthéon
3. Jardin du Luxembourg
4. St-Sulpice
5. La Sorbonne
6. Musée du Moyen-Age
7. Boulevard St-Germain
8. Boulevard St-Michel
9. Quai de la Tournelle
10. Musée Maillol

1 Musée d'Orsay

See pp12–15.

2 Panthéon

See pp28–9.

3 Jardin du Luxembourg

This 25-ha (60-acre) park is a wathe of green paradise on the ery urban Left Bank. The formal ardens are set around the 'alais du Luxembourg *(see p43)*, vith broad terraces circling the entral octagonal pool. A ighlight of the garden is the ɪeautiful Fontaine de Médicis *see p30)*. Many of the garden's tatues were erected during the 9th century, among them the nonument to the painter Eugène)elacroix and the statue of Ste ;eneviève, patron saint of Paris. 'here is also a children's play-ɪround, open-air café, a band-tand, tennis courts, a puppet heatre and even a bee-keeping ;chool *(see p38)*. ✆ *Map L6*

4 St-Sulpice

Begun in 1646, this enor-nous church unsurprisingly took 34 years to build. Its Classical açade by the Florentine architect Giovanni Servandoni features a wo-tiered colonnade and two ncongruously matched towers. Notice the two holy water fonts by the front door, made from nuge shells given to François I by he Venetian Republic. *Jacob*

Fontaine de Médicis, Jardin du Luxembourg

Clock, La Sorbonne

Wrestling with the Angel and other splendid murals by Delacroix (1798–1863) are in the chapel to the right of the main door. ✆ *Pl St-Sulpice, 75006 • Map L5 • Open 7:30am–7:30pm daily • Free*

5 La Sorbonne

Paris's world-famous univer-sity *(see p43)* was founded in 1253 and was originally intended as a theology college for poor students but it soon became the country's main centre for theo-logical studies. It was named after Robert de Sorbon, confes-sor to Louis IX. Philosophers Thomas Aquinas (c.1226–74) and Roger Bacon (1214–92) taught here; Italian poet Dante (1265–1321), St Ignatius Loyola (1491–1556), the founder of the Jesuits, and church reformer John Calvin (1509–64) are among its impressive list of alumni. Its tradition for conservatism led to its closure during the Revolution (it was re-opened by Napoleon in 1806) and to the student riots of 1968 *(see p45)*. ✆ *47 rue des Ecoles, 75005 • Map M5 • 01 40 46 21 11 • Group tours only, 9:30am & 2:30pm Mon–Fri (advance booking) • Admission charge*

Jazz on the Left Bank

Jazz has been played in Paris, especially on the Left Bank, since the 1920s. Numbers of black musicians moved here from the US as they found France less racially prejudiced, and Paris became a second home for many jazz musicians such as Sidney Bechet *(see p63)*. The city has never lost its love of jazz, nor jazz its love for the city.

6 Musée National du Moyen-Age

This impressive mansion, one of the oldest in Paris, was built by the abbots of Cluny in 1330 and now houses a magnificent collection of medieval art, from Gallo-Roman antiquity to the 15th century. It adjoins the ruins of 2nd-century Roman baths *(thermes)* with their huge vaulted *frigidarium* (cold bath). Nearby are the 21 carved stone heads of the kings of Judea from Notre-Dame, decapitated during the Revolution. The museum's highlight is the exquisite *Lady and the Unicorn* tapestry series, representing the five senses *(see p34)*. *6 pl Paul-Painlevé, 75005 • Map N5 • Open 9:15am–5:45pm Wed–Mon • Admission charge*

7 Boulevard St-Germain

This famous Left Bank boulevard runs for more than 3 km (2 miles) anchored by the bridges of the Seine at either end. At its heart is the church of St-Germain-des-Prés, established in 542, although the present church dates from the 11th century. Beyond the famous cafés, Flore and Les Deux Magots *(see p125)*, the boulevard runs west past art galleries, bookshops and designer boutiques to the Pont de la Concorde. To the east, it cuts across the Latin Quarter through the pleasant street market in the place Maubert, to join the Pont de Sully which connects to the Ile St-Louis *(see p69)*. *Map J3*

8 Boulevard St-Michel

The main drag of the Latin Quarter was created in the late 1860s as part of Baron Haussmann's city-wide makeover *(see p45)*, and named after a chapel that once stood near its northern end. It's now lined with a lively mix of cafés, clothes shops and cheap restaurants. Branching off to the east are rues de la Harpe and de la Huchette, which date back to medieval times. The

Boulevard St-Germain

Quai de la Tournelle

latter is an enclave of the city's Greek community, with many *souvlaki* stands and Greek restaurants. In the place St-Michel is a huge bronze fountain that depicts St Michael killing a dragon. ✎ *Map M4*

9 Quai de la Tournelle

From this riverbank, just before the Pont de l'Archevêché there are lovely views across to Notre-Dame. The main attraction of this and the adjacent Quai de Montebello, however, are the dark-green stalls of the *bouquinistes (see p122)*. The Pont de la Tournelle also offers splendid views up and down the Seine. ✎ *Map P5*

10 Musée Maillol

Dina Vierny, who modelled for the artist Aristide Maillol (1861–1944) from the ages of 15 to 25, went on to set up this foundation dedicated largely to his works. Set in an 18th-century mansion, it features his sculpture, paintings, drawings, engravings and terracotta works. A wonderful collection of works by other 20th-century artists, many of whom worked in Paris, including Picasso, Matisse, Dufy, Duchamp, Kandinsky and Poliakoff, is also on show.
✎ *59–61 rue de Grenelle, 75007 • Map J4 • Open 11am–6pm Wed–Mon • Admission charge*

A Day on the Left Bank

Morning

This area is as much about atmosphere as sightseeing, so take time to soak up some of that Left Bank feeling. Begin on the **Quai de la Tournelle**, strolling by the booksellers here and on the adjacent Quai de Montebello. As well as admiring the views of Notre-Dame, you might find an unusual souvenir.

From here head south down any street away from the river and you will meet the busy **Boulevard St-Germain**. Turn right in the direction of two famous cafés, the **Flore** and the **Deux Magots**, and stop for a break in either of them *(see p125)* amid the locals talking the morning away.

Cut your way south to the rue de Grenelle and the **Musée Maillol**, a delightful lesser-known museum. Then enjoy lunch at L'Oeillade *(10 rue St-Simon • 01 42 22 01 60)*, a bistro full of Gallic atmosphere.

Afternoon

The later you reach the **Musée d'Orsay** *(see pp12–15)* the less crowded it will be. Spend an hour or two exploring the collection. By far the most popular displays are the Impressionists on the upper level.

After admiring the art, enjoy tea and a cake at **Christian Constant**, one of the best chocolate-makers in Paris *(see p123)*. It's the ideal place for a special present or just a piece of self-indulgence for yourself.

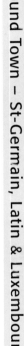

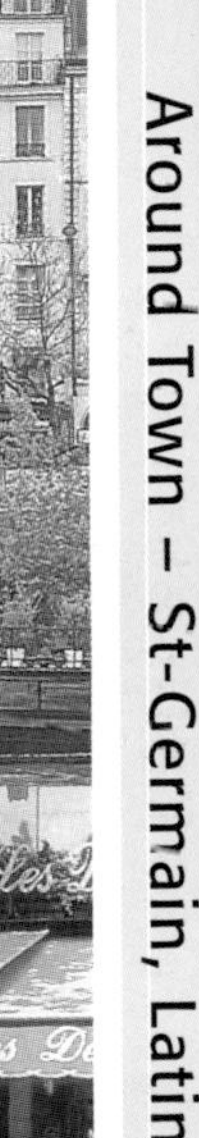

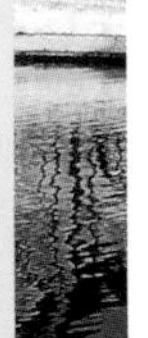

Left **Bouquinistes** Right **The Village Voice**

TOP 10 Booksellers

1 Shakespeare and Co
Bibliophiles spend hours in the rambling rooms of Paris's renowned English-language bookshop. There are books in other languages too and poetry readings most Mondays at 8pm. *37 rue de la Bûcherie, 75005 • Map N5*

2 Bouquinistes
The green stalls of the booksellers *(bouquinistes)* on the quays of the Left Bank are a Parisian landmark. Pore over the posters, old postcards, magazines, hardbacks, paperbacks, comics and sheet music. *Map N5*

3 Musée d'Orsay Bookshop
As well as its wonderful collections, the museum has a bewilderingly large and busy art bookshop *(see pp12–15)*.

4 La Hune
Landmark literary hangout. Good collections on art, photography and literature. *170 blvd St-Germain, 75006 • Map K4*

5 Librairie Gourmande
Foodies should head for this haven, where cookbooks in several languages are available, along with posters and other food-related items. *4 rue Dante, 75005 • Map L4*

6 Album
Specialist in comic books, which are big business in France, from Tintin to erotica. *8 rue Dante, 75005 • Map L4*

7 Librairie Présence Africaine
Specialist on books on Africa, as the name suggests. Good information point, too, if you want to eat African food or hear African music. *25 bis rue des Écoles, 75005 • Map P6*

8 Tea & Tattered Pages
An excellent venue for a relaxed afternoon's browsing among thousands of English-language books; you can have a cuppa, too. *24 rue Mayet, 75006 • Map P6*

9 Librairie Maeght
Specialist in books on art adjoining the Maeght art gallery, with a good collection of posters postcards and other items. *42 rue du Bac, 75007 • Map N5*

10 The Village Voice
North American bias, but works by writers from around the world as well. *6 rue Princesse 75006 • Map L4*

For more on shopping in Paris **See p169**

Left **Paris *chocolatier*** Right **Patisserie**

10 Specialist Food Shops

1 Christian Constant
Christian Constant is arguably the best *chocolatier* in Paris and spends much of his time globetrotting in search of ever-more exotic flavours. *37 rue d'Assas, 75006 • Map K5*

2 Cacao et Chocolat
Rue de Buci and the streets around are home to some smart food shops, not least this *chocolatier* specializing in unusual flavours such as chilli pepper. *29 rue de Buci, 75006 • Map L4*

3 Jean-Paul Hévin
Another of the distinguished *chocolatiers* of Paris, where it is regarded as an honoured profession. Also sells pastries and cakes. *3 rue Vavin, 75006 • Map E6*

4 Carton
For a sweet treat this patisserie provides great cakes, sharp lemon tarts, mouth-watering chocolate and strawberry creations. *6 rue de Buci, 75006 • Map P5*

5 Jadis et Gourmande
Specialists in fun chocolates, in the shape of the Eiffel Tower and other Parisian landmarks. *88 blvd du Port-Royal, 75005 • Map F6*

6 Debauve & Gallais
This shop dates from 1800 when chocolate was sold for medicinal purposes. The window displays would tempt anyone. *30 rue des Sts-Pères, 75007 • Map K4*

7 Pierre Hermé Paris
Here are some of the city's very finest cakes and pastries, including what is said to be the best chocolate gâteau in Paris. *72 rue Bonaparte, 75006 • Map L5*

8 RystDupeyron
A specialist wine shop, selling French wines, spirits and liqueurs and champagne. *79 rue du Bac, 75007 • Map N5*

9 Caves Miard
This splendid wine shop is based in a late 19th-century dairy, worth seeing in its own right. The owners will happily advise you on good bargains and vintage wines. *9 rue des Quatre Vents, 75006 • Map L4*

10 Gérard Mulot
Here you'll find some of the finest pastries in Paris, along with some truly miraculous macaroons. *76 rue de Seine, 75006 • Map L4*

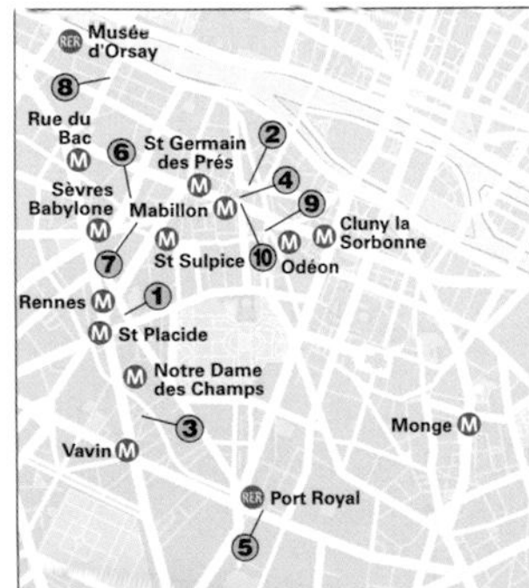

Left **Le Bar Dix** Right **Café Mabillon**

TOP 10 Late-Night Bars

1 Le Bar Dix
Incredibly lively bar, aimed at people who like to talk, smoke and drink. Happy hour 6–9pm. ⊗ *10 rue de l'Odéon, 75006 • Map L5*

2 La Gueuze
One for the beer lovers, with a dozen or so ales available on tap, including many Belgian brews, and another 100–150 by the bottle. Belgian-biased food as well. ⊗ *19 rue Soufflot, 75005 • Map M6*

3 El Palenque
This lively Argentinian place brings Latin America to the Latin Quarter. As well as drinks, also serves great meat dishes. ⊗ *5 rue de la Montagne-Ste-Geneviève, 75005 • Map N4*

4 Café Mabillon
The place that never closes. Hang out on the terrace with a few drinks and watch the world go by. Happy hour 7–9pm. ⊗ *164 blvd St-Germain, 75006 • Map N4*

5 L'Assignat
Pleasant, bright family-run bar, full of regulars propping up the bar with a beer or a glass of wine. ⊗ *7 rue Guénégaud, 75006 • Map L3*

6 Mezzanine
The place to see and be seen. The beer, wine and cocktails are not expensive given the buzz and the wonderful location. ⊗ *Alcazar, 62 rue Mazarine, 75006 • Map L3*

7 Petit Gaulois
Just the place to wind dow after a night of *joie de vivre.* ⊗ *184 rue St-Jacques, 75005 • Map N5*

8 Le Bob Cool
On a quiet backstreet, this shabby-chic bar plays host to thirsty local nighthawks as well as trendier partygoers on late-night cocktails. ⊗ *15 rue des Grands Augustins, 75006 • Map M4*

9 Coolin
An Irish bar that doesn't try too hard. Appeals to drinkers, talkers and listeners of all ages, who like their draught Guinness with a blarney chaser. ⊗ *15 rue Clément, 75006 • Map L4*

10 Le Mauzac
Friendly wine bar with a terrace for the summer, and there's a bistro too if you want t eat. Plenty of inexpensive wines by the glass, carafe or bottle. ⊗ *rue de l'Abbé de l'Épée, 75005 • Map F6*

For more cafés and bars in Paris **See pp52–3**

ɜft **Café de Flore** Right **Shakespeare and Co**

10 Literary Haunts

1 La Palette

This café has been patroned by the likes of Henry Miller pollinaire and Jacques Prévert. *43 rue de Seine, 75006 • Map L4 Open 8am–1am Mon–Sat*

2 Les Deux Magots

This was home to the literary nd artistic élite of Paris as well s a regular haunt of Surrealists uch as François Mauriac *(see 52). ✆ 6 pl St-Germain-des-Prés, 5006 • Map K4 • Open 8am–2am daily*

3 Café de Flore

Guillaume Apollinaire founded is literary magazine, *Les Soirées 'e Paris*, here in 1912 *(see p52).) 172 blvd St-Germain, 75006 • Map K4 Open 7am–1:30am daily*

4 Le Procope

The oldest café in Paris, this vas a meeting place for writers uch as Voltaire, Hugo, Balzac and ola. *✆ 13 rue de l' Ancienne-Comédie, 5006 • Map L4 • Open noon–1am daily*

5 Brasserie Lipp

Ernest Hemingway pays omage to this café in *A Moveble Feast*. It was also visited by symbolist novelist André Gide. *) 151 blvd St-Germain, 75006 • Map L4 Open 12:15pm–1am daily*

6 Hotel Pont Royal

Henry Miller drank here at he time of writing his *Tropic of Capricorn* and *Tropic of Cancer*. *) 5–7 rue de Montalembert, 7500/ Map J3 • Open 8am–midnight daily*

7 Shakespeare and Co

This bookshop has played host to many celebrated writers including Hemingway, Fitzgerald, Gide and Stein *(see p122)*.

8 Le Sélect

F Scott Fitzgerald and Truman Capote were among many American writers who drank in this café-restaurant. *✆ 99 blvd du Montparnasse, 75014 • Map E6 • Open 8am–2pm Mon–Fri, 8am–3:30pm Sat, Sun*

9 La Coupole

Opened in 1927, this former coal depot was transformed by artists into a lavish, Art Deco brasserie. It attracted such luminaries as Louis Aragon and François Sagan *(see p157)*.

10 Le Petit St-Benoît

Camus, de Beauvoir and James Joyce are among the many writers who once took their daily coffee here. *✆ 4 rue St Benoît, 75006 • Map K3 • Open noon–midnight daily*

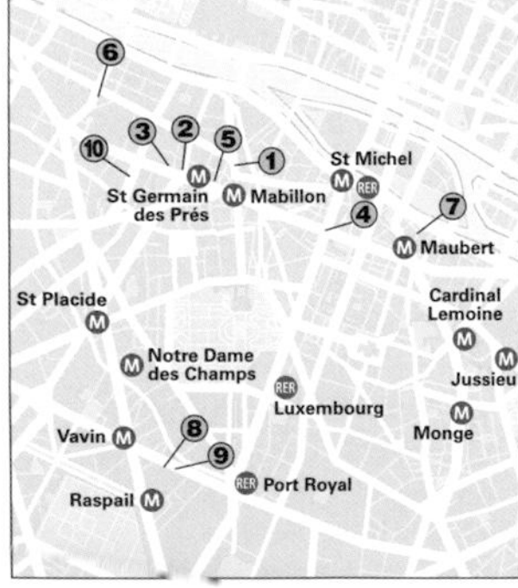

For more on writers in Paris **See p47**

Left **Rue de Buci market** Right **Parisian patisserie**

TOP 10 Picnic Providers

1 Rue de Buci Market
If your tastes are refined, head for this chic daily market where you'll find the very best regional produce, wine, pastries and everything else for the perfect picnic *(see p54)*. *Map L4*

2 Poilâne
Get the best bread for your picnic, made from the recipe of the late king of bread-makers, Lionel Poilâne. *8 rue du Cherche-Midi, 75006 • Map J5*

3 Carmes Market
A small market specializing in organic produce every Tuesday, Thursday and Saturday morning. A good place to pick up olives, cheese, tomatoes and fruit. *Pl Maubert, 75006 • Map N5*

4 Charcuterie Alsacienne
If you like strong tastes, try this shop which features produce from Alsace, including cold meats, cheese and wines. *8 rue de Buci, 75006 • Map L4*

5 Charcuterie Charles
This award-winning charcuterie shouldn't be missed. Flavoured sausages and *boudin blanc* are specialities, and the cold meats are ideal for picnics. *10 rue Dauphine, 75006 • Map M4*

6 Marché Biologique
This organic Sunday morning market brings together some of the best farmers in the region. *Blvd Raspail, 75006 • Map J4*

7 Bon
Wonderful patisserie, with an especially good line in small fruit tarts, such as lemon and strawberry. Fat-free cheesecake for the health-conscious, too. *159 rue St-Jacques, 75005 • Map N5*

8 Barthélémy
Cheese fans should not miss this shop, selling cheese from all over France, with a chance to taste before you buy. *51 rue de Grenelle, 75007 • Map J4*

9 Charcuterie Coesnon
Produce from Normandy is sold at this charcuterie – pâtés, ham, cheese and cider too. *30 rue Dauphine, 75006 • Map M4*

10 Kayser
If you don't want to make up your own picnic then try a ready-made sandwich from this bakery. Mouthwatering combinations include goat's cheese with pear. *14 rue Monge, 75005 • Map P6*

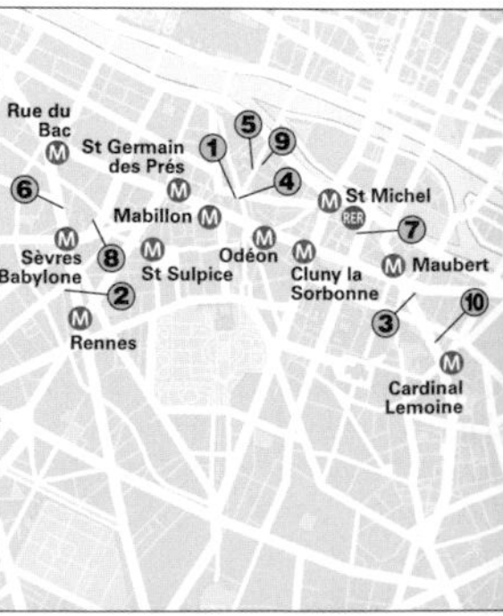

For more shops and markets in Paris **See pp54–5**

Price Categories

For a three-course meal for one with half a bottle of wine (or equivalent meal), taxes and extra charges	
€	under €30
€€	€30–€40
€€€	€40–€50
€€€€	€50–€60
€€€€€	over €60

eft **Alcazar** Right **Relais Louis XIII**

10 Places to Eat

1 L'Épi Dupin

The dishes are sublime, such as cod with saffron leeks *(see p64)*. *11 rue Dupin, 75006 • Map J5 • 01 42 22 64 56 • Closed Sat–Sun, Mon L, Aug • €€*

2 La Tour d'Argent

This two-star Michelin restaurant has views of Notre-Dame and duck *à l'orange* as the speciality. *15 quai de la Tournelle, 75005 • Map P5 • 01 43 54 23 31 • Closed Mon • No disabled access • €€€€€*

3 Les Bookinistes

This bistro, owned by Guy Savoy, offers creative cooking at affordable prices. *53 quai des Grands-Augustins, 75006 • Map M4 • 01 43 25 45 94 • Closed Sat L, Sun • No disabled access • €€€*

4 Alcazar

A stylish brasserie with a mix of French, Asian and British food. *62 rue Mazarine, 75006 • Map L3 • 01 53 10 19 99 • €€€*

5 Lapérouse

Classic French cuisine including fabulous desserts. *51 quai des Grands-Augustins, 75006 • Map M4 • 01 43 26 68 04 • Closed Sat L, Sun, Aug • €€€€€*

6 Le Relais Louis XIII

A 16th-century house with classic cooking. Try lobster ravioli. *8 rue des Grand-Augustins, 75006 • Map M4 • 01 43 26 75 96 • Closed Sun–Mon, Aug • No disabled access • €€€€€*

7 La Bastide Odéon

A taste of Provence, with rich and hearty dishes. Try risotto with scallops. *7 rue Corneille, 75006 • Map L5 • 01 43 26 03 65 • Closed Sun–Mon, Aug • No disabled access • €€€*

8 Aux Charpentiers

Archetypal Left Bank bistro. *Blanquette* (veal in cream) is one house speciality. *10 rue Mabillon, 75006 • Map L4 • 01 43 26 30 05 • €€*

9 Le Coupe-Chou

Romantic candlelit atmosphere. *Boeuf bourguignon* is one of the typical traditional dishes. *9 rue de Lanneau, 75005 • Map N6 • 01 46 33 68 69 • Closed Sun L • No disabled access • €€*

10 Au Moulin à Vent

One of the best bistros in Paris, with frogs' legs, *escargots* and Châteaubriand on the menu. *20 rue des Fossés-St-Bernard, 75005 • Map P6 • 01 43 54 99 37 • Closed Sat L, Sun–Mon, Aug • €€€*

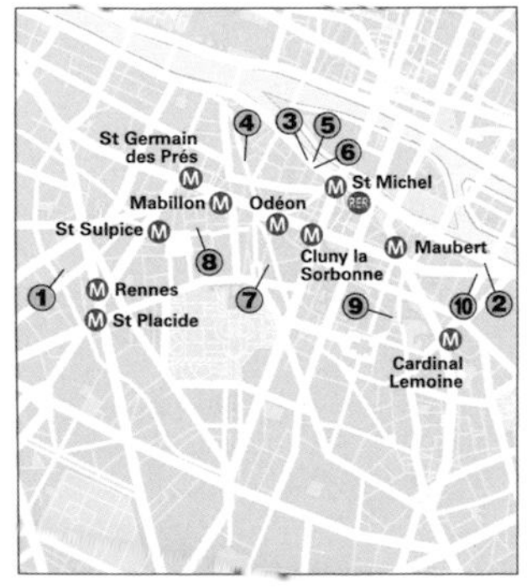

***Note:** Unless otherwise stated, all restaurants accept credit cards and serve vegetarian meals*

Left **Jardin des Plantes** Centre **Natural History Museum** Right **Institut du Monde Arabe exhibit**

Jardin des Plantes Quarte

TRADITIONALLY ONE OF THE MOST PEACEFUL *areas of Paris, the medicinal herb gardens which give the quarter its name were established here in 1626. It retained a rural atmosphere until the 19th century, when the city's population expanded and the surrounding streets were built up. Near the gardens is the Arènes de Lutèce, a well-preserved Roman amphitheatre. The rue Mouffetard, winding down the hill from the bustling place de la Contrescarpe, dates from medieval times and has one of the best markets in the city. The area is also home to a sizeable Muslim community, focused on the Institut du Monde Arabe cultural centre and the Paris Mosque. In contrast to the striking Islamic architecture are the grey slab 1960s buildings of the Paris university Jussieu campus.*

Riding a stone hippopotamus at the Ménagerie

TOP 10 Sights

1. Jardin des Plantes
2. Muséum National d'Histoire Naturelle
3. Ménagerie
4. Institut du Monde Arabe
5. Mosquée de Paris
6. Rue Mouffetard
7. Arènes de Lutèce
8. Place de la Contrescarpe
9. St-Médard
10. Manufacture des Gobelins

1 Jardin des Plantes

The 17th-century royal medicinal herb garden was planted by Jean Hérouard and Guy de la Brosse, physicians to Louis XIII. Opened to the public in 1640, it flourished under the curatorship of Comte de Buffon in the mid-18th century. It contains some 10,000 species, including the first Cedar of Lebanon planted in a French tropical greenhouse, and Alpine, rose and winter gardens *(see p132)*. *57 rue Cuvier, 75005 • Map G6 • 01 40 79 30 00 • Open times vary, so phone to check*

2 Muséum National d'Histoire Naturelle

Separate pavilions in the Jardin des Plantes house exhibits on anatomy, fossils, geology, mineralogy and insects. The Grande Galerie de l'Evolution *(see p60)* is a magnificent collection of stuffed African mammals, a giant whale skeleton and an endangered species exhibit *(see p34)*. *57 rue Cuvier, 75005 • Map G6 • Pavilions: open 10am–5pm Wed–Mon; Evolution Gallery: open 10am–6pm (10pm Thu) Wed–Mon • Admission charge*

3 Ménagerie

The country's oldest public zoo was founded during the Revolution to house the four surviving animals from the royal menagerie at Versailles. Other animals were donated from circuses and abroad, but during the Siege of Paris in 1870–71 *(see p45)* the unfortunate creatures were eaten by hungry citizens. A favourite with children *(see p60)*, the zoo has since been rehoused with monkeys, large cats, birds and reptiles. *Jardin des Plantes, 75005 • Map G6 • Open 9am–6pm daily • Admission charge*

Minaret, Mosquée de Paris

4 Institut du Monde Arabe

This institute was founded in 1980 to promote cultural relations between France and the Arab world. The stunning building (1987) designed by architect Jean Nouvel features a southern wall of 1,600 photo-sensitive metal screens that open and close like a camera aperture to regulate light entering the building. The design is based on the latticed wooden screens of Islamic architecture. Inside are seven floors of Islamic artworks, from 9th-century ceramics to contemporary art, and ancient astrolabes used by astronomers of old. *1 rue des Fossés-St-Bernard, 75005 • Map G5 • Open 10am– 6pm Tue–Sun • Admission charge*

5 Mosquée de Paris

Built in 1922–6, the mosque complex is the spiritual centre for Parisian Muslims *(see p41)*. The beautiful Hispano-Moorish decoration, particularly the grand patio, was inspired by the Alhambra in Spain. The minaret soars nearly 33 m (100 ft). There is also an Islamic school, tea room and Turkish baths, open to men and women on separate days. *2 bis pl du Puits-de-l'Ermité, 75005 • Map G6 • Tours: 9am–noon, 2– 6pm Sat–Thu; closed Islamic hols • Admission charge*

French North Africa

France has always had close connections with North Africa, though not always harmonious. Its annexation of Algeria in 1834 led to the long and bloody Algerian war of Liberation (1954–62). Relations with Tunisia, which it governed from 1883 to 1956, and Morocco, also granted independence in 1956, were better. Many North Africans now live in Paris.

6 Rue Mouffetard

Although the rue Mouffetard is famous today for its lively street market held every Tuesday to Sunday *(see p54)*, it has an equally colourful past. In Roman times this was the main road from Paris to Rome. Some say its name comes from the French word *mouffette* (skunk), as a reference to the odorous River Bièvre (now covered over) where waste was dumped by tanners and weavers from the nearby Gobelins tapestry factory. Though no longer poor or Bohemian, the neighbourhood still has lots of character, with its 17th-century mansard roofs, old-fashioned painted shop signs and affordable restaurants. In the market you can buy everything from Auvergne sausage to horse meat to ripe cheeses. *Map F6*

7 Arènes de Lutèce

The remains of the 2nd-century Roman amphitheatre from the settlement of Lutetia *(see p44)* lay buried for centuries and were only discovered in 1869 during construction of the rue Monge. The novelist Victor Hugo, concerned with the preservation of his city's historic buildings, including Notre-Dame *(see p21)*, led the campaign for the restoration. The original arena would have had 35 tiers and could seat 15,000 spectators for theatrical performances and gladiator fights. *49 rue Monge, 75005 • Map G6 • Open 9am–10pm daily (summer); 8am–5pm daily (winter) • Free*

8 Place de la Contrescarpe

This bustling square has a village community feel, with busy cafés and restaurants and groups of students from the nearby university hanging out here after dark. In medieval

Arènes de Lutèce

·imes it lay outside the city valls, a remnant of which still ·tands. Notice the memorial ·laque above the butcher's at No. 1, which marks the site of he old Pine Cone Club, a café vhere François Rabelais and ·ther writers gathered in the 6th century. *Map F5*

9 St-Médard

The church at the bottom of ue Mouffetard dates back to the ·th century, when it was a parish ·hurch dedicated to St Médard, ·ounsellor to the Merovingian ·ings. The present church, ·ompleted in 1655, is a mixture ·f Flamboyant Gothic and ·enaissance styles. Among the ·ine paintings inside is the 17th-·entury *St Joseph Walking with he Christ Child* by Francisco de ·urbarán. The churchyard was he scene of hysterical fits in the 8th century, when a cult of "*convulsionnaires*" sought miracle cures at the grave of a ·ansenist deacon. *141 rue ·Mouffetard, 75005 • Map G6 • Open ·am–noon, 2:30–7pm Tue–Sat, 9am–noon ·un • Free*

10 Manufacture des Gobelins

This internationally renowned apestry factory was originally a ·yeing workshop, founded by he Gobelin brothers in the mid-·5th century. In 1662, Louis ·IV's minister Colbert set up a ·oyal factory here and gathered he greatest craftsmen of the ·ay to make furnishings for the ·alace at Versailles *(see p151)*. ·ainters such as Charles Le Brun ·irected 250 Flemish weavers in ·reating the tapestries. You can ·ee the traditional weaving ·rocess on a guided tour. *42 ·ve des Gobelins, 75013 • Metro Gobelins • Tours: 2pm Tue–Thu (arrive 30 minutes ·rior) • Admission charge*

A Day in the Gardens

Morning

If it's a fine morning get an early start and enjoy a stroll in the **Jardin des Plantes** *(see p129)* before the city gets truly busy. The **Muséum National d'Histoire Naturelle** *(see p129)* doesn't open until 10am, but the garden is close enough to **rue Mouffetard** to enable you to enjoy the fabulous market, which gets going by about 8am. Don't forget to take your eyes off the stalls every now and then to see the splendid old buildings on this medieval street. Then return to the museum and its Evolution Gallery.

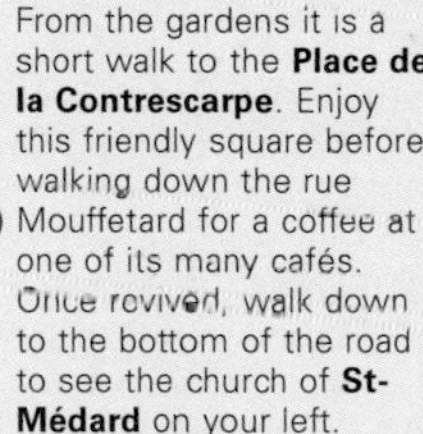

From the gardens it is a short walk to the **Place de la Contrescarpe**. Enjoy this friendly square before walking down the rue Mouffetard for a coffee at one of its many cafés. Once revived, walk down to the bottom of the road to see the church of **St-Médard** on your left.

Turn left along rue Monge to the **Arènes de Lutèce**. A couple of minutes away is a little bistro, Le Buisson Ardent *(25 rue Jussieu • 01 43 54 93 02)*, which is ideal for lunch.

Afternoon

You can spend part of the afternoon at the **Institut du Monde Arabe** *(see p129)*, exploring its beautiful Islamic artworks, before walking down to admire the Moorish architecture of the **Mosquée de Paris** *(see p129)*. Finish the day with a mint tea at the Café de la Mosquée *(pl du Puits-de-l'Ermité • 01 45 35 97 33)*.

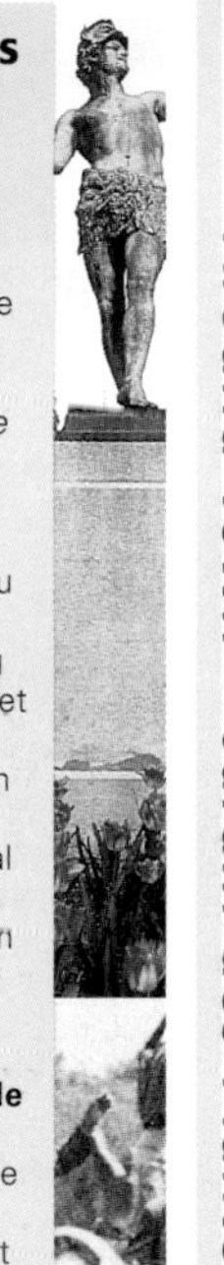

Left **Flowers in the Jardin des Plantes** Right **Dinosaur model**

Top 10 Jardin des Plantes Sights

1 Dinosaur Tree
One of the trees in the Botanical Gardens is the *Ginkgo biloba*, which is 150 years old but the species is known to have existed in exactly the same form in the days of the dinosaurs, 125 million years ago.

2 Cedar of Lebanon
This magnificent tree was planted in 1734, and came from London's Botanic Gardens in Kew, although a story grew up that its seed was brought here all the way from Syria in the hat of a scientist.

3 Rose Garden
Although only a fairly recent addition, being planted in 1990, the beautiful *roserie* has some 170 species of roses and 180 rose bushes on display. Spectacular when they are in full bloom in spring and summer.

4 Alpine Gardens
One of the stars of the Botanical Gardens, with more than 3,000 plants from the world's many diverse Alpine regions. There are samples from Corsica to the Caucasus, from Morocco to the Himalaya.

5 Sophora of Japan
Sent to Paris under the label "unknown seeds from China" by a Jesuit naturalist living in the Orient, this tree was planted in 1747, first flowered in 1777, and still flowers today.

6 Iris Garden
An unusual feature is this designated garden which brings together more than 400 differen varieties of iris.

7 Dinosaur Model
Outside the Palaeontology Gallery, which is crammed with precious dinosaur skeletons, is a huge dinosaur model, specificall designed for children to climb or *(see p60)*.

8 Nile Crocodile
The crocodile in the Reptile House now has a better home than he once did. This creature was found in a Paris hotel room, left behind as an unwanted pet! It has yet to reach its full size of 5 m (16.5 ft).

9 Microzoo
Within the zoological gardens, founded in 1794 and the oldest public zoo in the world, is a Microzoo, where microscopes are available to get a close-up look at the bugs of the world, both wild and household varieties.

10 Young Animal House
One of the zoo's most popular features for children is this house where young creatures, which for one reason or another cannot be looked afte by their natural parents, are raised. Once they reach adulthood they are returned to their natural habitat.

For the Jardin des Plantes **See p129**

Above **L'Avant-Goût**

Price Categories		
For a three-course meal for one with half a bottle of wine (or equivalent meal), taxes and extra charges	€	under €30
	€€	€30–€40
	€€€	€40–€50
	€€€€	€50–€60
	€€€€€	over €60

Top 10 Places to Eat

1 Le Terroir
The kind of place locals like to keep secret, because it's good, inexpensive and has a great atmosphere. The charcuterie and beef are recommended. *11 blvd Arago, 75013 • Metro Gobelins • 01 47 07 36 99 • Closed Sat–Sun, Easter, Aug • €€€*

2 L'Aimant du Sud
A new bistro with dishes such as tuna steak with toasted almonds. Pavement terrace in the summer. *40 blvd Arago, 75013 • Metro Gobelins • 01 47 07 33 57 • Closed Sun, Aug • €*

3 Au Petit Marguery
One for game lovers, with *lièvre à la royale* (hare in a wine sauce) the house speciality. Boisterous atmosphere. *9 blvd de Port-Royal, 75013 • Map F6 • 01 43 31 58 59 • Closed Sun–Mon, Aug • No vegetarian options • €€€€*

4 Anacréon
Bistro with an inventive and inexpensive changing menu. *53 blvd St-Marcel, 75013 • Metro Gobelins • 01 43 31 71 18 • Closed Sun–Mon, Aug • €€*

5 La Truffière
A 17th-century building, a wood fire and welcoming staff all make for a great little bistro. The menu features truffles. *4 rue Blainville, 75005 • Map F6 • 01 46 33 29 82 • Closed Mon • €€€€*

6 Les Vieux Métiers de France
Medieval decor, but there's nothing old about dishes such as squid in parsley and lemon. *13 blvd Auguste-Blanqui, 75013 • Metro Gobelins • 01 45 88 90 03 • €€*

7 Chez Paul
Not the best place for vegetarians, with *pot au feu*, tongue and other meaty delights, but there is also fish. *22 rue de la Butte-aux-Cailles, 75013 • Metro Place d'Italie • 01 45 89 22 11 • €€€*

8 Au Coco de Mer
Spicy Seychelles cuisine, such as octopus curry or smoked swordfish. Vegetarians should book ahead. *34 blvd St-Marcel, 75005 • Map G6 • 01 47 07 06 64 • Closed Sun, Mon L, Aug • €€*

9 L'Avant-Goût
Small and noisy with tables crammed together. Try the pork *pot au feu* or apple flan, if available, though the menu changes daily. *26 rue Bobillot, 75013 • Metro Place d'Italie • 01 53 80 24 00 • Closed Sat–Mon • €€*

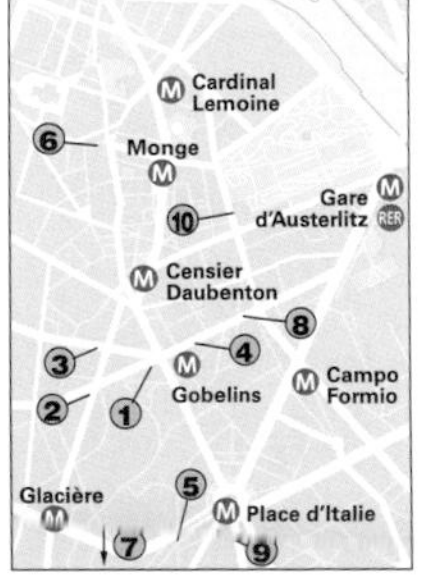

10 Le Zyriab
Fabulous views of Notre-Dame in this North African restaurant. Try the chicken *tagine*. *Institut du Monde Arabe, 1 rue des Fossés-St-Bernard, 75005 • Map G6 • 01 53 10 10 20 • Closed Sun D, Mon • €€€*

***Note:** Unless otherwise stated, all restaurants accept credit cards and serve vegetarian meals*

Left **Jardins du Trocadéro** Centre **Debussy's grave, Cimetière de Passy** Right **Café Carette**

Chaillot Quarter

CHAILLOT WAS A SEPARATE VILLAGE *until the 19th century, when it was swallowed up by the growing city and bestowed with wide avenues and lavish mansions during the Second Empire building* spree (see p45). *Its centrepiece is the glorious Palais de Chaillot which stands on top of the small Chaillot hill, its wide white-stone wings embracing the Trocadéro Gardens and its terrace gazing across the Seine to the Eiffel Tower. Behind the palace is the place du Trocadéro, laid out in 1858 and originally called the place du Roi-de-Rome (King of Rome), the title of Napoleon's son. The square is ringed with smart cafés, overlooking the central equestrian statue of World War I hero Marshal Ferdinand Foch. Many of the elegant mansions in this area now house embassies, and there are numerous fine dining spots. To the west are the exclusive residential neighbourhoods of the Parisian* bourgeoisie *(middle-classes).*

Top 10 Sights

1. Palais de Chaillot
2. Musée de l'Homme
3. Musée de la Marine
4. Musée du Patrimoine et de l'Architecture
5. Musée d'Art Moderne de la Ville de Paris
6. Cimetière de Passy
7. Jardins du Trocadéro
8. Musée du Vin
9. Maison de Balzac
10. Musée National des Arts Asiatiques Guimet

Exhibit at the Musée du Vin

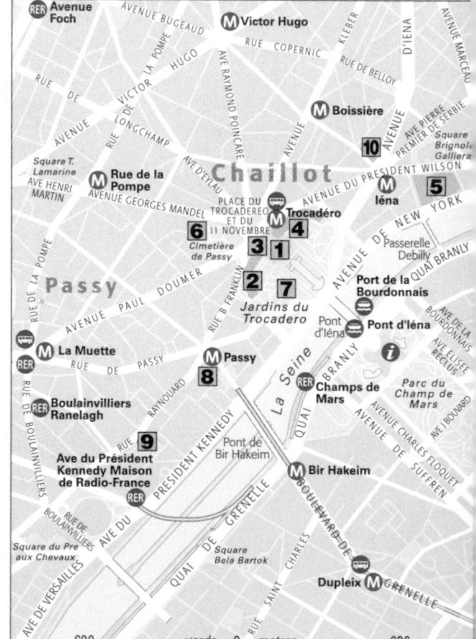

1 Palais de Chaillot

The fall of his empire cuppered Napoleon's plans for n opulent palace for his son on haillot hill, but the site was ter used for the original Trocaéro palace, built for the Univeral Exhibition of 1878. It was eplaced by the present Neolassical building with its huge olonnaded wings for another xhibition in 1937. The two avilions house three museums see below). The broad terrace etween the wings is the omain of souvenir sellers and kate-boarders by day, while at ight it is crowded with busloads f tour groups stopping off for he splendid view of the Eiffel ower across the Seine. Two ronzes, *Apollo* by Henri Bouhard and *Hercules* by Pommier, tand to the front of the terrace. eneath the terrace is the 1,200-eat Théâtre National de Chaillot. *⊗ 17 pl du Trocadéro, 75016 • Map B4*

2 Musée de l'Homme

This fascinating collection of nthropological and ethnological xhibits from around the world lates from prehistoric times to he present. All the African collections (soon to be followed y those from Oceania and the Americas) are in the process of eing transferred to the Musée u Quai Branly, which is due to e opened in 2006. High-tech, nteractive displays further xplore such subjects as genetics *(see p35)*. *⊗ Palais de Chaillot, 75016 • Map B4 • Open 9:45am–5:15pm Wed–Mon • Admission charge*

3 Musée de la Marine

French naval history is the ocus of this museum, whether n war, trade and commerce, or ndustries such as fishing. The displays range from naval art to

Cave art, Musée de l'Homme

science to maritime adventure and popular legends and traditions. Among the highlights is an outstanding collection of model ships, from the feluccas of ancient Egypt, to medieval galleys to nuclear submarines. You can also watch craftsmen at work on the models in the workshop. Napoleon's opulent royal barge is also on show *(see p35)*. *⊗ Palais de Chaillot, 75016 • Map B4 • Open 10am–6pm Wed–Mon • Admission charge*

4 Musée du Patrimoine et de l'Architecture

Formerly called the Musée des Monuments Français, this museum opened in 1879 and was the brainchild of Eugène Viollet-Le-Duc, the architect who restored Notre-Dame *(see p21)*. It showcases French architectural development from the early Romanesque to Gothic periods (1000–1500) through drawings, models and expert copies of columns, archways, monumental sculpture, frescoes, murals and ceiling paintings. Portions of churches and great French cathedrals such as Chartres and

General Foch

General Ferdinand Foch (1851–1929), whose statue stands in the centre of place du Trocadéro, was the commander-in-chief of the Allied armies by the end of World War I. His masterful command ultimately led to victory over the Germans in 1918, whereupon he was made a Marshal of France and elected to the French Academy.

Cahors have been re-created. The new collections of the Institut Français d'Architecture continue the timeline up to the present day. *Palais de Chaillot, 75016 • Map B4 • Closed for renovation until 2006*

5 Musée d'Art Moderne de la Ville de Paris

This modern art museum is housed in the east wing of the Palais de Tokyo, built for the 1937 World Fair. Its striking permanent collection includes such masters as Chagall, Picasso, Modigliani and Léger; further highlights include Raoul Dufy's enormous mural *The Spirit of Electricity* (1937), and Matisse's *The Dance* (1932). Much interesting and innovative contemporary work is shown here, and in the Site de Création Contemporaine, a huge arts space in the west wing, hot on installation art and on 'educating ordinary people' in the arts. *11 ave du Président-Wilson, 75016 • Map B4 • Open 10am–5:30pm Tue–Fri, 10am–6:45pm Sat–Sun • Admission charge*

6 Cimetière de Passy

This small cemetery covers only 1 ha (2.5 acres), yet many famous people have been laid to rest here with the Eiffel Tower as their eternal view *(see p138)*. It is worth a visit just to admire the striking sculptures on the tombs. *Pl du Trocadéro (entrance rue du Commandant Schloessing), 75016 • Map A4*

7 Jardins du Trocadéro

Designed in 1937, the tiered Trocadéro Gardens descend gently down Chaillot Hill from the palace to the Seine and the Pont d'Iéna. The centrepiece of this 10-ha (25-acre) park is the long rectangular pool lined with stone and bronze statues, including *Woman* by Georges Braque (1882–1963). Its illuminated fountains are spectacular at night. With flowering trees, walkways and bridges over small streams, the gardens are a romantic place for a stroll *(see p38)*. *Map B4*

Cimetière de Passy

8 Musée du Vin

The vaulted 14th-century ellars where the monks of assy once made wine are an :mosphere setting for this wine useum. Waxwork figures epict the history of the wine-naking process, and there are isplays of old wine bottles, lasses and instruments. Tours nclude a tasting session and vine for sale. *5 square Charles-ickens, 75016 • Map A4 • Open 0am–6pm Tue–Sun • Admission charge*

9 Maison de Balzac

The writer Honoré de Balzac see *p48)* rented an apartment ere from 1840–44, and ssumed a false name to avoid is many creditors. He worked n several of his famous novels ere, including *La cousine Bette* nd *La comédie humaine*. The ouse is now a museum display-ng first editions and manuscripts, ersonal mementoes and letters, nd paintings and drawings of is friends and family. There is lso a reference library. *47 rue aynouard, 75016 • Map A4 • Open 0am–6pm Tue–Sun • Admission charge*

10 Musée National des Arts Asiatiques-Guimet

)ne of the world's foremost nuseums of Asiatic and Oriental rt, founded by industrialist :mile Guimet in Lyon in 1879. 'he Khmer Buddhist temple culptures from Angkor Wat are he highlight of the finest ollection of Cambodian art in he west. Guimet's original ollection tracing Chinese and apanese religion from the 4th to 9th centuries is also on display, s are artifacts from India, ndonesia and Vietnam. *6 pl l'Iéna, 75016 • Map B3 • Open 10am–5pm Wed–Mon • Admission charge*

A Day in Chaillot

Morning

It would be hard to imagine a better start to a day in Paris than going to the **Palais de Chaillot** *(see p135)* and seeing the perfect view it has across the Seine to the **Eiffel Tower** *(see pp16–17)*. Then tour the fascinating collections of the **Musée de l'Homme** *(see p135)* and, if marine history is your thing, the **Musée de la Marine** *(see p135)*, both in the palace. Outside the palace, take a break in the Café du Trocadéro *(8 pl du Trocadéro • 01 44 05 37 00)* and watch the comings and goings in the square.

Afterwards, head along rue Benjamin Franklin and rue Raynouard, where you will find first the **Musée du Vin** and the **Maison de Balzac**. Walk to the far side of the Maison de Radio France building for a brunch or lunch at **Zebra Square** *(see p139)*.

Afternoon

Revived, walk back along the Seine towards the Palais de Chaillot, and head up to the place d'Iéna to the recently refurbished and much improved **Musée National des Arts Asiatiques-Guimet** for its spectacular Eastern artworks.

By now you will definitely be in need of a rest, so return to the place du Trocadéro for a coffee at the excellent Carette café at No. 4 *(01 47 27 88 56)*. End the day in the peaceful **Cimetière de Passy** and admire its ornate tombs, before heading back to your hotel.

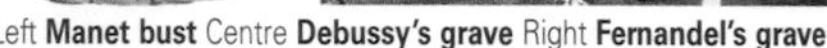

Left **Manet bust** Centre **Debussy's grave** Right **Fernandel's grave**

TOP 10 Graves in Cimetière de Passy

1 Edouard Manet
Born in Paris in 1832, Manet became the most notorious artist in the city when works such as *Olympia* and *Le Déjeuner sur l'Herbe (see p12)* were first exhibited. He died in Paris in 1883.

2 Claude Debussy
The French composer (1862–1918) achieved fame through works such as *Prélude à l'Après-midi d'un Faune* and *La Mer*, and was regarded as the musical equivalent of the Impressionist painters.

3 Berthe Morisot
The French Impressionist artist was born in Paris in 1841, posed for Edouard Manet and later married his lawyer brother Eugène. She never achieved the fame of the male Impressionists, and died in Paris in 1895.

4 Fernandel
The lugubrious French film actor known as Fernandel was born in Marseille in 1903 and made more than 100 films in a career that lasted from 1930 until his death in Paris in 1971.

5 Marie Bashkirtseff
This Russian artist was more renowned as a diarist after her death from tuberculosis in 1884. Despite living for only 24 years she produced 84 volumes of diaries and their posthumous publication created a sensation due to their intimacy.

6 Henri Farman
The French aviator was born in Paris in 1874 and died here in 1958. He was the first man to make a circular 1-km (0.5-mile) flight, and the first to fly across the Atlantic to New York. His gravestone shows him at the controls of a primitive plane.

7 Antoine Cierplikowski
The grave of this fairly obscure artist of the 1920s attracts attention because of its immensely powerful sculpture of a man and woman joined together and seeming to soar from the grave to the heavens.

8 Comte Emanuel de las Cases
Born in 1766, this historian and friend of Napoleon shared the emperor's exile on the island of St Helena and recorded his final thoughts. The Comte himself died in Paris in 1842.

9 Gabriel Fauré
The French composer, probably best known today for his *Requiem*, was a great influence on the music of his time. He died in Paris in 1924, at the age of 79.

10 Octave Mirbeau
The satirical French novelist and playwright was also an outspoken journalist. Born in 1848, he died in Cheverchemont in 1917 and his body was brought to Passy for burial.

For Cimetière de Passy **See p136**

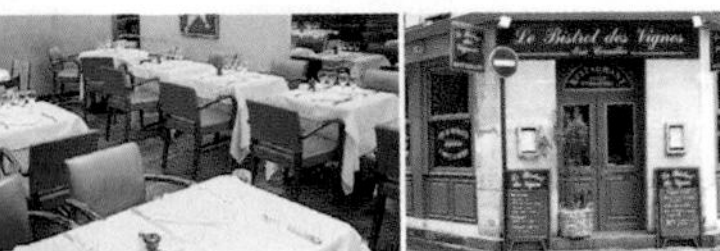

Price Categories		
For a three-course meal for one with half a bottle of wine (or equivalent meal), taxes and extra charges	€	under €30
	€€	€30–€40
	€€€	€40–€50
	€€€€	€50–€60
	€€€€€	over €60

Left **La Butte Chaillot** Right **Le Bistrot de Vignes**

10 Places to Eat

1 59 Poincaré

The fixed-price lunch menu is a bargain, offering the cuisine of superchef Alain Ducasse in a fine setting. *59 ave Raymond Poincaré, 75016 • Map B3 • 01 47 27 59 59 • Closed Sat L, Sun Mon • €€€€€*

2 Jamin

If you don't mind what you eat, go for the no-choice menu as it can halve the price of your meal. If you choose à la carte instead, try fricassé of lobster with dried cherry sauce. *32 rue de Longchamp, 75016 • Map A3 • 01 45 53 00 07 • Closed Sat–Sun, Aug • €€€€€*

3 La Butte Chaillot

This arty bistro from super-chef Guy Savoy is a winner. Dishes such as chicken with whipped mashed potatoes belie the price. *110 bis ave Kléber, 75016 • Map B3 • 01 47 27 88 88 • Closed Sat L • No disabled access • €€€*

4 Le Relais du Parc

Cuisine by Alain Ducasse. The menu is a fusion of east and west. *Sofitel Victor Hugo, 55–7 ave Raymond Poincaré, 75016 • Map B3 • 01 47 27 59 59 • Closed Sun & Mon • €€€€€*

5 Maison Prunier

Fish dishes reign at this restaurant with 1930s decor. *16 ave Victor-Hugo, 75016 • Map B3 • 01 44 17 35 85 • Closed Sun, Aug • No disabled access • €€€€€*

6 Le Scheffer

Superb food, friendly service and reasonable prices, so book well ahead. Try the red mullet Provençale, if available. *22 rue Scheffer, 75016 • Map B3 • 01 47 27 81 11 • Closed Sat–Sun, Jul–Aug • €€*

7 Le Petit Rétro

Cosy atmosphere in this 1900s bistro and affordable prices. Goat's cheese pasta is one option. *5 rue Mesnil, 75016 • Map B3 • 01 44 05 06 05 • Closed Sat L, Sun, Mon D, Aug • No disabled access • €€€*

8 Le Bistrot des Vignes

Unpretentious little bistro of the type everyone hopes to find in Paris. Simple but good food – try the garlic potatoes and the apple tart. *1 rue Jean-Bologne, 75016 • Map B4 • 01 45 27 76 64 • Closed Sun • No disabled access • €€*

9 Brasserie de la Poste

Chic but inexpensive brasserie with a fashionable clientele, offering delicious oysters, snails, duck in pepper sauce, and other staples. *54 rue de Longchamp, 75016 • Map A3 • 01 47 55 01 31 • €€*

10 Zebra Square

Media hang-out as it's close to a Paris radio station. Noted for its steak tartare. Weekend brunches are popular. *3 pl Clément-Ader, 75016 • Map A4 • 01 44 14 91 91 • €€€*

***Note:** Unless otherwise stated, all restaurants accept credit cards and serve vegetarian meals*

Left **Sacré-Coeur** Centre **Espace Montmartre Salvador Dalí** Right **Place Pigalle**

Montmartre and Pigalle

PAINTERS AND POETS, *from Picasso to Apollinaire, put the "art" in Montmartre, and it will forever be associated with their Bohemian lifestyles of the late 19th and early 20th centuries. There are plenty of artists around today too, painting quick-fire portraits of tourists in the place du Tertre. Some say the name comes from "Mount of Martyrs", commemorating the first bishop of Paris, St Denis, who was decapitated here by the Romans in AD 250. Parisians, however, call it the "Butte" (knoll) as it is the highest point in the city. Throngs of tourists climb the hill for the stupendous view from Sacré-Coeur, crowding the main square, but you can still discover Montmartre's charms along the winding back streets, small squares and terraces. Below the hill, Pigalle, once home to dance halls and cabarets, has largely been taken over by sleazy sex shows along the boulevard de Clichy.*

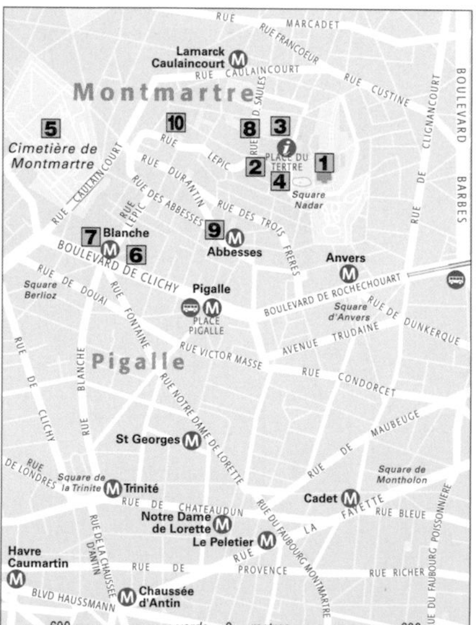

Streetside painter, Montmartre

Top 10 Sights

1. Sacré-Coeur
2. Espace Montmartre Salvador Dalí
3. Musée de Montmartre
4. Place du Tertre
5. Cimetière de Montmartre
6. Musée d'Erotisme
7. Moulin Rouge
8. Au Lapin Agile
9. Place des Abbesses
10. Moulin de la Galette

1 Sacré-Coeur

See pp22–3.

2 Espace Montmartre Salvador Dalí

ne Dalí works here may not be ne artist's most famous or best, ut this museum is still a must r any fan of the Spanish urrealist *(see p144)*. More than 00 of his drawings and sculp- ires are on display amid high- ech light and sound effects, ıcluding Dalí's voice, meant to reate a "surreal" atmosphere. here are also bronzes of his nemorable "fluid" clocks *(see 37)*. *⊗ 11 rue Poulbot, 75018 Map F1 • Open 10am–6pm daily Admission charge*

3 Musée de Montmartre

The museum is set in 1ontmartre's finest townhouse, nown as Le Manoir de Rose de osimond after the 17th-century ctor who once owned it. From 875 it provided living quarters nd studios for many artists. sing drawings, photographs nd memorabilia, the museum resents the history of the 1ontmartre area, from its 12th- entury convent days to the resent, with an emphasis on ne Bohemian lifestyle of the *elle époque*. There is even a e-created 19th-century bistro. *) 12 rue Cortot, 75018 • Metro Pigalle Open 10am–6pm Tue–Sun Admission charge*

4 Place du Tertre

At 130 m (430 ft), Mont- nartre's old village square, vhose name means "hillock", is ne highest point in the city. Any icturesque charm it might once ave had is now sadly hidden nder the tourist-trap veneer of ver-priced restaurants and ortrait artists hawking their services, although the fairy lights at night are still atmospheric. No. 21 houses the Old Montmartre information office, with details about the area. Nearby is the church of St-Pierre de Montmartre, all that remains of the Benedictine abbey which stood here from 1133 until the Revolution. *⊗ Map F1*

5 Cimetière de Montmartre

The main graveyard for the district lies beneath a busy road in an old gypsum quarry, though it's more restful than first appears when you actually get below street level. The illustrious tombs, many with ornately sculpted monuments, packed tightly into this intimate space reflect the artistic bent of the former residents, who include composers Hector Berlioz and Jacques Offenbach, writers Stendhal and Alexandre Dumas, German poet Heinrich Heine, Russian dancer Nijinsky and the film director François Truffaut. *⊗ 20 ave Rachel, 75018 • Map E1*

Street art, Montmartre

The Montmartre Vineyards

It's hard to imagine it today, but Montmartre was once a French wine region said to match the quality of Bordeaux and Burgundy. There were 20,000 ha (50,000 acres) of Parisian vineyards in the mid-18th century, but today just 1,000 bottles of wine are made annually from the remaining 2,000 vines in Montmartre, and sold for charity.

6 Musée de l'Erotisme

With more than 2,000 items from around the world, this museum presents all forms of erotic art from painting, sculpture, photos and drawings to objects whose sole purpose seems to be titillation. It's all tastefully presented, however, reflecting the sincere interest of the three collectors who founded the museum in 1997 to explore the cultural aspects of eroticism. The displays range from spiritual objects of primitive cultures to whimsical artworks by contemporary artists. *72 blvd de Clichy, 75018 • Map E1 • Open 10am–2am daily • Admission charge*

7 Moulin Rouge

The Moulin Rouge ("red windmill") is the most famous of the *belle époque* dance halls which scandalized respectable citizens and attracted Montmartre's artists and Bohemians. Henri de Toulouse-Lautrec immortalized the era with his sketches and posters of dancers such as Jane Avril, some of which which now grace the Musée d'Orsay *(see p13)*. Cabaret is still performed here *(see p58)*. *82 blvd de Clichy, 75018 • Map E1*

8 Au Lapin Agile

This *belle époque* restaurant and cabaret was a popular hangout for Picasso, Renoir, and poets Apollinaire and Paul Verlaine. It took its name from a humorous painting by André Gill of a rabbit *(lapin)* leaping over a cooking pot, called the "Lapin à Gill". In time it became known by its current name ("nimble rabbit"). It is still a popular and atmospheric nightclub *(see p58)*. *22 rue des Saules, 75018 • Map F1 • Open 9:15pm–2am Tue–Sun*

Au Lapin Agile

oulin de la Galette

9 Place des Abbesses

This pretty square lies at the ase of the Butte, between galle and the place du Tertre. each it via the metro station of e same name to appreciate ne of the few original Art ouveau stations left in the city. esigned by the architect Hector uimard, it features ornate green rought-iron arches, amber nterns and a ship shield, the mbol of Paris, on the roof. ong with Porte Dauphine, it is e only station to retain its iginal glass roof. A mural ainted by local artists winds ound the spiral staircase at the ntrance. But don't walk to the atform, take the elevator – it's e deepest station in Paris, with 35 steps. *Map E1*

0 Moulin de la Galette

Montmartre once had more an 30 windmills, used for essing grapes and grinding heat; this is one of only two till standing. During the siege of aris in 1814 its owner, Pierre-harles Debray, was crucified on s sails by Russian soldiers. It ecame a dance hall in the 19th entury and inspired paintings by enoir and Van Gogh *(see p144)*. is now closed to the public, ut it can be admired from utside and rue Lepic is worth a sit for its street market. *79 rue epic, 75018 • Map E1*

A Day in Montmartre

Morning

As with all the city's busy attractions, the sooner you get to **Sacré-Coeur** *(see pp22–3)* the more you will have it to yourself – it opens at 6am. Later in the morning, enjoy the bustle of Montmartre with tourists having their portraits painted by the area's street artists in the place du Tertre. There are plenty of places to choose for a coffee, but the one most of the artists frequent is the Clairon des Chasseurs *(3 pl du Tertre • 01 42 62 40 08)*.

For art of a more surreal kind, pay a visit to the **Espace Montmartre Salvador Dalí** *(see p141)*. Head down rue des Saules to continue the artistic theme with lunch at La Maison Rose *(2 rue de l'Abreuvoir • 01 42 57 66 75)*. Utrillo once painted this pretty pink restaurant.

Afternoon

After lunch, the **Musée de Montmartre** *(see p141)* is nearby, as are the Montmartre Vineyards, and the little Cimetière St-Vincent where you will find Maurice Utrillo's grave.

Head back up to rue Lepic to see the **Moulin de la Galette** before heading towards the boulevard de Clichy. Here you will see the sleazy side of Pigalle life, although the **Musée de l'Erotisme** is a more tasteful interpretation.

To the east is a great bar for an apéritif, La Fourmi *(74 rue des Martyrs • 01 42 64 70 35)*. Then end the day with a show at the world-famous **Moulin Rouge** cabaret.

Left **Dalí sculpture** Centre **Pablo Picasso** Right ***Moulin de la Galette,* Renoir**

TOP 10 Artists who Lived in Montmartre

1 Pablo Picasso

Picasso (1881–1973) painted *Les Demoiselles d'Avignon* in 1907 while living at the Bateau-Lavoir. It is regarded as the painting which inspired the Cubism movement, which he launched with fellow residents Georges Braque and Juan Gris.

2 Salvador Dalí

The Catalan painter (1904–89) came to Paris in 1929 and held his first Surrealist exhibition that year. He kept a studio in Montmartre, and his work is now celebrated in the Espace Montmartre Salvador Dalí *(see p141)*.

3 Vincent Van Gogh

The Dutch genius (1853–90) lived on the third floor of 54 rue Lepic. Many of his paintings were inspired by the Moulin de la Galette windmill *(see p143)*.

4 Pierre-Auguste Renoir

Renoir (1841–1919) is another artist who found inspiration in the Moulin de la Galette, when he lived at 12 rue Cortot. For a time he laid tables at Au Lapin Agile *(see p142)*.

5 Edouard Manet

Manet (1832–83) spent a lot of time in Montmartre and scandalized the art world with his paintings of nudes, including the famous *Olympia* *(see p13)*.

6 Maurice Utrillo

Utrillo (1883–1955) often painted the Auberge de la Bonne-Franquette, an atmospheric depiction of old Montmartre. His mother was the artis Suzanne Valadon and they both lived at 12 rue Cortot, now the Musée de Montmartre *(see p14*

7 Henri de Toulouse-Lautre

More than any other artist, Toulouse-Lautrec (1864–1901) i associated with Montmartre fo his sketches and posters of dancers at the Moulin Rouge ar other dance halls. They epitomi the era to this day *(see p13)*.

Toulouse-Lautrec

8 Raoul Dufy

The painter Dufy (1877–1953) lived at Villa Guelma c the boulevard de Clichy fror 1911 to 1953, when he was at the height of his career.

9 Amedeo Modiglian

The Italian painter (1884–1920) and sculptor arrived in Paris in 1906, when he was 22, and wa greatly influenced by Toulouse-Lautrec and the other artists on the Montmartre scene.

10 Edgar Degas

Edgar Degas was born in Paris in 1834 and lived in the city for the whole of his life, most of the time in Montmartre He died here in 1917 and is buried in the Montmartre cemetery *(see p141)*.

ft Le Placard d'Erik Satie Right Rue de Poteau market

10 Places to Escape the Crowds

1 St-Jean l'Evangéliste de Montmartre

his 1904 church is a clash of tyles, from Moorish to Art Nou-eau. ✎ *21 rue des Abbesses, 75018 Map E1 • Open daily • Free*

2 Montmartre City Hall

On display in this fine uilding are two Utrillo paintings, which he bequeathed to his local own hall on his death. ✎ *1 pl ules-Joffrin, 75018 • Metro Jules Joffrin*

3 Hameau des Artistes

This little hamlet of artists' tudios is private, but no one will nind it you take a quiet look ound. ✎ *11 ave Junot, 75018 • Map E1*

4 Musée de la Vie Romantique

Vriter George Sand frequently isited the owner of this house, rtist Ary Scheffer. The building is ıow devoted to her works. ✎ *16 ue Chaptal, 75009 • Map E1 • Open 0am–6pm Tue–Sun • Admission charge*

5 Musée Gustave Moreau

The former home of symbol-st artist Moreau now displays a arge collection of his works. ✎ *14 rue de La Rochefoucauld, 75009 • Map E2 • Open 10am–12:45pm, 2–5:15pm Wed–Mon • Admission charge*

6 Le Placard d'Erik Satie

A *placard* (cupboard) is how he composer referred to his dim-nutive studio. ✎ *6 rue Cortot, 75018 • Map E1 • 01 42 78 15 18 • Closed until urther notice • Admission charge*

7 Cité Véron

This cul-de-sac is home to the intriguing Ophir, a warehouse of theatre costumes and stage props. ✎ *92 blvd de Clichy, 75018 • Map E1*

8 Square Suzanne-Buisson

Named after a World War II Resistance fighter, this square is a romantic spot. ✎ *Map E1*

9 Rue de Poteau Market

This great food market is a long way from the tourist crowds. ✎ *Metro Jules Joffrin*

10 Chapelle des Martyrs

Also known as the Martyr-ium, this 19th-century chapel is said to be on the spot where St Denis was beheaded by the Romans in AD 250. ✎ *11 rue Yvonne-Le-Tac, 75018 • Map E1 • Chapel: open 10am–6pm Tue–Sun; crypt: open 3–6pm Fri • Admission charge*

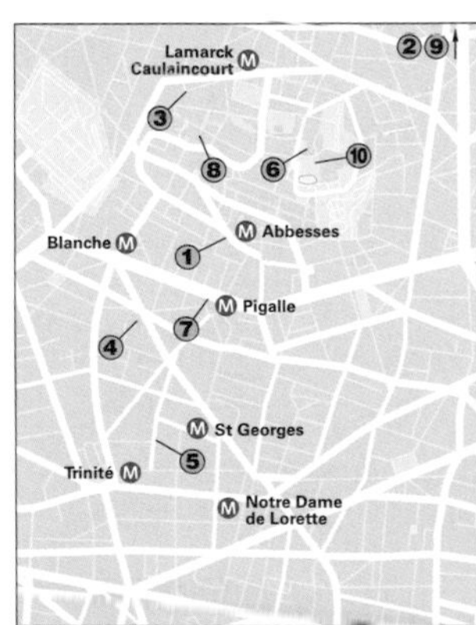

Left **Au Lapin Agile** Right **Moulin Rouge**

TOP 10 Cabarets and Clubs

1 Au Lapin Agile

Poets and artists not only drank in this cabaret club, some such as Renoir and Verlaine also laid tables. Picasso even paid his bill with one of his Harlequin paintings *(see p142)*.

2 Moulin Rouge

As old as the Eiffel Tower (1889) and as much a part of the Parisian image, today's troupe of 60 Doriss Girls are the modern versions of Jane Avril and La Goulue *(see p142)*. *82 blvd de Clichy, 75018 • Map E1*

3 Haynes

As well as being an American-style restaurant, there's often live music or some other entertaining events *(see p147)*.

4 Chez Madame Arthur

The entertainment at this club is provided by drag artists and transsexuals, and you won't need much French to understand some of the acts. *75 bis rue des Martyrs, 75018 • Map E1*

5 La Nouvelle Eve

One of the lesser-known cabaret venues. Its intimate nature does not undermine the professionalism of the shows. *25 rue Fontaine, 75009 • Map E1*

6 Hammam Club

This North African-style restaurant turns into a late-night club with DJ and a dance floor. *94 rue d'Amsterdam, 75009 • Map E1*

7 Cabaret Michou

Outrageous show of drag artists and a compère whose behaviour can never be predicted, this is close to the original spirit of Montmartre cabaret. *80 rue des Martyrs, 75018 • Map E1*

8 Folies Pigalle

This former strip club is now a leading dance venue and popular among the gay community. *11 pl Pigalle, 75018 • Map E1*

9 La Locomotive

Next to the Moulin Rouge, this vast club couldn't be more different, attracting young dancers who want to dance all night. *90 blvd de Clichy, 75018 • Map E1*

10 Le Divan du Monde

World music is played here, live and DJ, with regular dance events and concerts too. *75 rue des Martyrs, 75018 • Map E1*

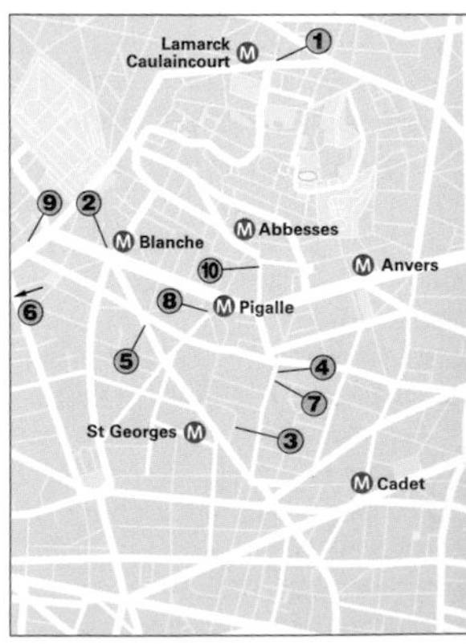

For more jazz clubs in Paris **See pp62–3**

Left **Café Burq**

Price Categories

For a three-course meal for one with half a bottle of wine (or equivalent meal), taxes and extra charges		
	€	under €30
	€€	€30–€40
	€€€	€40–€50
	€€€€	€50–€60
	€€€€€	over €60

10 Places to Eat

1 Café Burq

A genuine Montmartre bistro. Hearty southern French cuisine, such as duck *à l'orange*. *6 rue Burq, 75018 • Map E1 • 01 42 52 81 27 • Closed Sun–Mon L, Aug • No disabled access • €€*

2 Le Barramundi

The emphasis is on relaxation in this intriguingly decorated spot, just by the grands boulevards, and on unpretentious international cuisine. *3 rue Taitbout, 75009 • Map E3 • 01 47 70 21 21 • Closed Sat L, Sun • €€*

3 L'Alsaco

This Alsatian bar restaurant is a boisterous place. Noted for its charcuterie and regional wines. *10 rue Condorcet, 75009 • Map E1 • 01 45 26 44 31 • €*

4 Chez Jean

Home-baked bread starts the meal well and the quality continues with dishes such as red mullet with saffron. *8 rue St-Lazare, 75009 • Map E1 • 01 48 78 62 73 • Closed Sat L, Sun, Aug • €€*

5 Fuxia

Fabulous Italian-styled fare and its plentiful) is on offer at this relaxed and friendly venue. *25 rue des Martyrs, 75009 • Map E1 • 01 48 78 93 25 • Closed Aug • €€€*

6 Haynes

American restaurant-bar, with loud music and Mexican food. *3 rue Clauzel, 75009 • Map E1 • 01 48 78 40 63 • Closed L Mon–Sat, Sun • €€*

7 Charlot "Roi des Coquillages"

Art Deco brasserie, specializing in seafood. *81 blvd de Clichy, 75009 • Map E1 • 01 53 20 48 00 • No disabled access • €€€*

8 L'Entracte

Off-the-beaten-track bistro. Simple dishes like pepper steak. *44 rue d'Orsel, 75018 • Map E1 • 01 46 06 93 41 • Closed Aug • €€*

9 La Table de la Fontaine

Smart bistro with a changing menu. Oxtail stew is one offering. *5 rue Henri-Monnier, 75009 • Map E1 • 01 45 26 26 30 • Closed Sat–Sun, 2 weeks Aug • €€*

10 Aux Négociants

A cross between bar, pub and restaurant. Simple dishes such as pâté or potato pie. *27 rue Lambert, 75018 • Map E1 • 01 46 06 15 11 • Closed Sat–Sun, Aug • €*

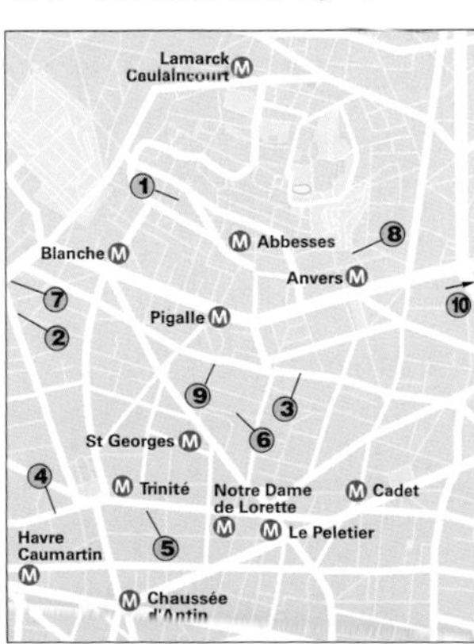

Note: *Unless otherwise stated, all restaurants accept credit cards and serve vegetarian meals*

Left **Bois de Boulogne** Centre **Cimetière Père-Lachaise** Right **Parc Monceau**

Greater Paris

CENTRAL PARIS HAS MORE THAN ENOUGH *on offer to keep any visitor occupied, but if time permits you should make at least one foray out of the centre, whether your interest is in the sumptuous Palace of Versailles, former home of the "Sun King" Louis XIV, or in the Magic Kingdom of Disneyland Paris. The excellent metro system makes for easy day trips to the area's two main parks, the Bois de Boulogne and the Bois de Vincennes, for a wide range of outdoor activities, from boating to riding or in-line skating, or just strolling amid pleasant greenery. In contrast to these bucolic pleasures is the cutting-edge modern architecture of La Défense. Visually stunning, it comprises Paris's stylish new business district to the west of the city, with added attractions in its exhibition centres. Two large cemeteries outside the centre are worth a visit for their ornate tombs.*

Top 10 Sights

1. Versailles
2. Disneyland Resort Paris
3. La Défense
4. Bois de Vincennes
5. Bois de Boulogne
6. Parc de la Villette
7. Montparnasse
8. Cimetière du Père Lachaise
9. Parc Monceau
10. Musée Marmottan-Claude Monet

Sculptures, Versailles

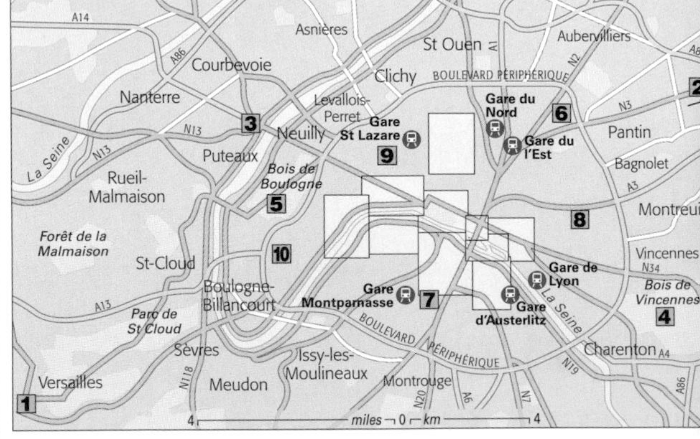

Preceding pages **Versailles gardens**

1 Versailles

The top day-trip from Paris as to be Versailles. This stunning chateau, begun by Louis XIV 1 1664, is overwhelming in its pulence and scale. Plan care-ılly what you want to see as ven a full day may not be long nough to take it all in. Much of ıe palace is only accessible on guided tour, so arrive early as n sunny days the queues can e incredibly long *(see p42)*.
) Versailles 78000 • RER line C to ersailles-Rive Gauche • Open Apr–Oct: am–6:30pm Tue–Sun; Nov–Mar: 9am–:30pm Tue–Sun • Admission charge

2 Disneyland Resort Paris

Visitors with children will robably have no choice about vhether they visit the Paris branch f Disneyland or not. However, ny parents who are sceptical ıight be pleasantly surprised, as ıe hi-tech workings and imagin-tion behind such attractions as Pirates of the Caribbean" and The Haunted House" are xtremely impressive *(see p60)*. 'he new Walt Disney Studios ıvolve visitors interactively hrough film, with a professional tunt show at the end. *Marne-la-'allée • RER line A to Marne-la-Vallée :hessy/Disneyland Open Sep–Jun: 9am–8pm 'aily; Jul–Aug: 9am–11pm 'aily (Studios Sep–Jun: 9am–:pm daily; Jul–Aug 9am–8pm 'aily) • Admission charge*

3 La Défense

The flair of French ırtistic vision and 'arisian style are both :learly shown by this nodern urban devel-pment. This new usiness and govern-nent centre was urposely built to the west of the city to allow the centre to remain unmarred by skyscrapers. More than just offices, however, the area is also an attraction in its own right, with stunning modern architecture including the Grande Arche, a cube-like structure with a centre large enough to contain Notre-Dame, and surrounded by artworks, a fountain, cafés and restaurants.
Metro Esplanade de la Défense or RER line A to Grande-Arche-de-la-Défense

4 Bois de Vincennes

To the southeast of the city centre lies the vast parkland of the Bois de Vincennes. Amid its greenery are three lakes, including a boating lake, along with the "Parc Floral" and its Four-Seasons Garden, a zoo, Buddhist Centre, and a summer amusement park. The beautiful Château de Vincennes, surrounded by a wall and a moat, was the French royal residence prior to the building of Versailles. After the Revolution Napoleon converted it into an arsenal. *Vincennes, 94300 • Metro St-Mandé Tourelle or Porte-Dorée • Park: open dawn– dusk daily; chateau: open 10am–noon, 1:15–6pm daily (until 5pm in winter)*

Grande Arche, La Défense

The Treaty of Versailles

France, Great Britain, the USA, Italy and the German Republic negotiated this agreement after World War I at Versailles, which required Germany to demilitarize parts of its territory, reduce the size of its army, abolish conscription, cease trading in military equipment and to pay compensation. The Treaty was signed on 28 June 1919.

5 Bois de Boulogne

This enormous park is the Parisians' favourite green retreat, especially on summer weekends when its 865 ha (2,135 acres) can become crowded. There is plenty to do, apart from simply walking and picnicking, such as cycling, riding, boating or visiting the various attractions. These include parks within the park, two race courses *(see p51)* and an art and folk museum. The park is open 24 hours a day, but it should be avoided after dark. *Map A2*

6 Parc de la Villette

More than just a park, this landscape to the northeast of the city was created in 1993 to a futuristic design. It provides the usual park features of paths and gardens, but modern sculptures, zany park benches and several major hi-tech attractions offer a different edge. These include the interactive science museum, the Cité des Sciences et de l'Industrie, a 60-seater mobile hydraulic cinema, an Omnimax cinema, play areas for younger children and a music museum *(see p60)*. *30 ave Corentin-Cariou, 75019 • Metro Porte de la Villette • Open 11am–6:30pm Tue–Sun • Admission charge*

7 Montparnasse

Though many visitors never venture as far south as Montparnasse, its location is highly visible due to the 209-m (685-ft) Tour du Montparnasse which dominates the southern skyline and naturally affords spectacular views. Five minutes' walk away is the area's main draw for visitors, the Cimetière du Montparnasse, where the great writer Maupassant, Sartre, de Beauvoir Baudelaire and Samuel Beckett are buried *(see p156)*. *Metro Gar Montparnasse • Tour du Montparnasse: open 9:30am–11pm daily (winter until 10:30pm Sun–Thu); admission charge • Cemetery: open 8:30am–5:30pm daily; fre*

Parc de la Villette

8 Cimetière du Père Lachaise

his is the most visited ceme-
ry in the world, largely due to
ck fans who come from around
e world to see the grave of the
gendary singer Jim Morrison of
e Doors. There are about one
illion other graves here, in
me 70,000 different tombs,
cluding those of Chopin, Oscar
ilde, Balzac, Edith Piaf, Colette,
olière and Delacroix *(see
156)*. There are maps posted
ound the cemetery to enable
u to find these notable resting
aces, or a more detailed plan
n be bought at the kiosks
ound the grounds. *16 rue du
epos • Metro Père Lachaise • Open
m–5:45pm Mon–Sat, 9am–5:45pm Sun,
t phone to check • Free*

9 Parc Monceau

This civilized little park is no
rther from the city centre than
ontmartre, yet it goes unnoticed
y many visitors. It was created
1778 by the Duc de Chartres
nd is still frequented by well-
eeled residents. Its flowerbeds
re colourful, while the grounds
re full of statues and an air of
ell-being *(see p38)*. *Blvd de
ourcelles, 75008 • Metro Monceau*

10 Musée Marmottan-Claude Monet

aul Marmottan was an art his-
orian and his 19th-century
ansion now houses the world's
rgest collection of works by
laude Monet *(see p13)*, includ-
g his *Impression Soleil Levant*
hich gave the Impressionist
ovement its name. The collec-
on was donated by the artist's
on in 1971, and includes the
rtist's collection of works by
enoir and Gauguin. *2 rue Louis-
oilly, 75016 • Metro Muette • Open
0am–6pm Tue–Sun • Admission charge*

A Taste of Greater Paris

Morning

You won't cover Greater Paris in a day, and **Disneyland Resort Paris** and **Versailles** *(see p161)* both need at least a day.

If you want variety, go to **Montparnasse** by métro and, in front of the busy mainline station, is the Tour Montparnasse – take a trip to the top. Return to the station and take a coffee break in one of its cafés, to see Parisians going about their business.

Back at the Tour Montparnasse, walk down boulevard Edgar Quinet. On your right is the entrance to the **Cimetière du Montparnasse**. An hour should be plenty of time here.

Walk towards the Vavin metro station to the café/brasserie **La Coupole** *(see p157)*, to have lunch.

Afternoon

Take the metro at Vavin, changing at Réaumur-Sébastopol, to **Cimetière du Père Lachaise** and explore the city's other great cemetery. Spend one or two hours searching out the famous names buried here and admiring the architecture of some of the monuments. Have a coffee afterwards at a good little neighbourhood café, Le Saint Amour *(2 ave Gambetta • 01 47 97 20 15 • Metro Père-Lachaise)*. From Père-Lachaise it is again just one change on the metro, at Nation, to the **Bois de Vincennes**, where you can spend the late afternoon in the park.

Left **Marble courtyard** Right **Palace gardens**

TOP 10 Versailles Sights

1 The Hall of Mirrors

The spectacular 70-m (233-ft) long Galerie des Glaces (Hall of Mirrors) is one of the few rooms at Versailles that can be visited without a guide. It was in this room that the Treaty of Versailles was signed in 1919, to formally end World War I.

2 Chapelle Royale

The Royal Chapel is regarded as one of the finest Baroque buildings in the country. Finished in 1710, the elegant, white marble Corinthian columns and numerous murals make for an awe-inspiring place of prayer.

3 Salon de Venus

In this elaborate room decorated mainly in marble, a statue of Louis XIV, the creator of Versailles, stands centre stage, exuding regal splendour beneath the fine painted ceiling.

4 Queen's Bedroom

In this ornate room filled with white-and-gold woodwork, the queens of France gave birth to their children in public view: 19 royal infants were born here.

5 Marble Courtyard

Approaching the front of the palace across the vast open courtyard, visitors finally come to the splendour of the black-and-white marble courtyard. This is the original area of the palace, before the north and south wings were added.

6 L'Opéra

The stunningly opulent ope house was built in 1770, to be ready in time for the marriage c the *dauphin*, the future Louis XVI, to Marie-Antoinette. The floors were designed so that they could be raised to stage level during special festivals.

7 Grand Trianon

In the southeast corner of the gardens stands the Grand Trianon, a miniature palace built by Louis XIV to enable him to retreat from royal duties and enjo a little private female company.

8 Palace Gardens

The palace gardens are scattered with walkways, landscaped topiary, fountains, pools, statues and the Orangery where exotic plants were kept in the winter. The magnificent Fountain of Neptune is to the north of the North Wing.

9 Salon d'Apollon

Louis XIV's throne room is, naturally, one of the palace's centrepieces, and features a suitably regal portrait of the 18th-century king. Dedicated to the god Apollo, it reflects the divine way in which the French monarchy saw themselves.

10 Stables of the King

The magnificent stables have been restored and they now house the famous Zingaro equine training academy.

For more on Versailles **See p151**

ft **Boating on lake** Right **Cycling in the Bois de Boulogne**

10 Bois de Boulogne Features

1 Parc de Bagatelle

Differing garden styles ature in this park, including nglish and Japanese, though e major attraction is the huge se garden, best seen in June.

2 Pré Catelan Park

This park-within-a-park is at e very centre of the Bois. Its wns and wooded areas include 200-year-old beech tree said to ave the largest spread of ranches in Paris.

3 Jardin d'Acclimatation

The main children's area of e Bois incorporates a small musement park, a oo with a farm and pets' corner, and Herb Museum imed especially at hildren *(see p60)*.

4 Lakes

Two long, thin akes adjoin each ther. The larger of e two, confus- ngly called Lac nférieur (the other Lac Supérieur) as boats for hire nd a motor boat to ake you to the islands.

Shakespeare Garden

5 Musée National des Arts et Traditions Populaires

his small museum provides an nteresting look at day-to-day life n both rural and urban France rior to the Industrial Revolution.

6 Parc des Princes

This stadium has been host to many football cup finals and rugby internationals and is home to the National Sports Museum.

7 Château de Longchamp

At the same time as he re-designed central Paris *(see p45)*, Baron Haussmann created the Bois de Boulogne. This chateau was given to Haussmann as a thank-you from Napoleon III.

8 Shakespeare Garden

Inside Pré Catelan park is a little garden planted with all the trees, flowers and herbs men-tioned in the plays of Shakespeare. There's an open-air theatre nearby.

9 Jardin des Serres d'Auteuil

This 19th-century garden has a series of greenhouses where ornamental hothouse plants are grown. In the centre is a palm house with tropical plants.

10 Horse-Racing

The Bois is home to two race courses. To the west is the Hippo-drome de Longchamp, where flat racing takes place including the Prix de l'Arc de Triomphe *(see p57)*; in the east, the Hippodrome d'Auteuil holds steeplechases.

For more on the Bois de Boulogne **See p152**

Left **Père Lachaise cemetery** Centre **Jim Morrison's grave** Right **Edith Piaf's tomb**

Top 10 Graves

1 Jim Morrison, Père Lachaise Cemetery
The American lead singer of The Doors rock band spent the last few months of his life in Paris and died here in 1971. Fans still hold vigils at his grave, which is covered with scrawled messages from all over the world.

2 Oscar Wilde, Père Lachaise Cemetery
The Dublin-born author and wit died in 1900, after speaking his alleged last words in his Paris hotel room: "Either that wallpaper goes, or I do." His tomb is unmissable, with a huge monument by Jacob Epstein.

3 Fredéric Chopin, Père Lachaise Cemetery
The Polish composer was born in 1810 but died in Paris at the age of 39. The statue on his tomb represents "the genius of music sunk in grief".

4 Edith Piaf, Père Lachaise Cemetery
The "little sparrow" was born in poverty in the Belleville district of Paris in 1915, less than 1,500 m (5,000 ft) from where she was buried in 1963 in a simple black tomb *(see p63)*.

5 Marcel Proust, Père Lachaise Cemetery
The ultimate chronicler of Paris, the writer was born in the city in 1871. He is buried in the family tomb *(see p47)*.

6 Samuel Beckett, Montparnasse Cemetery
The Irish-born Nobel prize-winning writer settled in Paris in 1937, having previously studied here. He died in 1989 and his gravestone is a simple slab, reflecting the writer's enigmatic nature *(see p47)*.

7 Jean-Paul Sartre and Simone de Beauvoir, Montparnasse Cemetery
Joined together in death as in life, even though they never lived together, their joint grave is a remarkably simple affair. Both of these philosophers were born, lived and died in Paris *(see p47)*.

8 Guy de Maupassant, Montparnasse Cemetery
The great French novelist and short-story writer died in Paris in 1893, and his grave with its luxuriant growth of shrubs stands out because of the open book carving *(see p46)*.

9 Charles Baudelaire, Montparnasse Cemetery
The poet who shocked the world with his frank collection of poems *Les Fleurs du Mal* was born in Paris in 1821 and died here in 1867.

10 Charles Pigeon Family, Montparnasse Cemetery
This charming and touching grave shows Charles Pigeon and his wife in bed, reading by the light of the gas lamp he invented.

For Greater Paris cemeteries **See pp152–3**

Left **Le Dôme**

Price Categories

For a three course meal for one with half a bottle of wine (or equivalent meal), taxes and extra charges		
	€	under €30
	€€	€30–€40
	€€€	€40–€50
	€€€€	€50–€60
	€€€€€	over €60

Top 10 Places to Eat

1 Le Pré Catelan
Tucked away in the Bois de Boulogne *(see p152)* is this high-class dining pavilion. Romantic setting and elegant service. *Route de Suresnes, Bois de Boulogne, 75016 • Metro Porte Maillot • 01 44 14 41 14 • €€€€€*

2 Les Trois Marches
Eating in this two-Michelin star restaurant is a sublime experience. Leek and mushroom tart is just one speciality. *Hôtel Palais Trianon, 1 blvd de la Reine, Versailles • RER line C to Versailles • 01 39 50 25 08 • Closed Sun–Mon in Aug • €€€€€*

3 Marée de Versailles
Versailles may be a long way from the sea, but this restaurant serves whatever fish is fresh that day. Its terrace is the perfect place for oysters and white wine. *22 rue au Pain, Versailles • RER line C to Versailles • 01 30 21 73 73 • Closed Sun–Mon • €€€€*

4 La Coupole
Near the Cimetière du Montparnasse *(see p152)* is this Parisian landmark. Eclectic menu features dishes such as Welsh rarebit. *102 blvd du Montparnasse, 75014 • Map E6 • 01 43 20 14 20 • €€*

5 La Closerie des Lilas
With its piano bar and terrace, this is a Montparnasse institution. The brasserie is cheaper and steaks are good. *171 blvd du Montparnasse, 75006 • Map E6 • 01 40 51 34 50 • €€€€€*

6 Le Dôme
The prime fish restaurant in the area, once frequented by Sartre. Great food and grand decor. *108 blvd du Montparnasse, 75014 • Map E6 • 01 43 35 25 81 • Closed Sun–Mon in Aug • €€€€*

7 La Gare
If visiting the Bois de Boulogne, include La Gare on the itinerary. This stylish brasserie in a former railway station has a summer terrace and rotisserie-style food. *19 chaussée de la Muette, 75016 • Metro La Muette • 01 42 15 15 31 • €€*

8 Colimacon
Handy after a visit to Père Lachaise *(see p153)*. The food is first class, from ostrich and fish dishes to pastas and salads. *107 rue de Ménilmontant, 75020 • Metro Gambetta • 01 40 33 10 40 • Closed Sun • €*

9 Chez Jean
Not far from Père Lachaise is this family-run bistro. The food is standard yet the atmosphere is perfect. *38 rue Boyer, 75020 • Metro Gambetta • 01 47 97 44 58 • Closed Sun, Aug • €*

10 Relais d'Auteuil
At the southern end of the Bois de Boulogne is this gourmet restaurant. Sea bass in a pepper crust is just one delicious speciality. *31 blvd Murat, 75016 • Metro Boulogne Jean Jaurés • 01 46 51 09 54 • Closed Sun • €€€€€*

***Note:** Unless otherwise stated, all restaurants accept credit cards and serve vegetarian meals*

STELLA ARTOIS
BAR
TRAITEUR
AP
ASIE PRESTIGE
SUBLIME !

STREETSMART

Left **Parisian hotel** Centre **Parisian restaurant** Right **French perfume**

Top 10 Planning Your Trip

1 When to Go

April in Paris may be a cliché but it is still a good time to visit. Spring and autumn are both pleasant and there are plenty of parks and tree-lined boulevards to enjoy. Although certain places shut down in August, when most Parisians take their holidays, there is still plenty to see and do.

2 Choosing an Area

The Left Bank is a good choice if you like a Bohemian atmosphere of cafés and clubs. The Marais has many good museums and restaurants and the Opéra and Louvre quarters are central to everything. To save money, stay just outside the centre and use the excellent yet cheap metro.

3 Choosing a Hotel

If space is important, ask about the size of the rooms: some can be very cramped. It is also worth checking whether the rooms face busy, noisy roads and what is the hotel's nearest metro station. Ask if there is an elevator to all floors, as in some older buildings this may not be the case.

4 Choosing a Restaurant

If you like to eat well, or want to try a particular restaurant, phone and book a few weeks ahead of your visit. If you decide to take pot luck, however, the city is full of good places to eat and you should always be able to find a table.

5 What to See

Don't expect to see the whole of Paris on a weekend visit – you would not even see the whole of the Louvre in this time *(see pp8–11)*. Even on a longer visit, don't be over-ambitious: leave time for wandering the streets or relaxing in a bar or café, the way the Parisians do. It's all part of the experience.

6 What to Pack

The weather can be unpredictable, so allow for unexpected cold or wet spells at almost any time of year by bringing a pullover and an umbrella. Parisians are casual but chic, so take a few smart outfits for dining out. Only the most expensive restaurants require men to wear a tie.

7 How much Money to Take

You can use the major credit cards (Visa, MasterCard, American Express) almost everywhere, and there are cash dispensers (ATMs) all over Paris which display symbols of cards they accept. Make sure you have a few euros in cash when you arrive, however, to pay for metro tickets or a taxi. *Bureaux de change* offices also abound throughout the city.

8 Passports and Visas

No visa is required for citizens of EU countries, the USA, Canada, Australia or New Zealand if you are staying for less than three months, although your passport will need to be valid for at least three months beyond the end of your stay. Citizens of other countries should consult their French embassy or consulate for information before travelling.

9 Customs

For EU citizens there are no limits on goods that can be taken into or out of France, provided they are for your personal use. Outside the EU, you may import the following allowances duty-free: 200 cigarettes or equivalent in tobacco; 4 litres of wine, or 2 litres of wine plus 1 litre of spirits; 60ml of perfume and 250ml of eau de toilette; €350 worth of other items.

10 Travelling with Children

Some hotels allow children under a certain age to share their parents' room for free *(see p179)*, so check the arrangements. Most Parisians don't take children to restaurants, seeing them as places to drink, smoke and talk, but they won't be turned away and there are plenty of child-friendly options *(see pp60–61)*.

For hotels in Paris **See pp172–9**

Left **Metro exit sign** Right **Restaurant prices**

10 Things to Avoid

1 Crime
As long as you avoid the quieter areas after dark, you will find Paris a reasonably safe city. Crime in busy areas is rare, except for pick-pockets. Muggings are not common but theft is, so make sure your hotel room and car are locked and secure.

2 Health Costs
In case you fall ill, avoid expensive health care by taking out insurance. For any minor health problems, pharmacies are plentiful and marked by a green cross; if one is closed, the address of the nearest open pharmacy will be shown in the window.

3 Beggars
Avoid displaying large amounts of bank-notes in front of the many beggars and buskers who frequent the metro and some of the city streets. The choice of whether to offer them money is up to you, but do so with small change.

4 Pickpockets
Pickpockets do frequent busy tourist places and public trans-port so keep a watchful eye on your belongings. Men should never keep their wallet in a back pocket and women should make sure their handbags are closed and held firmly in front of them if possible.

5 Taking the Wrong Metro
To avoid taking the wrong route, check the number of the line you want on a map and the name of the end station for the direction in which you wish to travel. All signs in metro stations work in this way and the system is simple. There is always a panel on the wall just before you reach the platform; this panel will have a list of the train's destinations, so you can double check *(see p164)*.

6 Transport Fines
When using the metro, put your ticket through the machine as you enter, but remember to retrieve it as you should keep it with you until your journey is completed. You will be fined if you are not found to be carrying a validated ticket by an inspector. This also applies to travelling by bus.

7 Tourist Traps
It is more difficult to eat badly in Paris than in many cities, but there are places which look for a fast profit at the expense of the tourist who will never return. Avoid signs that say "*Menu Touris-tique*" – they may be fine, but places that attract local people are far better.

8 Hidden Charges in Cafés or Bars
When paying a bill, check if service is included – it usually is. If you want to save money, take your drink or snack at the counter. Prices are lower and no tip is expected.

9 Over-Tipping
Restaurants and cafés normally include a 10–15 per cent service charge, so only leave a further small gratuity for very good service. Taxi drivers should get 10–15 per cent. Porters are tipped €1.5–3 per bag and chambermaids a similar amount per day, usually left at the end of your stay.

10 Queues
Get to popular tourist attractions such as the Louvre a little while before they open: 15 minutes queuing then could save you an hour queuing later in the morning. Late afternoon is also a good time to avoid the queues.

Queues to enter Notre-Dame

Left **Eurostar train** Centre **Ice cream parlour in Gare du Nord** Right **Orlyval high-speed train**

TOP 10 Arriving in Paris

1 Eurostar
Eurostar trains arrive at Gare du Nord, slightly north of the city centre. The station is served by three metro lines and three RER lines, and has a taxi rank outside, usually manned by assistants to help newly arrived visitors.

2 Gare du Nord Facilities
Gare du Nord is a large station with several places to eat and drink and shops selling books, newspapers and snacks. The metro station is reached from the concourse and is clearly signposted. There is also a tourist office by the Grandes Lignes exit.

3 CDG Airport
Roissy-Charles-de-Gaulle Airport is the arrival point for most international flights, 23 km (14 miles) northeast of the city centre. Its main terminals are some distance apart, so check which one you require when returning. A 24-hour English-language information service is available. *CDG information: 08 92 68 15 15.*

4 Connections from CDG Airport
CDG is connected to central Paris by several bus services and (the easiest option) the RER train line B. This links with Gare du Nord, Les Halles and St Michel, among other central stations. Taxis take at least 30 minutes to the centre, sometimes more, and cost about €40.

5 Orly Airport
Orly is 14 km (8.5 miles) south of the city centre and is used by French domestic services and some international airlines. It also has two terminals: Orly-Sud is mainly for international flights; Orly-Ouest is for domestic flights. English-language information is available 6am–11:30pm. *Orly information: 01 49 75 15 15.*

6 Connections from Orly Airport
Air France and other bus services link Orly with the city centre and metro stations, while the high-speed and frequent Orlyval train runs to the Orlyval RER station, for onward RER links to central Paris. Taxis take about 30 minutes and cost about 40 euros.

7 Beauvais Tillé Airport
Beauvais Tillé Airport is some 70 km (43 miles) north of Paris and is not used by major airlines, with the exception of the Irish budget airline Ryanair, whose flights from Dublin and Glasgo land here. There is a connecting bus link wit Porte Maillot metro station; allow at least a hour for the journey.

8 Arriving by Road
All motorways from whichever direction eventually link with Pari Boulevard Périphérique (Outer Ring Road). Acces to central Paris is via different exits *(portes)*, so drivers should check their destination before setting off and know which exit they will nee

9 Parking
To park on the stree you will need the nerves and ability of a local: the often park illegally, seemingly with impunity Visitors are advised to use one of the official ca parks, which are plentiful

10 Arriving by Bus
The main operator, Eurolines, has services from the UK, Ireland, Germany and several other European countries. Coaches arrive at Gare Routière International, east of the city centre but linked to the metro from the Galliéni station on Line 3.

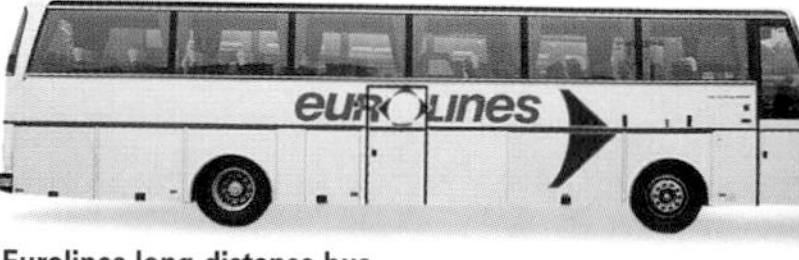

Eurolines long-distance bus

For information on getting around Paris **See p164**

ft Paris tourist office sign Right Parisian listings magazines

10 Sources of Information

1 French Tourist Offices

ne French Tourist Office as branches in many ajor international cities.

2 Office de Tourisme de Paris

he main office is near e Pyramides metro tation. It is well tocked with rochures, nd has otel and our reservation services, *bureau de change* and shop. *25 rue des Pyramides, 75001 • Map E3 08 92 68 30 00 • Open 0am–7pm Mon–Sat, 11am–pm Sun • Closed 1 May*

PARIS Convention and Visitors Bureau Tourist Office

3 Espace du Tourisme d'Ile de France

This tourist facility serves Paris and the wider Ile de France region. It has a good range of brochures, especially for outside Paris, and can book tours and accommodation. *99 rue de Rivoli, 75001 • Map M2 • 0826 166 666*

4 Websites

Two official sites are the state tourist office (www.paris.org) and the city tourist office (www.paris-touristoffice.com), both of which have vast amounts of information and links in French and English. Many major attractions such as the Musée du Louvre (www.louvre.fr) also have their own sites.

5 This City Paris

This bi-monthly magazine covers all aspects of Paris life, from places to eat and shop, to book reviews and festivals. You can buy it or pick up a free copy in some hotels and stores. Its website is www.thiscityparis.com

6 Officiel des Spectacles

Less comprehensive than *Pariscope* but slightly cheaper, and good enough if you want more general information about current exhibitions.

7 Paris Free Voice

This monthly magazine is published by the American Church and aimed at US residents in Paris. Available from English-language bookshops, it is a good source of information on what is happening in the city. It also has a website www.parisvoice.com

8 Francofile electronic newsletter

This monthly mailing available via the linked website (www.parisanglo.com) is sent out in English to visitors, residents and anyone interested in what's going on in Paris. It covers exhibitions, politics, restaurant openings and closings and offers a question-and-answer service.

9 Libraries

Public libraries are found all over Paris and all of them are free to enter. Most have selections of newspapers and magazines, as well as notices that may be useful to visitors. Only Paris residents, however, can borrow material.

10 Newspapers

Foreign newspapers are available on the day of publication in many newsagents. The *International Herald Tribune* is published from Paris. French-speakers can also keep in touch with world events via France's national publications such as *Le Monde* or *Le Figaro*, or the city's own paper, *Le Parisien*.

French Tourist Offices Overseas

UK
178 Piccadilly, London W1J 9AL • 0906 8244 123 (within UK only).

USA
444 Madison Ave, 16th Floor, New York, NY 10022 • 410 286 8310.

Australia
25 Bligh St, Level 20, Sydney, NSW 2000 • 02 9231 5244.

Canada
1981 McGill College, Suite 490, Montréal, QUE H3A 2W9 • 514 288 20 26.

Left **Metro sign** Centre **Locator map outside a metro station** Right **Walking in Paris**

TOP 10 Getting Around Paris

1 Metro

The Paris metro system is a cheap and efficient way of getting around the city. The network is comprehensive and the service is very frequent: you seldom have to wait more than a few minutes between trains. The service operates from roughly 5:30am–12:30am and exact times for each line are given at stations.

2 RER

The RER train system (5am–midnight) is less comprehensive than the metro, having only five lines, but the network goes further into the suburbs. Metro tickets are only valid on RER trains in the central zones (1 and 2). If travelling further, you must buy a separate RER ticket.

3 Buses

Buses run from approximately 6:30am–8:30pm, although some services operate until 12:30am. A *Grand Plan de Paris* available from metro stations shows all bus routes. Metro tickets are valid in Zones 1 and 2, but you cannot switch between bus and metro on the same ticket. Bus stops show the line route.

Parisian bus

4 Taxis

There are 470 taxi ranks in Paris and you can also call taxis from a hotel or restaurant. Fares are not expensive, but make sure the meter is switched on when you get on board. The final fare will be more than the metered fare if you have luggage with you or were picked up at a mainline station. Some drivers will not take more than three people in their taxi, to avoid passengers in the front seat.

5 Arrondissements

Paris is divided into 20 *arrondissements* (districts), which radiate out in a clockwise spiral from the centre. The first is abbreviated to 1er (Premier) and follow on as 2e, 3e (Deuxième, Troisième) etc. The postal address for the first district is 75001, and again these follow on – the second district is 75002.

6 Asking Directions

The Parisians' reputation for rudeness is unjustified. Most are polite and will try to help even if you do not speak French (many Parisians speak English). Politeness is all-important, however, so begin any enquiry with "*Excusez-moi*" ("Excuse me").

7 Cycling

In this city of heavy traffic cycling might seem like madness, but there is an ever-expanding network of cycle lanes. Get the free map *Paris à Vélo (Paris by Bike)* from tourist offices and bike shops. Several shops rent bikes, from about €14 per day.

8 Rollerblading

Parisians are mad about rollerblading and on Friday nights and Sunday afternoons organized *balades* (outings) often take place, usually beginning at Bastille.

9 Boat

The Batobus only runs from May to September, but its six stops link major attractions such as the Eiffel Tower, Louvre Museum and Notre-Dame. Boats run every 20 minutes, from 10am–7pm (until 9pm Jun–Aug). A day pass is advisable if you plan to make more than one journey. ✆ *01 44 11 33 99*

10 Walking

Central Paris is fairly compact, and even a walk from the Arc de Triomphe to the Bastille should only take just over an hour. Shorter walks are a pleasant way of getting around, but don't forget to look up to see the beautiful old buildings – and down to avoid the less-beautiful evidence of Parisian dogs.

ft **Canal tour boat** Centre **Pedestrian walk sign** Right **Bus tour**

10 Guided Tours

1 Boat Tours

The most popular urs in Paris are on the ver Seine and plenty of ›tions are available. The ng-established Bateaux-ouches operate daily ith regular daytime and vening dinner cruises ıt there are many other milar companies. *Bateaux-Mouches: 01 42 5 96 10 • Bateaux arisiens: 01 44 11 33 44 Vedettes de Paris: 01 47 5 71 29 • Les Vedettes du ont Neuf: 01 46 33 98 38*

2 Walking Tours

Tours are available on wide range of themes ıd in several languages; aris Contact and Paris Valks are two of the ading English-language ompanies. Also check ut the website www. aris-expat.com *Paris Contact: 01 42 51 3 40 • Paris Walks: 01 48 9 21 40 (www.paris-alks.com)*

3 Cycle Tours

Several companies ow offer guided cycling urs, with multilingual uides, including night-me tours, medieval aris and as far afield as ersailles. *Paris à Vélo: 1 48 87 60 01 • Mike's ike Tours: 01 56 58 10 54 • scapade Nature: 01 53 17 3 18*

4 Canal Tours

Less well-known ıan river trips, these ours take you into the ascinating backwaters of the Paris canal system. Commentaries will often only be in French, but they may include English if there happen to be many English speakers on board. *Canauxrama and Navettes de la Villette: 01 42 39 15 00 • Paris Canal: 01 42 40 96 97*

Sign for Paris canal tour

5 Bus Tours

Numerous bus tours are available – the main tourist office on the Champs-Élysées *(see p163)* is the best place to begin. It has all the brochures and can also book any of the tours for you. Tours usually last up to two hours but many of the companies allow you to hop on and off at any of their stops.

6 Gourmet Tours

Promenades Gourmandes offers tailor-made French- or English-language tours of the city's markets, food shops, kitchenware shops or anything else in Paris that is of food-related interest. *Promenades Gourmandes: 01 48 04 56 84 • www.promenadesgourmandes.com*

7 Parks and Gardens Tours

Paris City Hall organizes tours of parks, gardens and cemeteries, for groups or individuals with a specialist interest. Ask at the tourist office at Pyramides or telephone direct. *City Hall tours: 01 40 71 75 60*

8 Shopping and Fashion Tours

Pay a guide to direct you to the best shops and you can then choose from a range of themes. *Shopping Plus: 01 47 53 91 17*

9 Themed Tours

American company Paris Through Expatriate Eyes runs several tours through the streets of Paris and within some museums, revealing many secrets even Parisians don't know. *Paris Through Expatriate Eyes: www.paris-expat.com*

10 Sports Tour

Sports fans can take a guided one-and-a-half hour tour of the huge Stade de France, where the 1998 World Cup Final was played *(see p57)* and where numerous operas, rock concerts and other major sporting events take place throughout the year. *Stade de France: 01 55 93 00 00 • Tours 10am-5pm on the hour daily except on event days (English-language tour 10:30am & 2:30pm) • www.stadefrance.com*

Left **Paris bus** Centre left **Budget hotel** Centre right **Eating at the bar** Right **Museum passes**

TOP 10 Paris on a Budget

1 Public Transport

There is a bewildering array of discount travel passes available for use on the metro, buses and trains *(see p164 & 168)*, so be sure to study them to find the best one for you. You can buy one-, three- and five-day passes, as well as weekly and monthly passes, with options for different zones. Savings can be considerable, provided the pass gives you what you want.

2 Hostels and Camping

It is perfectly feasible to find acceptable accommodation in central Paris for €30–45 per night, especially if sharing. Even cheaper options include the following hostel groups. *YHA: 01 43 57 43 28 • CHEAP: 01 42 64 22 02 • Camping du Bois de Boulogne: 01 45 24 30 00*

3 Bed-and-Breakfast

Several companies offer rooms with Parisian families on a bed-and-breakfast basis. Most are located either centrally or close to a metro station, and can cost as little as €25 per person per night, if sharing. *Alcove & Agapes: 01 44 85 06 05 • Good Morning Paris: 01 47 07 28 29 • Tourisme chez l'Habitant: 01 34 25 44 44*

Paris metro sign

4 Cheap Eats

For a coffee or snack, standing at the bar is cheaper than sitting down. In restaurants, the *prix-fixe* (fixed-price) menus offer good deals and the *plat du jour* (dish of the day) is usually inexpensive. If you want to sample fine dining, do it at lunchtime when top restaurants usually offer a cheaper menu.

5 Cheap Seats

Half-price theatre and concert tickets are available for same-day performances only from kiosks at Place de la Madeleine *(see p97)*, Montparnasse station and Châtelet-Les Halles. Cinemas usually offer discounts in the mornings, and on Wednesdays.

6 Cheap Treats

Several attractions including the Louvre, Musée Picasso and Arc de Triomphe are free on the first Sunday of each month. The Louvre also reduces its admission price after 3pm *(see p8)*. Other attractions generally offer free admission on Wednesdays, so check when planning your sightseeing.

7 Paris Museum Pass

This gives free admissi to 70 museums and monuments and saves queuing and money if planning to visit a number of attractions. There are one-, three- and five day options: the one-da pass is cheaper if visitir both the Louvre and Musée d'Orsay on the same day. They are avai able at museums, main metro stations and tourist offices *(see p16*

8 Breakfast

Most hotels charge separately for breakfast and what is on offer varies widely. Some are excellent, but you can save money by opting out and choosing a sma snack in a café instead.

9 Churches

As well as being fre to visit, many churches also put on free or very inexpensive concerts, both at lunchtime and ir the evening. If passing church, take a look to se if any such concerts are being advertised.

10 Concessions

Many places offer free or discounted admi sion to various groups o people, particularly students, under-25s or over-60s. Always carry proof of your age, a student pass or some other means of identification to take advantage of these deals.

For budget hotels in Paris **See p175**

ft **Paris taxi** Right **Musée d'Orsay**

10 Paris for the Disabled

1 Tourist Office Leaflets
ıe main tourist office in ıris *(see p163)* carries a ıflet called *Touristes ıand Même* which has ıtailed information about cilities for the disabled roughout Paris.

2 Useful Organizations
ɔth the Association des ıralysés de France (APF) ıd the Groupement pour ısertion des Personnes andicappées Physiques ıIHP) provide information ı disabled facilities in ıris. *APF: 58 rue de 'onceau, 75008, 01 44 01 5 77 (www.apf.fr) GIHP: 32 rue du Paradis, 5010, 01 45 23 83 50 ww.gihpidf.asso.fr*

3 Guided Tours
The Paris City Hall ganizes numerous spec-ized tours of the city's ırks, gardens and ɜmeteries for people ith disabilities, including ɔecial visits for the blind. *City Hall: 01 40 71 75 60*

4 Itineraries
For those with wheel-ɔwer who want to go it one in central Paris, APF ave detailed information ı negotiating various ıarters of the city *(see bove for address). Paris omme sur des roulettes* also a useful guide with ıaps colour coding the ıality of the pavements ı given routes, access to ıblic conveniences etc. *Editions Dakota, 45 rue St-Sébastien, 75011 (€8.99), or from FNAC and large newsagents.*

5 Travel Agents
Holiday Care, in the UK, has a useful list of specialist tour operators, while APF Evasion, in Paris, can also organize your entire stay. *Holiday Care: 0845 1240 071 (www.holidaycare.co.uk) • APF Evasion: 17 blvd August Blanqui, 75013, 01 40 78 69 00*

6 Metro/RER
Few stations are easily accessible for wheelchairs and most require a station member of staff to operate lifts to avoid either stairs or escalators. The new Météor line, however, is wheelchair accessible. Main metro and RER stations have a leaflet on transport facilities, called *Handicaps et Déplacements en Région Ile-de-France.*

7 Buses
Paris buses are slowly being equipped with access for wheelchairs, and all buses already have seats reserved for disabled and elderly persons, war veterans and pregnant women.

8 Taxis
It is a legal requirement for taxi drivers to help people with disabilities to get in and out of their vehicle, and to carry guide dogs as passengers. This does not mean that all taxis are able to carry wheelchairs, so do check when booking. *Taxi G7 has a large fleet of cars: 01 47 39 47 39*

9 Hotels
Many older hotels are unsuitable for people with mobility problems as they are without elevators, so it is essential that you check before booking. Newer hotels and the modern hotel chains are usually wheelchair accessible, but always ask when making a reservation.

10 Attractions
While some of the older museums and monuments are not accessible for people in wheelchairs, most museums and galleries are, and they also increasingly cater for those with special needs. To be sure about the facilities on offer, get the relevant tourist office leaflet before you visit. APF publishes a guide to disabled access in Paris' museums, theatres and cinemas, *Guide 98 (see Useful Organizations).*

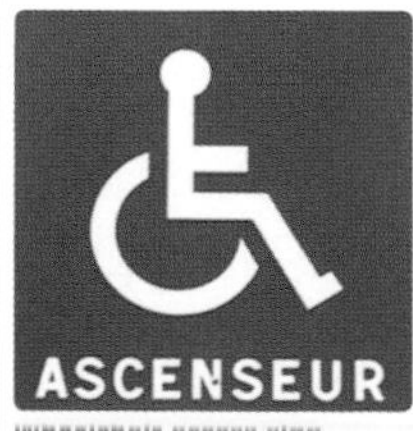

Wheelchair access sign

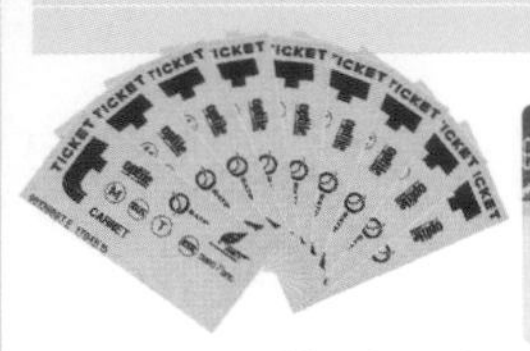

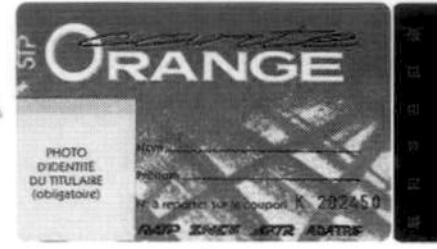

Left **Metro carnet tickets** Centre **Carte Orange** Right **Museum pass**

Top 10 Tickets

1 Metro Tickets

Metro tickets can be bought in batches of 10 *(un carnet)*, which offer considerable savings on the price of a single ticket. Each ticket is valid for one journey, no matter how many changes of route are made. They must be stamped when you enter the metro and retained until you leave *(see p161)*. If staying in Paris for a few days, consider buying a *Carte Orange*, a pass offering savings on all city transport *(see p166)*.

2 Bus Tickets

One type of ticket serves all bus and metro routes and Zones 1 and 2 of the RER network. As with the metro, time-stamp your ticket when boarding the bus and keep it until the end of the journey in case of inspection. This is infrequent, but will result in an automatic fine if you are not found in possession of a valid ticket.

3 RER Tickets

Using the purple metro and bus tickets on the central Zones 1 and 2 of the RER service makes for a convenient way of getting around. See the station maps for the extent of these zones.

4 SNCF Train Tickets

Tickets issued by the RATP (Régie Autonome des Transports Parisiens) are not valid on the mainline SNCF (Société Nationale des Chemins de Fer) services, France's national rail network. To find out about services to suburban stations, including Versailles *(see p151)*, ring the General Information and reservations line. *SNCF information: 08 92 35 35 35*

5 Theatre Tickets

These can be bought in the usual ways: at the box office of the theatre in question, by telephone or at ticket agencies. Some theatres offer reduced-price tickets for students or stand-by seats 15 minutes before the performance. There is also a half-price ticket kiosk *(see p166)*.

6 Cinema Tickets

Prices are average for a European city, but ask about discounts that may be available for students, over-60s and families. Note that admission prices on Wednesdays are also reduced. Larger cinemas will take credit card reservations over the telephone.

7 Clubs

Admission prices are high at all Paris clubs and are often increased at weekends or after midnight, but women can sometimes get in at a reduced rate. Although the admission charge may include a first drink, subsequent drinks will usually be very pricey.

8 Tickets for Attractions

Some concessionary an discount tickets are available *(see p166)*. Th Museum Pass saves queueing if you are planning to visit many c the major museums *(se pp34–5)*, but otherwise there is no facility for booking tickets for historical attractions in advance. Turning up ear is the best option. Mos museums admit visitors 30 minutes before their official opening time.

9 Ticket Touts

Like elsewhere, Par has its ticket touts, and the usual rules apply. It may get you tickets for an in-demand event, bu be wary of forgeries an exorbitantly increased prices. Some Parisians carry a sign saying "*cherche une place*" ("I'm looking for a seat" which might find a ticke at face-value from some one with one to spare.

10 Ticket Agencies

Tickets for concerts and theatre shows are sold at the main tourist information centre on th Champs-Elysées and at ticket agencies around the city, including at several branches of the FNAC chain of CD/book/ video stores, and at the Virgin Megastore. There is a booking fee for usin agencies. *52 ave des Champs-Elysées • Map C • 01 49 53 50 00*

eft Paris chocolate shop Centre Street market stall Right Souvenir biscuit tins

10 Shopping

1 What to Buy
Food and fashion are wo of the things that aris does supremely vell and at all kinds of rice ranges. Good wines an be found reasonably nexpensively. Galleries ffer artworks from the raditional to the avant-arde and stationery hops tempt buyers with eautiful displays.

2 Shopping Hours
These vary enor-nously, though typically hey will be from about :30am–7pm Monday to aturday. Thursday is ate-night shopping until pm in many shops. unday is very quiet but nany small shops do pen, especially food hops in the morning as eople stock up for unday lunch. Shops may vell close during August.

3 Taxes
Different rates of ales tax (TVA) apply to nost goods, varying etween 5 25 per cent nd are generally includ-d in the stated price. No efunds are available on urchases of food, wine r tobacco. On other oods, tax can be refund-d to non-EU citizens who pend more than €175 in ne shop. Ask the store or the appropriate form.

4 Clothes
Paris is still a fashion apital, for men and vomen, and a range of hopping options is available. There are the genuine *haute couture* stores, mostly on and near avenue Montaigne *(see p100)*, but many shops sell cut-price designer labels and there is a great choice of inexpensive fashion too.

5 Food and Drink
No visit to Paris is complete without going to one of the street markets. Don't let the stalls blind you to the shops, however, which are full of gastronomic delights. Place de la Madeleine has a high concentration of food stores *(see p98)*.

6 Lingerie
French fashion isn't all on the surface. Designers also produce stylish underwear, from subtly erotic to rather blatantly provocative.

7 Perfume and Cosmetics
Two more items to check out in Paris. There are many shops devoted to both, including the Sephora chain where you can sample hundreds of scents. Prices are usually favourable, too.

Fashion clothing

8 Department Stores
Paris's huge department stores come on a grand scale. You almost need a map to find your way round Galeries Lafayette, while Au Printemps has separate buildings for its various sections *(see p54)*. BHV sells household goods and a vast collection of DIY tools, as well as clothes.

9 Music
Parisians are into music in a big way, and the large music stores reflect this. Try any of the FNAC chain of shops, which stock a huge range of CDs alongside books, videos and computer software. The Virgin Megastore on the Champs-Elysées has several floors, and has shop-floor headphones to let you listen to the stock.

10 Stationery
French stationery can be exquisite and there are plenty of specialist shops with tempting window displays. Handmade papers sit alongside beautifully designed pens and cards that anyone would be pleased to receive. Diaries and address books make tasteful presents.

For more shops in Paris **See pp54–5**

Left **Bureau de change** Centre **Paris postbox** Right **Newspapers on sale**

TOP 10 Banking & Communications

1 Currency
The euro (€), the single European currency, is now operational in 12 of the 15 member states of the EU, including France. Euro banknotes have seven denominations: 5, 10, 20, 50, 100, 200 and 500. There are also eight coin denominations: €1 and €2, and 50, 20, 10, 5, 2 and 1 cents (also referred to as centimes!). Both notes and coins are valid and interchangeable within each of the 12 countries. Check on exchange rates against your own currency at the time of travel.

2 Credit Cards
These are widely accepted throughout Paris and you should have no difficulty paying for most things with plastic. The only possible exception is American Express because of the heavy commission it incurs. The Visa card is the most widely used.

Parisian public telephone

3 Cash Dispensers (ATMs)
There are cash dispensers all over Paris, and each one indicates the cards it accepts. Many of them also operate in several languages. If you know your PIN number, obtaining cash in this way is very easy.

4 Changing Money
Bureaux de Change exist throughout Paris, especially near tourist hotspots. Many banks also have either a *bureau de change* or foreign desk. "No commission" signs can be misleading, as they probably mean an unfavourable rate. If changing a large amount, a bank is usually best.

5 Post Offices
The main post offices in the heart of Paris are at 52 rue de Louvre (open 24 hours) and 71 ave des Champs-Elysées. They do not exchange currency or travellers' cheques but will exchange international postal cheques, giros and money orders.

6 Postcards
For simple letters and postcards home, you can buy stamps at a *tabac* (tobacconist) rather than try to find a post office. Not all of them advertise the service, but if they sell postcards it is worth asking. Some hotels and newsagents also sell postage stamps.

7 Telephones
Paris phone number begin with 01 and have eight subsequent digits, usually written in four sets of two digits. If calling Paris from overseas drop the zero from "01". Most public telephones require a *télécarte* (phonecard), which can be bought from post offices, metro stations, tobacconists and a few other outlets.

8 Internet Cafés
These aren't as common as in some cities but are rapidly on the increase and it should not be hard to track one down. easyEverything group recently opened a large 24-hour internet café on Boulevard Sébastopol, between Les Halles and the Pompidou Centre *(see pp26–7)*.

9 Newspapers and Magazines
A wide choice of the major foreign newspapers is available on the day of publication throughout Paris. The closer you are to the Champs-Elysées, the more you will see. The popular *International Herald Tribune* is published in Paris.

10 Television and Radio
Most hotels subscribe to multilingual cable and satellite channels, which vary the diet of French-language entertainment.

›ft **Pedestrian stop sign** Centre **Paris police car** Right **Pharmacy sign**

10 Security & Health

1 Crossing the Road

ake care when crossing aris's roads. French rivers are not known for espècting pedestrians, hough a red light will sually – although not ways – make them stop. edestrians do not have utomatic priority on a rossing, unless lights e also in their favour. n pedestrian crossings, otorists often have the ght to turn right, so ways look before you tart to cross.

2 Pickpockets

Gangs of pickpockets n frequent tourist spots uch as the Eiffel Tower nd the Arc de Triomphe, s well as wandering the netro system. Some are mateur gangs and easy o spot, but others are nore subtle so guard your elongings at all times.

3 Mugging

Mugging is less of a roblem in Paris than in ther big cities, but it can appen. Try not to travel lone late at night and void unlit streets. Try to void long interchanges etween metro stations oo: better a longer ourney than an unfortu-ate experience. The nain stations you should void at night are Les lalles and St Lazare.

4 Police

There are a number f police stations in entral Paris. These are listed in the phone book, or call the Préfecture Centrale for details. All crimes should be report-ed, if only for insurance purposes. ✆ *Préfecture Centrale: 01 53 71 53 71 • Open 24 hours*

5 Women Travellers

Parisian men are generally courteous. A firm rebuttal usually halts unwanted attention. If not, try to seek the help of another man: they do not like to see a woman being pestered.

6 Insurance

Paris medical treat-ment is very good but it can be expensive, so be sure to have good health insurance. Visitors from EU countries should be equipped with an E111 form to avoid emergency fees; instructions for use are on the form. All other nationalities should take out private insurance. Report all crimes or lost property, and keep a copy of the statement you make to the police.

7 Hospitals

English-speaking visitors might want to contact the British or the American Hospitals, both open 24 hours a day. Paris hospitals are listed in the phone book, or call Hôpital Assistance Publique. ✆ *British Hospital: 01 46 39 22 22 • American Hospital: 01 46 41 25 25 • Hôpital Assistance Publique: 01 40 27 30 00*

8 Ambulances

If you need an ambu-lance, dial the emergency number. Fire stations also have ambulances and are qualified to carry out first aid.

9 Pharmacies

A green cross indicates a pharmacy (chemist). They are usually open between 9am–7pm Monday to Saturday. At other times, each pharmacy will have the address of the nearest one open on the door or window. Phar-macies can tell you where the nearest doctor is.

10 Dentists

These are listed in the Paris *Pages Jaunes (Yellow Pages)* under *Médecins Qualifiés*. In a dire emergency, a service called SOS Dentistes will provide a house call, but be prepared to pay. A large dental practice is at the Centre Médical Europe. ✆ *SOS Dentistes: 87 blvd Port Royal, 01 43 37 51 00 • Centre Médical Europe: 44 rue d'Amsterdam, 01 42 81 93 33*

Emergency Numbers

Police
17

Ambulance (SAMU)
15

Fire Department
18

Left **Hôtel Intercontinental** Centre **Hôtel le Parc** Right **Ritz Hotel**

TOP 10 Luxury Hotels

1 Hôtel de Crillon

With one of the best locations in Paris, one of the best restaurants and one of the best reputations, the Crillon is for those who enjoy their comforts. From the marble lounge to the light and spacious rooms, the Crillon oozes class. *10 pl de la Concorde, 75008 • Map D3 • 01 44 71 15 00 • www.crillon.com • No disabled access • €€€€€*

2 Four Seasons George V

Recently modernized to great effect, all the rooms have been upgraded, while retaining certain features like the panelled Bar Anglais. The revamped restaurant, Le Cinq, has become one of "the" places to eat. *31 ave George V, 75008 • Map C3 • 01 49 52 70 00 • www.fourseasons.com/paris • reservations.paris@fourseasons.com • €€€€€*

3 Hôtel Inter-Continental

A world away from the usual anonymity of chain hotels, being set in a 19th-century building designed by Charles Garnier, also responsible for the Paris Opéra *(see p97)*. The original atmosphere has been retained, but the rooms offer everything you would expect from the name. *3 rue de Castiglione, 75001 • Map E3 • 01 44 77 11 11 • www.interconti.com • €€€€€*

4 Lotti

An intimate version of a grand hotel, with the atmosphere of a private club. Most rooms are spacious and well equipped, but it has resisted the thorough modernization that many of its rivals have undergone. *7 rue Castiglione, 75001 • Map E3 • 01 42 60 37 34 • hotel.lotti@wanadoo.fr • €€€€€*

5 Meurice

The sumptuous antique decor of the Meurice may not be original, but you would never know it. The fading hotel has been completely restored rather than just refurbished, creating spacious guest rooms and state-of-the-art facilities, while retaining a traditional feel. And the location could not be better. *228 rue de Rivoli, 75001 • Map E3 • 01 44 58 10 10 • www.meuricehotel.com • €€€€€*

6 Hôtel le Parc

The façade of this 1912 mansion conceals a beautiful flower-filled courtyard, while the interior decor combines the feel of the old with the design of the new. Superchef Alain Ducasse has his top restaurant, 59 Poincaré, right next door *(see p139)*. *55–7 ave Raymond Poincaré, 75016 • Map B3 • 01 44 05 66 66 • www.sofitel.com • h2797@accor.com • €€€€€*

7 Plaza Athénée

Surrounded by designer shops *(see p108)* is this venerable but modernized hotel. Alain Ducasse has a restaurant in the hotel *(see p109)*. *25 ave Montaigne, 75008 • Map C3 • 01 53 67 66 65 • www.plaza-athenee-paris.com • reservations@plaza-athenee-paris.com • €€€€€*

8 Hôtel Raphaël

One of the city's finest hotels. The antique decor is reflected in the rooms but they have been fully modernized in terms of facilities. Higher floors have stunning Parisian views. *17 ave Kleber, 75016 • Map B3 • 01 53 64 32 00 • www.raphael-hotel.com • €€€€€*

9 Ritz Hotel

The Ritz has never lost its glamour and still attracts visiting film stars royalty and politicians. Antique furniture is backed up by every modern requirement. *15 pl Vendôme, 75001 • Map E3 • 01 43 16 30 30 • www.ritz.com • resa@ritzparis.com • €€€€€*

10 Westminster

This hotel was built in the 18th century and has only been a hotel for 20 years, combining modern facilities with English-style furnishings. *13 rue de la Paix, 75002 • Map E3 • 01 42 61 57 46 • www.warwickhotels.com • resa-westminster@warwickhotels.com • €€€€€*

***Note:** Unless otherwise stated, all hotels accept credit cards, have en-suite bathrooms and air conditioning*

Price Categories

For a standard, double room per night (with breakfast if included), taxes and extra charges.		
	€	under €100
	€€	€100–€150
	€€€	€150–€250
	€€€€	€250–€350
	€€€€€	over €350

ɪft **Brighton** Right **Hôtel du Panthéon**

10 Hotels in Great Locations

1 Hôtel Edouard VII

An elegant boutique otel with eclectic design atures and oodles of harm. Most rooms have e bonus of breath-king balcony views ver the spectacular péra National de Paris arnier *(see p97)*. *✆ 39 venue de l'Opéra, 75002 Map E3 • 01 42 61 56 90 www.edouard7hotel.com infos@edouard7hotel.com No disabled access €€€€€*

2 Brighton

Enjoy the rue de ivoli location without aying the usual prices. his old hotel is slowly eing renovated, so try get one of the newer ooms with a view over e Tuileries opposite *see p95)*. *✆ 218 rue de ivoli, 75001 • Map K1 • 01 7 03 61 61 • www.esprit-e-france.com • hotel. righton@wanadoo. fr No air conditioning • No isabled access • €€*

3 Bristol

Prices reflect the ıxury standards and ɔcation, close to the ashionable shops of St-onoré, and near the lysée palaces *(see p103–104)*. Rooms are ırge and fitted out with ntique furniture and narble bathrooms. *112 rue du Faubourg-St-Honoré, 75008 • Map D3 01 53 43 43 00 www.lebristolparis.com resa@lebristolparis.com €€€€€*

4 Hôtel du Jeu de Paume

Tucked away on the Ile St-Louis is this beautiful old building with beams. Rooms are small but the friendly atmosphere makes up for everything. *✆ 54 rue St-Louis-en-l'Ile, 75004 • Map Q5 • 01 43 26 14 18 • info@jeudepaume hotel.com • No air conditioning • No disabled access • €€€*

5 Hôtel des Deux-Iles

To stay on one of the Seine islands is a treat, and to do it in this hotel is a double treat. The bed-rooms may be small, due to the building's 17th-century origins, but the cheerful decor, the inti-macy (only 17 rooms) and the hidden patio with its flowers and fountain more than compensate. *✆ 59 rue St-Louis-en-l'Ile, 75004 • Map Q5 • 01 43 26 13 35 • www.deuxiles-paris-hotel. com • hotel.2iles@free.fr • No disabled access • €€€*

6 Hôtel d'Orsay

Art-lovers will enjoy this hotel, right by the Musée d'Orsay *(see pp12–15)*. The hotel's modern bright colours are strikingly offset with antique furniture here and there. Several more expensive suites are also available. *✆ 93 rue de Lille, 75007 • Map J2 • 01 47 05 85 54 • www.esprit-de-france.com • orsay@ espritfrance.com • No air conditioning • €€*

7 Hôtel du Panthéon

A small, family-run hotel set in an 18th-century building right by the Panthéon *(see pp28–9)*. *✆ 19 place du Panthéon, 75005 • Map N6 • 01 43 54 32 95 • www.hoteldu pantheon.com • reservation @hoteldupantheon.com • €€€*

8 Pavillon de la Reine

The best hotel in the Marais, convenient for all the attractions of the area *(see pp84–7)*. Lovely rooms and a quiet court-yard. *✆ 28 pl des Vosges, 75003 • Map R3 • 01 40 29 19 19 • www.pavillon-de-la-reine.com • contact@ pavillon-de-la-reine.com • €€€€€*

9 Hôtel de la Place du Louvre

A hotel with a great view of the Louvre *(see pp10–13)*. Rooms cleverly mix the historical with the modern. *✆ 21 rue des Prêtres-St-Germain-l'Auxerrois, 75001 • Map M2 • 01 42 33 78 68 • www.esprit-de-france.com • hpl@espritfrance.com • No disabled access • €€*

10 Hôtel Castille

This sumptuous hotel is located close to many main attractions. It also boasts a renowned res-taurant. *✆ 33 rue Cambon, 75001 • Map E3 • 01 44 58 44 58 • www.starhotels.com • reservations@castille. com • €€€€€*

Left **Hôtel Favart** Centre **Aviatic Hôtel** Right **Hôtel de l'Elysée**

TOP 10 Romantic Hotels

1 Hôtel d'Aubusson

The rooms in this 17th-century building are spacious and many of them have beams. In winter there is a log fire in the guests' lounge. ✆ *33 rue Dauphine, 75006 • Map M4 • 01 43 29 43 43 • www.hoteldaubusson.com • reservationselim@hoteldaubusson.com • €€€€*

2 Hôtel Favart

A venerable hotel with modern bedrooms. Mirrored bathrooms and beams in the first-floor rooms make for a romantic setting. ✆ *5 rue Marivaux, 75002 • Map E3 • 01 42 97 59 83 • www.hotel-paris-favart.com • favart.hotel@wanadoo.fr • €€*

3 Aviatic Hôtel

A homely hotel that bubbles with the atmosphere of the Left Bank. Ask them to pack a picnic for you for a romantic stroll around the nearby Jardin du Luxembourg *(see p119)*. ✆ *105 rue de Vaugirad, 75006 • Map D6 • 01 53 63 25 50 • www.aviatic.fr • welcome@aviatic.fr • No disabled access • €€€*

4 Hôtel Pergolèse

The Pergolèse manages to be both modern and welcoming. Couples seeking romance should book the best room, also called the Pergolèse, with its pale colours, skylight roof and luxurious open-plan bathroom. ✆ *3 rue Pergolèse, 75016 • Map A2 • 01 53 64 04 04 • www.hotelpergolese.com • hotel@pergolese.com • No disabled access • €€€*

5 Hôtel de l'Elysée

Some of the rooms at the Elysée have four-poster beds, so if planning a romantic getaway be sure to specify one of these. The public rooms are plush and the hotel is around the corner from the Presidential Palace. ✆ *12 rue des Saussaies, 75008 • Map D3 • 01 42 65 29 25 • www.france-hotel-guide.com • hotel.de.le.elysee @wanadoo.fr • No disabled access • €€*

6 Hôtel du Danube

Book a slightly more expensive superior room for the old furnishings, low lighting and other touches that make guests feel pampered. All rooms are of a good size, and the hotel is in the heart of St-Germain *(see pp118–121)*, just the right location for a truly Parisian getaway. ✆ *58 rue Jacob, 75006 • Map K3 • 01 42 60 34 70 • www.hoteldanube.fr • info@hoteldanube.fr • No air conditioning • No disabled access • €€*

7 Hôtel Costes

Book a first-floor room overlooking the courtyard for a romantic place to stay. Low lighting and dark furniture add to the mood, as does the Oriental-style swimming pool and trendy restaurant. ✆ *239 rue St-Honoré, 75001 • Map E3 • 01 42 44 50 00 • hotel.costes@wanadoo.fr • €€€€*

8 Le Relais Christin

This 17th-century mansion offers a back-street haven from the St-Germain bustle. Opt for a terraced room overlooking the seclude garden and take breakfast in the vaulted room which was once an abbey's refectory. ✆ *3 ru Christine, 75006 • Map M • 01 40 51 60 80 • www.relais-christine.com • No disabled access • €€€€*

9 Hôtel Lancaster

Pampering is paid fc here, but the investmen pays off with huge roon in a 19th-century mansic just a stroll from the Champs-Elysées. ✆ *7 ru de Berri, 75008 • Map C3 • 01 40 76 40 76 • www.hotel-lancaster.fr • reservations@hotel-lancaster.fr • No disabled access • €€€€€*

10 Hôtel Caron de Beaumarchais

If you find your romance in the days of the 18th-century, then this hotel will be perfect. Period furniture and classical music attempt to captur that era. Rooms are beautiful and guests are truly pampered. ✆ *12 rue Vieille-du-Temple, 75004 • Map R2 • 01 42 72 34 12 • www.carondebeaumarcha .com • hotel@carondebeaumarchais.com • No disabled access • €€*

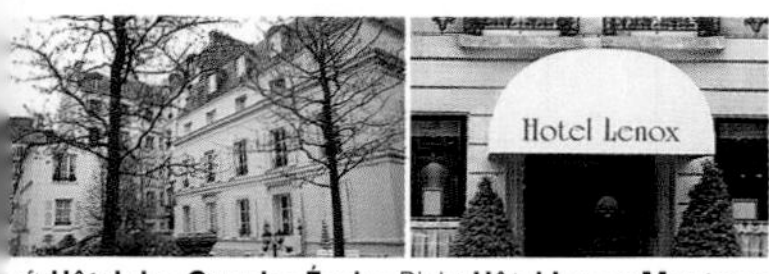

Left **Hôtel des Grandes Écoles** Right **Hôtel Lenox Montparnasse**

Price Categories

For a standard, double room per night (with breakfast if included), taxes and extra charges.

€	under €100
€€	€100–€150
€€€	€150–€250
€€€€	€250–€350
€€€€€	over €350

10 Budget Hotels

1 Hôtel des Grandes Écoles

A secret hideaway in a lovely part of Paris, the two buildings that make up this 51-room hotel are set around a garden. The rooms are attractively decorated and the location is perfect for exploring the Latin Quarter. *75 rue du Cardinal-Lemoine, 75005 • Map P6 • 01 43 26 79 23 • www.hotel-grandes-ecoles.com • No air conditioning • €€*

2 Hôtel Lenox Montparnasse

The flower-filled Lenox is close to Montparnasse cemetery *(see p151)*, and despite the price, rooms are clean, with modern facilities. Some are on the small side so ask for a larger room: there is also a top-floor suite. *15 rue Delambre, 75014 • Map D6 • 01 43 35 34 50 • www.hotellenox.com • hotel@lenoxmontparnasse.com • No disabled access • €€*

3 Hôtel Saint-André-des-Arts

This charmingly modest hotel offers unique character and a Left Bank location at bargain prices. The rooms are tiny, but for a cheap bolt-hole and truly Parisian Bohemian feel, it can't be beaten. *66 rue St-André-des-Arts, 75006 • Map M4 • 01 43 26 96 16 • hsaintand@wanadoo.fr • No air conditioning • No disabled access • €*

4 Hôtel Keppler

Book well ahead for a room in the Keppler, with its inexpensive prices in an expensive part of Paris. Rooms are spacious and provide the basic comforts – a few have balconies. The management ensures that cheap prices do not mean cheap service. *12 rue Keppler, 75016 • Map B3 • 01 47 20 65 05 • www.hotelkeppler.com • hotel.keppler@wanadoo.fr • No air conditioning • No disabled access • €€*

5 Grand Hôtel Lévêque

The only thing grand about this hotel is its name, but it remains a favourite with those needing budget accommodation in Paris. Despite the price, almost all rooms have fans, phone, TV, hairdryer and even a modem socket. *29 rue Cler, 75007 • Map C4 • 01 47 05 49 15 • www.hotel-leveque.com • No disabled access • €*

6 Hôtel de Lille

If you want a cheap central hotel, they come no cheaper nor more central than the Lille, just a minute's walk from the Louvre Museum. Rooms are clean but basic, and there is no breakfast and no elevator serving the five floors. *8 rue du Pélican, 75001 • Map M2 • 01 42 33 33 42 • No credit cards • No air conditioning • No disabled access • €*

7 Le Caulaincourt Square Hôtel

You may not get luxury but you do get a friendly atmosphere and access to the sights of Montmartre. *2 square Caulincourt, 75018 • Map E1 • 01 46 06 46 06 • www.caulincourt.com • No air conditioning • No disabled access • €*

8 Hôtel Plessis

Delightful hotel in an untouristed area of Paris. Rooms are compact but clean. Fifth-floor rooms have balconies; all have TV and phone. *25 rue du Grand Prieuré, 75011 • Metro République • 01 47 00 13 38 • hotel.plessis@club-internet.fr • No air conditioning • No disabled access • €*

9 Hôtel du Globe

Set in a 17th-century building near the Jardin du Luxembourg, flowers fill the rooms and some have four-poster beds. *15 rue des Quatre Vents, 75006 • Map E6 • 01 43 26 35 50 • www.hotel-du-globe.fr • No air conditioning • No disabled access • €*

10 Ermitage Hôtel

A wonderful family-run hotel in Montmartre. Some rooms have views over the city, others overlook a garden, and the furniture is antique or repro. *24 rue Lamarck, 75018 • Map E1 • 01 42 64 79 22 • www.ermitage-sacrecoeur.fr • No credit cards • No air conditioning • No disabled access • €*

***Note:** Unless otherwise stated, all hotels accept credit cards, have en-suite bathrooms and air conditioning*

Left **Hôtel de Seine** Right **Hôtel de Banville**

Top 10 Medium-Priced Hotels

1 La Régence Étoile Hôtel

Very reasonably priced for its standard and location (a short walk from the Arc de Triomphe), the Régence has plush public areas and modern bedrooms with TVs, direct-dial phones, mini-bars and safe. *24 ave Carnot, 75017 • Map B2 • 01 58 05 42 42 • hotelregenceetoile-paris@wanadoo.fr • No disabled access • €€*

2 Hôtel d'Angleterre

Hemingway once stayed in this long-established hotel. Most rooms are a good size with high ceilings, and some are decorated with antiques. The standard rooms are small so book a superior one at extra cost. *44 rue Jacob, 75006 • Map N5 • 01 42 60 34 72 • www.hotel-dangleterre.com • No air conditioning • No disabled access • €€*

3 L'Abbaye Saint-Germain

This 16th-century former convent has a cobbled courtyard in a quiet location near St-Sulpice *(see p41)*. It is perfect for exploring much of the Left Bank, and is a haven to return to afterwards. The 46 rooms are all different, the best being the top-floor suites with their rooftop views. A delightful experience. *10 rue Cassette, 75006 • Map K5 • 01 45 44 38 11 • www.hotel-abbaye.com • No disabled access • €€€*

4 Hôtel de Seine

Timbered rooms indicate the old-world nature of this mansion, close to the Jardin du Luxembourg. Some rooms have balconies. *52 rue de Seine, 75006 • Map L5 • 01 46 34 22 80 • www.hotel-de-seine.com • hotel-de-seine@wanadoo.fr • No air conditioning • No disabled access • €€€*

5 Hôtel Ferrandi

This bargain hotel combines old-fashioned comfort with modern convenience. A bonus is the hotel's car park. *92 rue du Cherche-Midi, 75006 • Map J6 • 01 42 22 97 40 • www.123france.com • hotel.ferrandi@wanadoo.fr • No disabled access • €€*

6 Hôtel Le Clos Médicis

Built in 1773 for the Médici family, ancient beams and artworks now combine with modern design for a special place to stay. Rooms are small, but compensations are the garden, adjacent bar, and the location in a quiet street off boulevard St-Michel. *56 rue Monsieur-le-Prince, 75006 • Map M5 • 01 43 29 10 80 • www.closmedicis.com • message@closmedicis.com • 1 room suitable for disabled guests • €€€*

7 Hotel des Trois Poussins

In the Pigalle area but well away from the sleazy side. Some rooms are small, but the higher they go, the better the view. *15 rue Clauzel, 75009 • Map E1 • 01 53 32 81 81 • www. les3poussins.com • h3p@les3poussins.com • No disabled access • €€*

8 Hôtel Saint-Merry

This hotel is unlike any other – one room even sports its own flying buttress. Carved bedboards and other features ensure an historical experience. *78 rue de la Verrerie, 75004 • Map P2 • 01 42 78 14 15 • www.hotelmarais.com • hotelstmerry@wanadoo.fr • No air conditioning • No disabled access • €€€*

9 Hôtel Saint-Paul

This 17th-century building has antique furniture and some rooms have four-poster beds. Some also overlook the Jardin du Luxembourg. *43 rue Monsieur-le-Prince, 75006 • Map M5 • 01 43 26 98 64 • www.hotelsaintpaulparis.com • hotel.saint.paul@wanadoo.fr • €€*

10 Hôtel de Banville

This wonderful 1928 mansion may be away from the centre but it oozes class and is filled with antiques. Several rooms have four-poster beds. *166 blvd Berthier, 75017 • Metro Porte de Clichy • 01 42 67 70 16 • www.hotelbanville.fr • hotelbanville@wanadoo.fr • No disabled access • €€€*

***Note:** Unless otherwise stated, all hotels accept credit cards, have en-suite bathrooms and air conditioning*

Price Categories

For a standard, double room per night (with breakfast if included), taxes and extra charges.	
€	under €100
€€	€100–€150
€€€	€150–€250
€€€€	€250–€350
€€€€€	over €350

Left **Hotel Résidence Lord Byron** Right **Hôtel Chopin**

TOP 10 Famous-Name Hotels

1 Hôtel Esmeralda

The proximity to Notre-Dame gives the hotel its name. Ask for a room with a cathedral view, and be prepared for a Bohemian atmosphere. The area is noisy and the rooms are not modernized, though most have en suite bathrooms. *4 rue St-Julien-le-Pauvre, 75005 • Map P4 • 01 43 54 19 20 • No air conditioning • No disabled access • €*

2 Résidence Lord Byron

An inexpensive hotel in an expensive area, with a pleasant courtyard garden for summer breakfasts. Top floor rooms are cheaper because the elevator doesn't go that far, but they do have good views. *5 rue Chateaubriand, 75008 • Map C2 • 01 43 59 89 98 • www.escapade-paris.fr • lord.byron @escapade-paris.fr • No disabled access • €€€*

3 Balzac

Fashionably chic, this luxurious hotel has a restaurant and a basement bar, both popular with locals. The 56 rooms and 14 apartments are simply but tastefully decorated, with terraced suites offering great views of the Eiffel Tower. *6 rue Balzac, 75008 • Map C2 • 01 44 35 18 00 • www.hotelbalzac.com • reservation@hotelbalzac.com • No disabled access • €€€€€*

4 Hôtel Chopin

Hidden away in one of the city's *passages* *(see p50)*, the Chopin opened in 1846. At this price don't expect the best facilities, but it is a pleasant place to stay and the rooms are comfortable. Ask for an upper room for more light. *46 passage Jouffroy, 10 blvd Montmartre , 75009 • Map F2 • 01 47 70 58 10 • No air conditioning • No disabled access • €*

5 Hôtel Daguerre

Surprisingly smart hotel at the budget end of the market. Rooms are brightly decorated, if a little small, but some of the upper ones have views as far as Sacré-Coeur and others overlook the patio garden. *94 rue Daguerre, 75014 • Metro Gaîté • 01 43 22 43 54 • www.hoteldaguerre.net • €*

6 Hôtel Flaubert

Terrific value, slightly out of the centre but not far from the metro. New owners have smartened it up, and bamboo furniture works well with the lush garden. Rooms vary in size. *19 rue Rennequin, 75017 • Map C1 • 01 46 22 44 35 • www.hotelflaubert.com • €€*

7 Hôtel Baudelaire Opéra

The French writer Baudelaire lived here in 1854, and today it makes a good bargain find in this central area. Rooms are brightly decorated, although most of them are small. *61 rue St-Anne, 75002 • Map H4 • 01 42 97 50 62 • www.paris-hotel.net • No air conditioning • No disabled access • €€*

8 Hôtel Victor Hugo

This long-established hotel has some delightful features, including a vegetable cart that's used for the buffet in the garden breakfast room. *19 rue Copernic, 75016 • Map B3 • 01 45 53 76 01 • www.victorhugohotel.com • paris@victorhugohotel.com • No disabled access • €€€*

9 Hôtel Galileo

Tasteful decor throughout, and a walled garden, all just a short walk away from the Arc de Triomphe. *54 rue Galilée, 75008 • Map B2 • 01 47 20 66 06 • www.hotel-ile-saintlouis.com • hotelgalileo@wanadoo.fr • No disabled access • €€€*

10 Grand Hôtel Jeanne d'Arc

You could pass a whole weekend in without wandering far from this well-equppied hotel, surrounded as it is by Marais attractions. *3 rue de Jarente, 75004 • Metro St-Paul • 01 48 87 62 11 • www.hoteljeannedarc.com • information@hoteljeannedarc.com • No air conditioning • No disabled access • €*

Left **Hotel Square** Centre **Hôtel du Quai Voltaire** Right **Le Notre-Dame**

Top 10 Rooms with a View

1 Hôtel Bourgogne et Montana

Stylish hotel, with the Musée d'Orsay *(see pp12–15)* and the Invalides close by. Top floor rooms have great views across the Seine. Paintings line the walls, antique furniture and gilt-lined mirrors abound. *3 rue de Bourgogne, 75007 • Map D4 • 01 45 51 20 22 • www.bourgogne-montana.com • bmontana@bourgogne-montana.com • No disabled access • €€€*

2 ArtusHôtel

Indulge yourself in the food shops of the Rue de Buci *(see p123)*, then indulge yourself back in this hotel – especially if you have booked the suite with a Jacuzzi from which there are great views of the Latin Quarter. *34 rue de Buci, 75006 • Map L4 • 01 43 29 07 20 • www.artushotel.com • info@artushotel.com • No disabled access • €€€*

3 Hotel Square

Boutique-style hotel with 22 rooms and views down the Seine to the Eiffel Tower. Slightly out of the centre, but makes up for it with style. *3 rue de Boulainvilliers, 75016 • Map A5 • 01 44 14 91 90 • www.hotelsquare.com • €€€€*

4 Hôtel du Quai Voltaire

Impressionist artist Camille Pissarro (1831–1903) painted the view of the Seine and Notre-Dame visible from most of the guest rooms here. Rooms are small, but the warm welcome and the location more than make up for that. *19 quai Voltaire, 75007 • Map K2 • 01 42 61 50 91 • www.quaivoltaire.fr • info@quaivoltaire.fr • No air conditioning • No disabled access • €€*

5 Hôtel des Grands Hommes

Great views of the Panthéon *(see pp28–9)* from this intimate 32-room family hotel in an 18th-century house. The rooms are reasonably sized. *17 pl du Panthéon, 75005 • Map N6 • 01 46 34 19 60 • www.hoteldesgrandshommes.com • No disabled access • €€€*

6 Terrass Hôtel

The Terrass has fabulous views over Paris which can be enjoyed from its rooftop terrace. Most rooms in this early 19th-century building are now air-conditioned; all are comfortable. There is a bar, restaurant and other facilities. *12–14 rue Joseph-de-Maistre, 75018 • Map E1 • 01 46 06 72 85 • www.terrass-hotel.com • terrass@francenet.fr • No disabled access • €€€€*

7 Le Notre-Dame

Right by the Seine with magnificent views of Notre-Dame, the bright decor here makes up for the size of the rooms. There are three suites. *1 quai St Michel, 75005 • Map N4 • 01 43 54 20 43 • www.paris-hotel-notredame.com • hotel.lenotredame@libertysurf.fr • No disabled access • €€€*

8 Les Rives de Notre-Dame

The view of Notre-Dame from this 10-room hotel is arguably the best in Paris. The decor is modern and the rooms are fairly spacious. *15 quai St-Michel, 75005 • Map N4 • 01 43 54 81 16 • www.rivesdenotredame.com • hotel@rivesdenotredame.com • No disabled access • €€€*

9 Hôtel Régina

Across the rue de Rivoli from the Louvre *(see pp8–11)* with views of the Tuileries, this is a splendid old hotel. *2 pl des Pyramides, 75001 • Map K1 • 01 42 60 31 10 • www.regina-hotel.com • €€€€€*

10 Hôtel du Rond-Point de Longchamp

A view of the Eiffel Tower from the top floors of this charming hotel. Rooms are equipped for business travellers, but there are family rooms. *86 rue de Longchamp, 75018 • Map A3 • 01 45 05 13 63 • www.rd-pt-longchamp.fr • abla@rd-pt-longchamp.fr • No disabled access• €€€*

***Note:** Unless otherwise stated, all hotels accept credit cards, have en-suite bathrooms and air conditioning*

Price Categories		
For a standard, double room per night (with breakfast if included), taxes and extra charges.	€	under €100
	€€	€100–€150
	€€€	€150–€250
	€€€€	€250–€350
	€€€€€	over €350

Left **Relais St-Germain** Right **Fleurie**

Top 10 Family-Friendly Hotels

1 Hôtel Baltimore
Part of the Sofitel hotel chain and situated between the Trocadéro and the Arc de Triomphe, the Baltimore caters well for families with good facilities and a friendly attitude. Rooms are being refurbished, so ask for one of the revamped ones. *88 bis avenue Kléber, 75016 • Map B3 • 01 44 34 54 54 • www.accorhotels.com • No disabled access • €€€€€*

2 Relais St-Germain
There are four apartments for rent in this hotel, close to the Jardin du Luxembourg for when the children simply want to play in the park. All have their own cooking facilities, which will help keep down the cost of a family holiday. *9 carrefour de l'Odéon, 75006 • Map L4 • 01 44 27 07 97 • No air conditioning • No disabled access • €€€€*

3 Relais du Louvre
Right by the Louvre museum and therefore with easy access to many of the city's main sights, several rooms can be combined, and some suites too. Decor varies from traditional to bright and modern, so state which you prefer. *19 rue des Prêtres-Saint-Germain-l'Auxerrois, 75001 • Map M2 • 01 40 41 96 42 • www.relaisdulouvre.com • contact@relaisdulouvre.com • No disabled access • €€€*

4 Fleurie
Children under-12 stay free in this smart but lively St-Germain hotel, and those over 12 can have an extra bed in their parents' room for a small charge. Satellite TV and PC connections in each room, and a huge buffet breakfast. *32–4 rue Grégoire de Tours, 75006 • Map L4 • 01 53 73 70 00 • www.fleurie-hotel-paris.com • bonjour@hotel-de-fleurie.fr • No disabled access • €€€*

5 Méridien Montparnasse
Facilities here are what you would expect from a large chain hotel. Children's entertainment is laid on during Sunday brunch. *19 rue du Commandant René Mouchotte, 75014 • Map D6 • 01 44 36 44 36 • www. lemeridien-montparnasse.com • meridien.montparnasse@lemeridien.com • €€€*

6 Hôtel de l'Université
In this 17th-century St-Germain mansion, there is a discount for children sharing a room with their parents. *22 rue de l'Université, 75007 • Map K3 • 01 42 61 09 39 • www.hoteluniversite.com • hoteluniversite@wanadoo.fr • No disabled access • €€€*

7 Hôtel des Arts
A good choice for families on a budget, with triple rooms and cots available. The hotel is in one of Paris's *passages* (see p50). *7 Cité Bergère, 6 rue du Faubourg Montmartre, 75009 • Map F2 • 01 42 46 73 30 • hda9@free.fr • No air conditioning • No disabled access • €*

8 Hôtel St-Jacques
Numerous Left Bank attractions are near this comfortable hotel with family rooms and cots available. Almost all rooms are en-suite and have telephone and TV. *35 rue des Écoles, 75005 • Map N5 • 01 44 07 45 45 • www.paris-hotel-stjacques.com • No air conditioning • No disabled access • €€*

9 Résidence Hôtel Malesherbes
A collection of intriguing studios makes up for the slightly out-of-centre location. Parc Monceau and a good market are nearby. *129 rue Cardinet, 75017 • Map D1 • 01 44 15 85 00 • http://malesherbes.hotel.free.fr • malesherbes.hotel@free.fr • No air conditioning • No disabled access • €*

10 Hotel Ibis Bastille Faubourg Saint Antoine
Right in the heart of the Bastille district, this no-frills hotel may be a chain but it's handy for some of the city's best markets. Rooms are cheaper at weekends. *13 rue Trousseau, 75011 • Map H5 • 01 48 05 55 55 • www.ibishotel.com • €*

For Paris for children **See pp60–61**

General Index

D

N

O

P

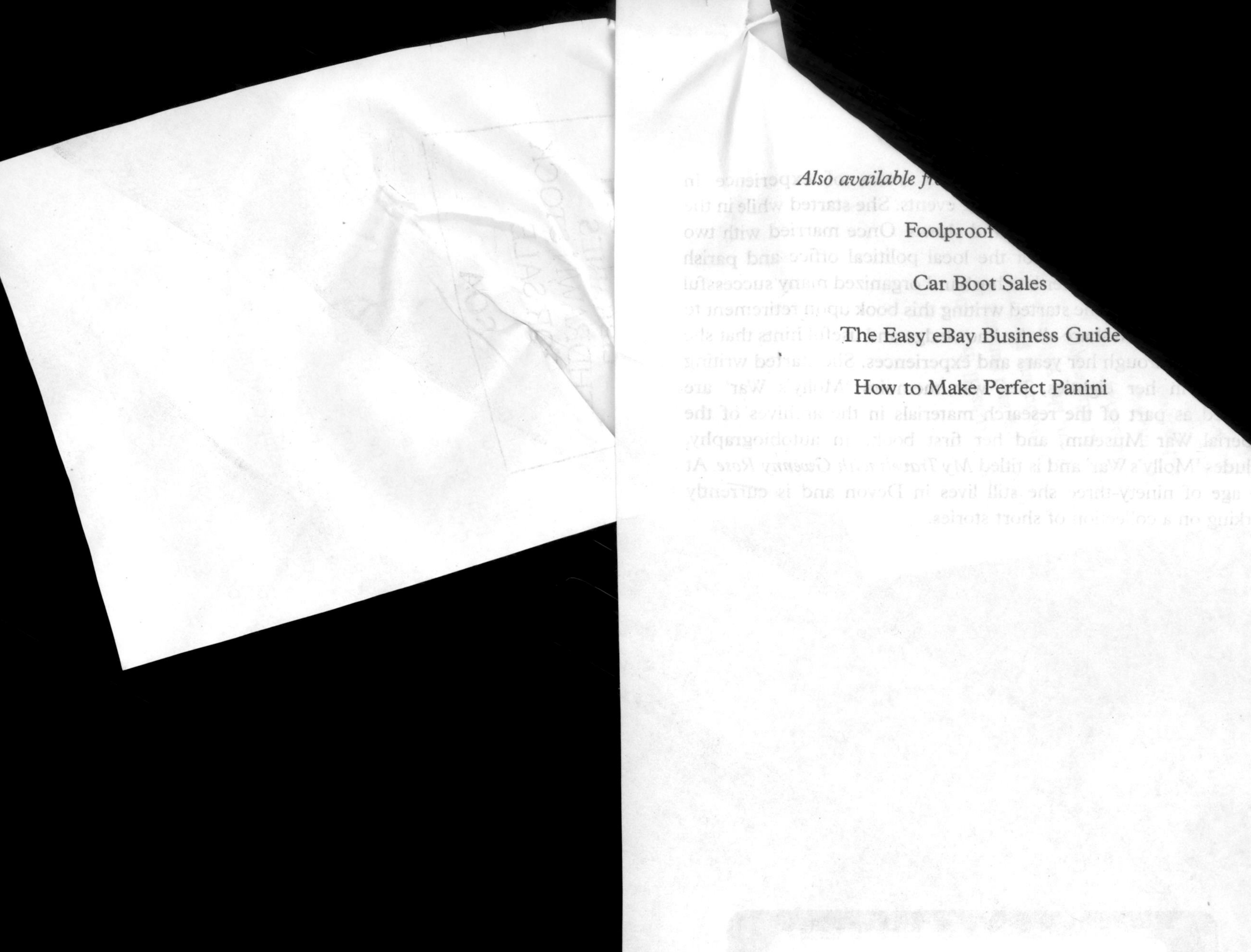

Also available fr

Foolproof

Car Boot Sales

The Easy eBay Business Guide

How to Make Perfect Panini

FUNDRAISING IDEAS

Plan and run events to raise money for good causes

Molly Russell

ROBINSON

First published in Great Britain in 2014 by Robinson

1 3 5 7 9 10 8 6 4 2

A CIP catalogue record for this book is available from the British Library.

ISBN: 978-0-71602-394-4 (paperback)
ISBN: 978-0-71602-395-1 (ebook)

The material contained in this book is set out for general guidance and does not deal with any particular and personal circumstances. Laws and regulations are complex and liable to change, and readers should check the current position with relevant authorities before making individual arrangements and where necessary take appropriate advice.

Typeset in Great Britain by Ian Hughes, www.mousematdesign.com
Printed and bound in Great Britain by
Clays Ltd, St Ives plc

Robinson
is an imprint of
Constable & Robinson Ltd
100 Victoria Embankment
London EC4Y 0DY

An Hachette UK Company
www.hachette.co.uk

www.constablerobinson.com

Dedicated to my husband
Vincent Russell

Contents

Introduction

Contrary to popular belief, fundraising can be fun!

The thought of having to do something about raising funds can be a daunting prospect, particularly for the beginner, but once the first steps have been taken and plans start to take shape, the excitement of the challenge begins to take over. Working with a team of volunteers to raise money for others brings its own special rewards. As more people become involved with the venture it is heartwarming to discover how much helpfulness and generosity there is in the world. The real satisfaction comes at the end of the day when, after all the careful planning and hard work, the function has achieved maximum profit with a minimum amount of fuss and those who have parted with their money feel that it was worth every penny.

This book is written for those faced with fundraising for the first time, to share ideas and tips that will lead them around some of the pitfalls. Information about the legal aspects is accurate at the time of going to press, but laws are amended with such frequency that facts and figures soon get outdated and must be checked.

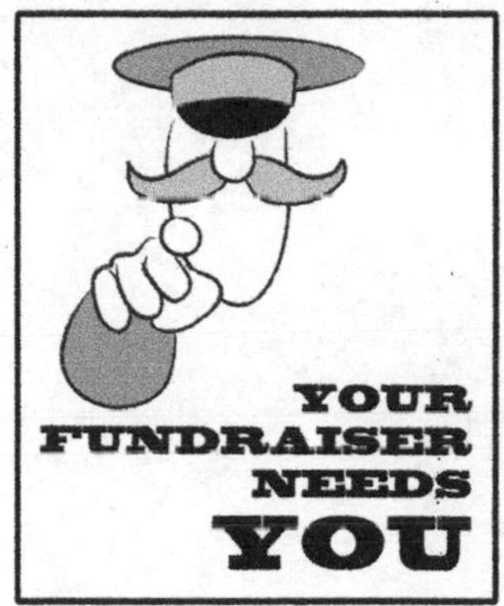

PART ONE
Getting Started

CHAPTER 1

Selecting and Planning an Event

When deciding the best way to raise money for your particular cause, it is worth taking a little time to list the various assets in your area and think about how they could be used. Consider not only the availability of a local celebrity, TV personality, member of the nobility or millionaire (more on this in Chapter 4), but also local features such as ruined castles, lakes, stately homes, waterways, disused airstrips or hangers, and municipal gardens.

Tactful enquiries will reveal if any of these notable people and amenities may be pressed into service, borrowed or hired, and at what cost. This list should give your committee a useful starting point for a discussion about the type and scope of event which could be run, and the possible number of people who could be accommodated there. Remember that access and parking space for cars, trailers, horseboxes, etc., may have to be considered, and you don't want to have to make special arrangements to transport your public to out-of-the-way places and then take them back again.

The planning and organization of a major event, when you hope to attract several thousand people, may take over a year. Popular attractions need to be booked well in advance and, if you plan to ask a celebrity to attend, you will need to offer them a number of possible dates. Again, this takes time to arrange.

At the other end of the scale it is possible to put together a small garden party during a period of lovely weather at very short notice, just as long as it takes to get the news on the 'grapevine' that you're holding it and to muster a band of helpers to provide goods for both eating and selling.

If you are short of time and helpers, there are some functions you can hold and make a profit when all you have to do is sell tickets. For example: dinner dances, coach trips, concert and theatre parties, river trips, day excursions and holidays abroad. See 'Group Bookings' for more information, page 67.

If you live in a part of the country attractive enough to appeal to the tourist trade, think about a scheme to invite tourists, from home or overseas, to stay as guests in the homes of those who support the cause. More details can be found in 'Paying Guests', page 78.

If raising money for your organization is a perennial problem, it is not necessary to try a new venture every time. Once you are fortunate enough to find something that goes well in your area, make it an annual event. When people enjoy themselves and don't get overcharged, they will come again, and nothing is more rewarding.

Before 'naming the day' of your major event, make enquiries to ensure that you are not planning to hold your do on a day when the whole population tramps off to some other established annual event. Diaries of forthcoming events are usually to be found in public libraries, with the mayor's secretary or in principal council offices. Check also that you don't pick a day when the great British public is going to be glued to the television, watching a major sporting event. Once you have picked a date which is reasonably free from other attractions, let the principal fundraising organizations in your area know what you're planning to do; this should avoid you having to make way for another event. Once yours is in the civic diary you should be sure of getting the local VIPs to attend.

Ideas and tips for all sorts of events can be found in Part Two of this book. All of these are ideas I have carried out over my fifty-plus years of fundraising.

Having decided on the type of event, the possible site and date, you now need to form a committee to run it. Creating a successful team out of a group of volunteers takes tolerance as well as good humour and drive. You may find some people volunteer with reluctance, but once they are caught up in the organization of the social event, and have become enthused with a common purpose to make the largest profit they can, they will soon find out how satisfying such a challenge can be.

CHAPTER 2

The Committee and its Duties

Whether you get an idea to run a fundraising event within the family or get together with several friends, it is essential for the smooth running of the show that you form a committee and allocate specific responsibilities to suitable people. The size of the committee will depend to a certain extent on the scale of the event. It is generally true that the larger the committee the less it achieves, so keep yours to between five and eight members.

A full committee might consist of:

Chair	Planning and overall supervision.
Secretary	Clerical, distribution and information.
Treasurer	Budgeting, cash transactions, security, cash floats and change, and night safe arrangements if necessary.
Assistant Treasurer	To help the Treasurer, but main function on the day is liaison with stalls, car parks, programme sellers, ticket office, etc.
Catering Officer	Refreshments for VIPs and public.
Bar Officer	Obtaining bar licence, bar staff and stock, and bar tending on the day.
Publicity Officer	Advance publicity, design of publicity materials, sites for posters, sign posting, liaison with police, etc.
Site Officer	Layout of site, obtaining ropes, poles, signs, working parties, siting of loos, water and electricity points if outside or if indoors, checking on existing facilities, layout of stalls, exhibitions, dressing rooms, etc., tables and chairs, and adequate lighting.

In addition to the main committee it may be found necessary to co-opt 'specialists' to help with any technical aspects of your event and form sub-committees to relieve the main committees from detailed planning.

The Chair

In all committees there are those who stand out as natural leaders in society. When looking for a suitable person to head up your committee, look for someone who has held a position of responsibility. Avoid the orator, the dictator and the tycoon. And we have all met the 'I must do it myself then I know it will get done' type, who gets thoroughly overtired and irritable as the event gets closer. They frequently end up by causing such an atmosphere of tension and frustration amongst fellow committee members that the whole show is affected.

At best find someone who is authoritative, decisive and tactful. Select someone who will organize and delegate and ensure that steady progress is being made by the other members of the committee with regular and tactful checks.

At worst, if you have to include someone who is not going to be a lot of help but can't be excluded, give them an honorary position such as Chair or even 'President' and make yourself the Secretary so that you can lead from behind.

The Secretary

The Secretary is the key member of the committee. Ideally, select someone who is keen, energetic and thorough with good organizing ability, own transport and some spare time. Computer abilities are an advantage but not essential.

The Secretary is responsible for all correspondence, arranging meetings, notifying members of the subjects to be discussed at the next meeting (this is called an agenda), making notes of all decisions made during meetings and confirming these in writing to members later, in the form of minutes. Specimen copies of an agenda and minutes can be found in Appendix C, pages 116–18.

The Treasurer

Ideally this should be someone connected with finance, banking or the law; a citizen above reproach who is both methodical and painstaking. It is no job for the scatterbrained volunteer who forgets to 'note it down', loses cheques, fails to acknowledge donations and produces unpaid bills long after the final balance has been distributed. All fundraising organizations must be seen to be completely reliable when handling other people's money.

The Treasurer is responsible for outline budgeting, all cash transactions, invoices, bills and accounts, arrangements for security, cash floats, supply of change, banking and night safe arrangements. Finally, when all accounts have been settled after the event, he or she is responsible for producing a detailed balance sheet.

Other Committee Members

These should be selected from those most suited to perform the duties required of them, not only because they bring that particular expertise to the task, but also because they are likely to have the contacts necessary to keep expenses down, obtain supplies at cost price and be able to find the 'man with the van' for that job when a car is too small. When trying to run a large function to raise substantial sums of money, get experts into the principal jobs. Enthusiastic amateurs, however keen and willing they may be, are more likely to involve your organization in costly problems.

CHAPTER 3

Charitable Giving

Before embarking on raising money it needs to be decided if your cause can legally be classified as a charity. A registered charity is exempt from paying taxes on its income and charitable donations are exempt from income tax, which might act as an incentive to possible givers.

To clarify the meaning of the word 'charity', the Charities Act 2011 has a list of thirteen charitable purposes that includes the following:

- The relief of poverty.
- Advancement of education.
- Advancement of health or saving of lives.
- Advancement of citizenship or community development.
- Advancement of arts, culture, heritage or science.
- Advancement of amateur sport.
- Advancement of human rights.
- Conflict resolution or reconciliation or the promotion of religious or racial harmony or equality and diversity.
- Advancement of environmental protection or improvement.
- Relief of those in need by reason of youth, age, ill-health, disability, financial hardship or other disadvantage.
- Advancement of animal welfare.
- Promotion of efficiency of the armed forces of the Crown or the efficiency of the police, fire and rescue or ambulance services.
- Any other purposes recognized as charitable under the Act – this last item covers a charitable purpose that is within the spirit of the above purposes and is a mechanism for future development of the list of charitable purposes.

A group of people forming an organization to raise funds on behalf of an individual cannot register as a charity, however worthwhile the cause. Don't let this put you off; just because you are not a charity, doesn't mean you can't organize a successful event. If you have a worthy cause that people feel they would like to support, a lot of money can still be raised.

The Charity Commission registers and regulates charities in England and Wales: www.charitycommission.gov.uk or call 0161 798 9999.

CHAPTER 4

Advertising, Promoting and Funding

The VIP

If the event you plan to run is big enough and is being held for a cause in which you know a member of the Royal Family has a special interest, write to ask if they would be prepared to open or attend the event. Suggest any Saturday from May to September during the next three years. If you are lucky, and you may well be if you are prepared to plan ahead, the news of visiting royalty will soon take care of your recruitment of helpers, sponsors, sales of tickets and patrons' passes, as well as ensuring the full cooperation of press and local radio, both before and on the day of the event.

A local celebrity, TV personality or political figure will also ensure good local press and radio coverage, although naturally they will not draw the crowds in quite the same way. It may help if you try to think up some eye-catching press-worthy gimmick. For example, 'Visiting Bishop goes up in a hot air balloon after opening grand fête' or 'Army General to be fired as human cannonball at opening of carnival' are more likely to hit the headlines of your local paper than simply 'Local MP opens garden party'.

Advertising Media

To attract the general public, notify the 'What's on' section of local papers and radio. Prepare banners, posters, leaflets, car stickers, etc. Make sure your event is listed on your website and through other social media outlets.

It pays to advertise, but only if your material is well-designed, eye-catching and informative. 'Many stalls, attractions and side-shows' does not actually set one alight with desire to attend, but 'Stock up the deep-freeze with home-baked bread or *cordon bleu* TV dinners', may well attract the hostess who wants the mostest. 'A chance for the motorist to test his skill' or 'Fascinating contest for the skilled darts player' may attract the man of the family, and few children can resist the opportunity to crawl about in an army tank or fire engine. See my notes in 'The VIP' (above) too. Try to make your event sound exciting and different but be sure you can carry out your promises; you want the public to trust you and come again.

The sale in advance of lucky numbered programmes, car park tickets or vouchers to spend on the day will advertise the show as well as providing a much needed flow of cash to cover the initial outlay.

Direction signs on the roadside must be well made, weather proof and readable by passing motorists. They should be placed on key roads and junctions to the town or village where the event is to be held. Before your enthusiastic committee member goes blazing off with posters, posts and sledge hammer to awaken the sleeping public, or if you want to display a banner across a main road, do consult the local authority to ensure that you are not infringing any local by-laws or causing danger to motorists by obscuring turnings, etc.

If you wish to use a loudspeaker van to advertise the function, you must first obtain consent from the police.

Good publicity is costly but worthwhile. Plan the publicity campaign like a battle; put something out well in advance but keep some in reserve for use nearer the event. Find a local firm or factory to sponsor publicity materials to defray the cost (see below), but make sure that the firm's name appears on all the advertising materials you use.

Finally, see that the team that puts up any posters, banners and signs is also responsible for the removal as soon after the event as possible.

Social Media and the Internet

The internet has become the first place people go to seek information and has a host of advertising and promotion opportunities that can be taken advantage of with no or little cost to your organization. A website is good place to start. You don't have to get too fancy, but it gives people a place to go to find out about your organization, what your goals are and contact information, and – of course – how and when to get to your event. If you are lucky enough to have someone 'in the know' on your committee, designing a simple website is not too difficult. If you feel a more sophisticated website adds more legitimacy to your enterprise, the cost of design can be offset by offering advertising or getting sponsors who could be listed on the site. See Appendix G, page 131, for more details.

Funding

It is advisable to try to offset major expenditure before your event takes place by inviting sponsorship, patronage and sale of stall space for traders and exhibitors. If you can build up a healthy balance beforehand, all the money you take on the day will be clear profit and, should some disaster prevent your function from taking place, you won't have made a total loss.

Sponsorship

Most firms and industries put aside a sum of money each financial year to cover advertising and publicity, and if approached with a carefully presented and well-thought-out scheme they will often agree to become sponsors. The sponsor must be consulted about the layout of all publicity material and give final approval to the drafts before any printing is done. The following are some examples of advertising which can be offered in return for sponsorship:

- On your website.
- On large display boards, giving the firm's name and product, set at strategic points around the site.
- In the programme or catalogue, e.g.: '1st prize of £50 will be presented by Mr Green of The Lime Green Custard Company, who has kindly sponsored this exhibition'.
- At the foot of all notices, leaflets, etc., and on the reverse side of the entrance tickets: 'The cost of all printing and publicity materials has been kindly met by The Lime Green Custard Company'.
- In racecards and schedules: 'All the prize money and rosettes for classes 1 to 6 have been kindly given by The Lime Green Custard Company'.

- On the final page of the programme, etc.: 'We are indebted to the following for the generous sponsorship, without which this show would not have been possible.'
- On handouts, free or sold at low cost: biros, rain hats, book markers, balloons, etc., all giving the date of the show and the sponsor's name and product.
- Over the PA system when events and winners are being announced.

If you find private individuals who are willing to act as sponsors and do not wish to have any publicity in return, don't forget to include their names with other sponsors in the programme, catalogue or racecard.

Patronage

Large subscribers may be given the honorary title of Vice-President, and in many events it has become the practice to offer Honorary Vice-Presidencies in return for a donation. This entitles them to special car-parking and refreshment privileges and their names are recorded in the programme, with the thanks of the organizers.

Sale of Advertising Space

The sale of space in a magazine, catalogue or programme will defray the cost of the printing. Once you know how much the publication is going to cost it will be possible to calculate how much advertising is going to have to be sold – in quarter, half or full pages – to offset the expenses.

Important points are:

- Get the advertisers to submit their copy 'print ready', so that you don't have to design it yourself.
- Get payment from advertisers in advance.
- Send complimentary copies of the publication to the advertisers.
- List all who have bought advertising space at the back of the publication, with thanks from the organizers.

Sale of Exhibition and Trading Space

The sale of exhibition and trading space on a showground brings invaluable additional revenue as well as adding interest to the proceedings. In return, provision must be made for adequate electricity and water as well as refreshment and toilet facilities. Sites should be priced according to area, frontage onto spectator precincts and proximity to centres of attraction.

I have provided an example Conditions of Sale of Exhibition Sites form, see Appendix D (i), page 119 from a two-day equestrian event when an attendance of several thousand was expected. If only a few hundred spectators are expected, the range of spaces and prices should be drastically reduced to get traders to come at all, since one is not able to guarantee that it will be worth their while.

CHAPTER 5

Professional Support for your Event

Insurance

Ask yourself if you can afford to replace, repair or pay compensation for anything that might be broken, damaged, stolen, injured or killed as a result of the events that you are holding. You will probably decide that, except for very small gatherings when most of the guests are known to each other, the premium paid for insurance is a small price to pay for your peace of mind when using other people's property. Get estimates from two or three local insurance companies, you will be surprised how much they vary.

If you are running a function for a well-known charity or political party, check with their headquarters to see if they hold the general insurance policy for all functions held in their name, then check to see that the function you intend to hold is adequately covered. (The little matter of 'third party' is sometimes omitted.)

With our uncertain climate you may consider taking out a policy against rain. Cover is hard to find and cost varies according to the month, number of hours to be covered and area in which the function is to be held, but rainfall of half an inch has to be recorded before you can claim and the premium is usually too high to make it worth while.

If you are hiring a marquee, tent or other equipment, find out from the owners if their insurance extends to accidents caused by or to their property when on hire by your organization.

Public safety is important so check your public liability and insure your event as necessary. It may pay you to shop around for insurers, it also may pay to ask an expert to vet your policy to ensure that you are adequately covered and that there are no unacceptable exclusion clauses in the small print.

Medical and Veterinary Support

When running an event where there is an element of risk to life or limb, of man or beast, you must arrange for professional help to be available should the need arise. This must be taken into consideration when preparing your site plan. All first-aid points, ambulances, veterinary tents, etc., should be sited in such a way that easy access is available. Make sure that you have signs pointing to the first aid or veterinary posts.

St John's Ambulance Brigade will, when requested, set up a first-aid post and for larger events will also have ambulances in attendance. Write to your local medical and veterinary practices enclosing complimentary tickets, car passes, etc., asking if they would nominate someone to act as Honorary Medical/Veterinary Officer. They may not be able to attend for the entire time, but will ensure that an officer is on call and quickly available if requested.

Acknowledgement and thanks to all who assist in this way should be recorded in your programme or racecard, and a letter of thanks should be sent to them after the show. In the case of St John's Ambulance Brigade and other voluntary organizations of this kind, it is customary to send a donation to help cover their expenses.

Police and Local Government Involvement

Always consult the police, unless the function you plan to hold is in a private house or is too small to impede or increase the flow of traffic to the venue.

Write to the principal police officer in your area in the early stages of your plans, and suggest a meeting to find out what you may or may not do – before you put too much effort into something that is not permitted by law.

Such is the nature of local government, involvement may be needed from the county council, the district council and your local town council, as outlined below.

Highways

There are many bylaws and regulations governing events, such as car rallies, held on the public highways. As a general rule, when arranging any event to be held on a public highway, permission must be obtained from the local county council, but check with your local authority for their rules. Full details of guidance notes are given in Appendix A (ii), page 106. Permission to hold a cycle race or rally must also be obtained from the police.

If you applied to the police for permission to hold sponsored walks, or sponsored bed, pram or wheelchair pushes, they will say that, although there is nothing in law to prevent you from running such an event, they recommend most strongly on safety grounds that you should not do so. If you do go ahead in spite of their warning of the possible dangers to both competitors and other road users, the police will make it clear that full responsibility will lie with the organizers who must have plenty of easily identifiable stewards along the route.

Advertising

Sticking posters on anything you choose (known as fly posting) is not permitted by law. Outline your plans to the police and ask for their advice. Posters and hoardings may only be placed on private land after permission from the owner has been obtained. Should you wish to hang a banner across a road you must first get permission from the town clerk and satisfy the police that it will be hung high enough not to cause an obstruction and that permission from the owners of the property on either side has been obtained.

Security

Discuss with the police all aspects of security with particular reference to property which may have to be left unguarded for any length of time. While the police have not got the manpower to offer twenty-four hour surveillance, they will arrange for a patrol to make regular checks. They may recommend that you should employ a watchman or dog and handler, but they will still make regular routine calls as a backup service.

Traffic Control

When you have given the police all the details as to date, times and type of show being held, they will then make such arrangements for traffic control and policing as they consider necessary.

Bar
If you run a bar or beer tent, you will need to ensure you have a licence – see Appendix A (i), page 103. The police will make regular checks to ensure that you are complying with the rules governing the granting of the licence. These visits can be very reassuring to the bartender, especially if he anticipates trouble at closing time.

Public Address
PA equipment used in a moving vehicle as a form of advertisement is seldom effective and not recommended, but if you find that it is necessary to broadcast from a car on the public highways, permission must first be obtained from the police. Public address systems may be used on the site of your show without permission from the police.

* * * * *

Having covered all the points you wish to raise with the police you might consider offering them a free site for a static display or recruiting stand: But a word of caution: if they suggest a 'car accident display' do all you can to discourage it. One of these put on by the police at the entrance of a local horse show was so realistic and blood-stained, that members of the public entering by the gate scuttled passed white-faced and shaken. It is not the easiest thing to create an atmosphere of light-hearted entertainment after that.

Finally instruct the secretary to put the police and local government on the distribution list of any amendments to the plans.

Health and Safety

Although those three words may well cause a sharp rise in blood pressure in some potential fundraisers, Health and Safety is a fact of life which has to be taken into consideration for many forms of raising money.

Once you have decided on your event, think about all the safety issues that could arise and do some research to see what government regulations are in place that you might need to look into. It is also advisable to pick up the phone and ask your local district council to put you through to the department dealing with these matters, to make sure that you are not breaking any local regulations. For more detailed information about how Health and Safety regulations may affect the event you are planning, the Health and Safety Executive have a free book, *The event safety guide*, which you can download at www.hse.gov.uk.

Health and Hygiene

Food hygiene and food safety standards are overseen by the Food Standards Agency. Their website, www.food.gov.uk, has all the information on the regulations and has useful hygiene training videos that might make you think twice before offering to throw the hamburgers on the grill. Using common sense and following their guidelines should prevent any unpleasant 'gastric nasties'.

When serving food to the public, have a list of the ingredients and a sign to show that the item might contain nuts, dairy, shellfish, gluten or other allergenic ingredients.

Electrical Equipment

The days of grabbing the old coffee pot from the attic to press into service for the coffee morning are gone. There are now regulations that require all appliances used to be portable appliance tested on a regular basis. This includes things like floor heaters, coffee pots, water coolers, musical amplifiers, etc. This 'PAT' should be performed by someone qualified to perform the test and will also give you piece of mind that your equipment is safe to use and it won't let you down at an inconvenient moment.

Working with Children

Previously called CRB checks, a Disclosure and Barring Service (DBS) check may be necessary for fundraisers who are working with children. If in doubt your first port of call is www.gov.uk/disclosure-barring-service-check where you will find more information and the relevant forms. The DBS check is free for eligible volunteers. The Secretary should give them a form to fill in, which they return along with proof of identity. The Secretary then sends this off to the DBS. The form will be sent to the volunteer, and you should ask to see this when they receive it. See www.gov.uk for more information and the relevant forms.

PART TWO

Fundraising Ideas

Amateur Dramatics

Amateur dramatics, although great fun to take part in, are not normally considered to be great moneymakers. The key to success, as so often is the case, is to get someone with a really sound knowledge of the business to 'produce'. If you decide to put on a play, musical or variety show, it must always be as professional as you can possibly make it. No need to dwell on the lights that fail, the curtains that have their own unique action quite unrelated to the strings which control them, the scenery that falls over to reveal weird and wonderful goings-on backstage and the players that 'dry' and cannot hear the prompt – these happenings may leave the audience rolling in the aisles at your first night but will do little for box office takings at subsequent shows.

Requirements
An experienced producer, suitable venues for rehearsals and performances, and enthusiastic helpers and performers.

Time to arrange
This will depend on the producer but allow a minimum of six months.

Refreshments
Interval bar with light refreshments, confectionary acquired on a 'sale or return' basis.

Publicity
Local paper, parish magazine, posters, leaflets, car stickers, a website and via social media, local radio and by sale of tickets in advance.

Method
Leave the onstage activities to the producer but be prepared to liaise with him over scenery painting, lights and costume, etc., as required.

Expenditure
Hire of hall, printing, possible costumes and props, and royalties.

Income
Sale of tickets, bar and refreshments.

Notes

- Amateur dramatics are often a useful way to raise funds for the church. Think of the available talent often to be found within its choir stalls and in the congregation. Facilities for rehearsals and even for the performances themselves are often available, at no cost, in church halls.
- Musicals, with their large casts, usually do very well as you are assured large audiences of friends and relations.
- Costume plays have to be looked at carefully unless you have free access to period clothes, because costumes can be very costly to hire.
- Royalties have to be paid to the author of the play during his or her lifetime and for seventy years after death. These costs can vary, but it is not reasonable to expect authors to reduce or waive performing rights for charity.
- Should you wish to stage a copy of the panel game as seen on television, do check with the copyright department of the authority concerned before doing so.
- Some companies admit old-age pensioners and children to dress rehearsals at half price. This gives the performers valuable help getting the 'feel' of an audience and timing laughs, as well as bringing in extra money.
- Managers of some theatres are prepared to negotiate fees for amateur companies. They sometimes accept a share of the profit in lieu of the normal booking charge. It pays to call on them for a little chat early on in your planning stages.
- Copies of plays can be obtained from: Samuel French, Theatre Bookshop, 52 Fitzroy Street, London W1T 5JR Tel: 020 7387 9373
- The checklist in Appendix H, page 135, may be helpful.

Antique Valuations, Fairs and Auctions

Although there are a variety of ways of holding antique valuations, road shows and auctions, one which was held in aid of Barnardo's some years ago is well worth recommending.

The event lasted all day. It was held in a small theatre and conducted by a member of one of London's best salerooms. Members of the public brought items of interest to be identified and valued, and in some cases auctioned. The valuer was highly qualified and most amusing and it was mainly due to his expert appraisals that the day was so enjoyable and successful.

Requirements
A suitable location ideally with a stage and an area that can be locked for storage of items. An antique expert that in knowledgeable in all fields, PA system for the audience to hear the comments and insurance. If planning to combine with an auction see section on auctions on page 32.

Time to arrange
At least six months.

Refreshments
Provide a running buffet and arrange to take out a Temporary Events Notice so that a bar may be run throughout the day. See www.gov.uk/temporary-events-notice and read Appendix A(i), page 103, for further information.

Publicity
Principally by means of an introductory letter, which gives details of the event, together with an application form to be used by those wishing to have an item valued. Nearer to the date of the event, by posters, leaflets, car stickers, social media and notices in the local paper.

Method
Recruit plenty of helpers for this function. You will need to provide stacks of homemade food for the running buffet, have staff to serve all day and experienced bartenders. As the safety and security of items (some of which may be of great value) is most important, collect together a surefooted and careful team of porters to carry goods on and off the stage, returning them to a locked storage room after valuation. Divide the event into three sessions: valuations from 10 a.m. to 1 p.m. and from 2 to 5 p.m. and the auction from 5.15 onwards. Sell tickets to spectators for either the morning, afternoon or auctioning sessions.

Expenditure
Hire of hall or theatre, food, drink, insurance, expenses and fees for the valuer, printing and postage.

Income
Sale of tickets, from a charge made on each item valued (this might be a percentage of the value given) and a percentage of the price raised on any item auctioned, profit from the bar and buffet.

Notes

- The committee should consult a reputable antique dealer and get his advice on a reasonable percentage to be charged for the valuation and auction. These charges must be set out in the letter so that potential customers know the scale of charges before they place an item for valuation.
- Establish if the theatre where the event is to be held already holds a bar licence. If not, application should be made to obtain one at least ten working days before the date of the function.
- When items are handed in, prior to the show, have a detailed description made of each piece, noting major cracks, chips and scratches. The item could be digitally photographed, especially noting cracks and chips, etc.; as the photo is time and date stamped it could be very useful if a dispute later arises. Give the owner a receipt and ensure that the item is only handed back on production of that receipt.

- In order to maintain a smooth flow of goods to the valuer, it is essential that owners should hand in their property before the start of each session and not expect them to be accepted from the body of the theatre. Once the goods are in your charge, it is vital that they be handled as little as possible and that every care be taken for their safety and protection. Check on the insurance needed for an event of this kind.
- A useful checklist can be found in Appendix H, page 135.

Appeal Letters

Why is it that some appeal letters arouse interest and sympathy while others either irritate or make no impact at all?

When you sit down to compose an appeal letter try not to make the recipient feel guilty, don't take it for granted that their support will be forthcoming, don't suggest the size of their contribution and remember that not everyone has a bank account.

Nicholas Lowe, an appeals director for Barnardo's, had a knack of producing a winner every time. What was the secret of his success? In the example below, first he involves you emotionally with a simple human story which ends with more than a glimmer of hope so you read on, without skipping a word, as he shows you the wider picture of the work done by the whole organization and their continuing need for funds. Throughout the letter he holds your attention until finally he makes a direct appeal for money.

As postage can be a big drain on organizations funds, ask people to send a stamped addressed envelope if they wish for a receipt.

See Appendix B, page 115, for guidelines on bulk mailing.

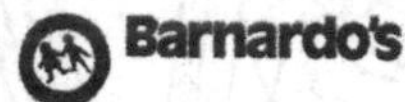

Ref: DU

'We never wanted her at home.'
A chilling comment from a mother as her small daughter entered hospital. For three-year-old Tessa, severely physically handicapped and rejected by her family, the future looked extremely bleak.

It was found that Tessa was in need – not only of specialist treatment – but also of protection. Parental resentment of her condition had led to ill-treatment and there were signs of bruising, both physically and emotionally.

Tessa lay in a hospital bed – a rather hopeless, unloved little form.

Some weeks later she was placed in the care of Barnardo's. Unable to walk and acutely apprehensive, Tessa seemed to live in a little world of her own. Day by slow day, however, she began to benefit from special caring, physiotherapy and kindly human contact. As she responded to the whole atmosphere of love and warmth, a new life was opening out for Tessa.

When she was older and stronger two operations were performed which improved both her physical handicap and personal appearance. With the aid of callipers Tessa took her first, hesitant steps and suddenly beamed at her achievement.

Tessa will always have a slight limp but now, at nine years old, she is completely mobile and attends an outside school. Her special flair is for cookery and recently, in Barnardo's, she helped to make her own birthday cake. Tessa was greatly elated at its success, especially as she had asked to bring some friends 'home to tea'. Now, Tessa has supervised visits to her own home, for after years of hard work by social workers, a better relationship is being built with her family and much damage is being repaired.

Over the last eleven years, Barnardo's has laid a new emphasis on the care of physically and mentally disabled children. So much can be done for their development and in our specialized units and schools we help to widen their horizons and bring hope to their lives. Can you imagine, perhaps, some of the costs involved in specialized care – the money needed for medical and educational purposes. Then we start to add the bills from our residential homes, day centres, play buses, community projects – **the needs are never ending**. That is why we are writing to you today. Your support really matters. Please, will you help? We should be so grateful if you would send us a donation for whatever sum you can afford.

With warmest thanks,

Yours sincerely,

Nicholas Lowe

Nicholas F. Lowe
Appeals Director

Art Exhibition

There may be many amateur artists in your locality who would never think of entering a competition or exhibiting their works unless attracted by an advertisement with a direct invitation that encourages them. If you can awaken the interest of these budding artists, you may be able to put on your own exhibition.

The small rural village of Instow, North Devon started an exhibition at the local yacht club over thirty years ago to support the local RNLI. This attracted amateur artists from all walks of life, and has developed into a most successful and popular annual event. Even with sponsorship for the prize money, you are unlikely to make much profit from your first year, but if you find genuine interest in the venture it should be worthwhile establishing it as an annual event.

Requirements
A suitable venue for exhibition, where pictures may remain on view for a week or two – a country house, civic or community centre, or school during the holidays. You will also need a panel of judges.

Refreshments
Are not advised except possibly at the preview.

Publicity
For exhibitors, by leaflet, notices, social media, articles and letters in the local paper. Nearer to the date of the exhibition, publicity to be aimed at viewers with a fresh batch of posters, leaflets and invitations to attend. Try to sell advertisements in the catalogues to help with the cost of printing.

Method
Send copies of the leaflet to local art classes, schools, colleges, senior citizens' clubs, public libraries and other organizations in the

area. Once application forms start coming back, the Secretary should begin to calculate the hanging space required and plan accordingly. (Structures on which the pictures can be hung can usually be borrowed from colleges or the council.) When items are handed in, prior to the show, have a detailed description made of each piece, also noting any damage. The item could be digitally photographed – as the photo is time and date stamped it could be very useful if a dispute later arises. Give the owner a receipt and ensure that the item is only handed back on production of that receipt.

Expenditure
Hire of premises, printing, expenses for judges, insurance, and prize money if not sponsored.

Income
Entry fees, sale of catalogues, admission and commission on sale of exhibits.

Auction Sale

Many people have surplus furniture and suchlike in their attics or garages which they are prepared to give to your cause if you can make use of it. You can make a lot of money from auctions, especially if you are prepared to spend a bit of time smartening up the goods prior to the sale. It takes a fair amount of organization but it does yield a very good return for the effort.

Requirements
A professional auctioneer, posters, a suitable hall or room with a rostrum, and a large storeroom where items can be kept and repaired prior to the sale.

Time to arrange
Three or four months.

Refreshments
These are not normally served although, if the sale is likely to go on all day, a coffee and sandwich bar might add to the profits.

Publicity
First by leaflet for distribution to the whole area to be canvassed, followed by posters, notices in the local paper, social media, leaflets, car stickers, etc., and finally by advance sale of catalogues.

Method
This event is easier to organize if the area to be canvassed is divided between members of your committee, each one to be responsible in his own area, for the distribution of leaflets, calling back to collect items and for arranging transport for larger pieces of furniture. Goods should be stored as collected in a place where minor repairs and renovations, if necessary, can be carried out. As goods are collected they should be listed and a catalogue prepared, giving

conditions of sale. Arrangements should be made with a local dealer for the removal of anything left over after the sale for an agreed price.

Expenditure

Hire of premises, fee or expenses of auctioneer, printing of the catalogue and publicity (although you might cover this by sale of advertisements in the catalogue or by sponsorship).

Income

Sale of catalogues, money received from goods auctioned and profit from the coffee bar if held. You may decide to charge an entry fee.

Notes

- A specimen leaflet is given in Appendix E, page 129. If people cooperate and display the reverse side of the leaflet in the window, it makes the job of calling back and collecting items for the sale a much easier one.
- The numbering of catalogues is recommended if they are to be sold prior to the event. They can then be issued to helpers in bulk and any unsold catalogues returned, together with the cash from those sold.
- Some very successful auctions are held on a 50/50 basis, when a percentage of the auction price is returned to the donor. But this does give additional work to those organizing the sale, as unsold goods have to be returned to their owners and arrangements have to be made to return the cash when a sale has been made.

Barbecue

This event is very easy to run and is popular with all age groups. If the barbecue is to be held in the grounds of a private house, for security reasons the host or hostess should be asked if they would like the sale of tickets restricted to people they know personally and members of the organization, rather than to members of the public. Catering is made easier when the number of those attending is known in advance.

Requirements
A suitable outdoor location with, if possible, open-fronted shed or barn or large garage for use in wet weather. Barbecue equipment with the correct fuel, outdoor lighting, music and a few tables and chairs or hay bales.

Time to arrange
A few weeks only.

Refreshments
The price of tickets can include one drink, after that additional drinks can be bought from a licensed bar. Partly cook the main ingredients to be ready for the 'fry-up' when required, allow about 1.5 soft baps per head. Cook onions and keep hot on the side and have mustard, tomato and barbecue sauces ready to 'paint on' as requested.

Publicity
By sale of tickets, email and social media.

Method
Try out and time the barbecue equipment before the day so that you know when to light it to give maximum heat when needed. Provide long tongs, oven gloves and an apron for the 'chef', and

have some cooking oil and paint brush to hand. Music will liven up the evening, especially if there is an area suitable for dancing. During hot weather an evening swim can be an added attraction although, with the right mixture of guests, a very happy evening can be held round the fire without additional facilities.

Expenses

Printing of tickets, food and drink, fuel and possible hire of barbecue, sound equipment and outside lights (although one can usually borrow these).

Income

Sale of tickets, profit from the bar, and raffle or tombola if one is held.

Notes

- If you intend to run a licenced bar apply for a Temporary Events Notice in plenty of time, see Appendix A (i), page 103.
- If you play music, you should also have a PPL Licence, see Appendix A (iv), page 113.
- Rules governing the holding of a raffle at a private function are given in Appendix A (iii), page 108.
- A checklist for this event is given in Appendix H, page 135.

Bridge Drive and Whist Drive

Whist Drive

Though not very remunerative, whist drives are a popular form of fundraising. In a village where players know each other they can come to regard the evenings as an important regular social event.

Requirements

A hall or room large enough to take about ten card tables and chairs, a master of ceremonies, sufficient packs of cards for the number of tables in use and scorecards for everyone taking part.

Time to arrange

A few weeks.

Refreshments

Tea, coffee, biscuits or cakes, to be served halfway through the evening.

Publicity

By posters, leaflets, social media and sale of tickets prior to the event. Once the evenings have become established as regular events the publicity will take care of itself.

Method

Arrange for someone who knows the rules of the game to act as master of ceremonies. He or she will display a card denoting trumps at the beginning of each game, keep an eye on the play and, when all the players have completed the game and recorded their score, move the winning couples on to another table. Prizes are awarded at the end of the evening for the highest scores, with a 'booby' prize awarded to the lowest. A raffle can be held during the interval.

Expenditure
Hire of hall, scorecards, refreshments and prizes (unless donated). In order to make as much money as you can from the evening, get local benefactors to donate gifts to be used as prizes for the winners as well as for a raffle.

Income
Entry fee and money taken on the raffle.

Bridge Drive

Most bridge clubs will be glad to cooperate with you in arranging a charity competition, in which couples play 'duplicate bridge' and prizes are given to the winning pair of players. Duplicate bridge differs completely from contract or auction bridge in that the couples, who stay together for the whole evening, play with cards which have been dealt before the games begin and arranged so that the N, S, E and W players at each table are playing with the identical hands or cards. Rotation of players will have been worked out in advance to give each couple the opportunity to play against every other couple competing.

The correct procedure for this game is complicated, so you are recommended to ask the bridge club to nominate an expert to work out the hands and the moves for you in advance and supervise play during the evening.

The amount of money raised in this way will depend on the number of pairs you invite to take part. For example: eight tables with each player paying a table fee of £5 will bring in £160. From this it is apparent that you can't expect to raise a great deal of money in one evening but, if you have enthusiastic bridge players in your area, perhaps you can arrange to hold a series of competitions. Naturally it will help if you can get the prizes donated, and not paid out of the table fees.

Car or Motorcycle Rally, Proficiency Tests and Competitions

The most popular events for raising money are car rallies, treasure hunts and navigational scatters, although events held on the public highways are generally not so popular with the police. However, if you have an area suitable to accommodate a large number of cars and motorcycles, plus a level space where proficiency tests and competitions can be held, an event of this sort can be both entertaining and lucrative.

Requirements

Suitable location (for example, a disused airstrip), PA system, trailers, caravans or tents for use by the organizers, flags and stopwatches. Get plenty of volunteers to act as marshals, stewards, etc. Get stakes, ropes and hay bales for use as barriers to separate the competitors from the spectators, and cones and barrels for use as obstacles on the course.

Time to arrange

Up to six months.

Refreshments

Provide refreshments appropriate to the time of the year; a cold drinks and ice-cream stall or a hot dog and coffee stall or, if you intend to run this event on a large scale, have a refreshment marquee and a beer tent.

Publicity

By notices in the local paper (including entry forms), social media, posters, leaflets, car stickers and large billboards on the site where the function is to be held.

Method

Invite a member of the police, the AA or RAC to join your

committee to decide on a schedule of events, tests and competitions. This co-opted member can also be asked to provide a panel of judges. Copies of this schedule with entry forms can be then sent to colleges, appropriate clubs and others. Rosettes, cash prizes or certificates of proficiency can be awarded to the winners. Invite local traders to set up appropriate stalls and have a play area for small children at a safe distance from the competitions. Ask members of the committee to set up and run sideshows and stalls to entertain those not taking part in the contests. Play lively music on the PA equipment to help to create a carnival atmosphere.

Expenditure

This will vary with the size of the enterprise but, for a small show, if you beg, borrow or 'find' the props needed to set up the various tests and competitions, the main costs will be the hire of the PA equipment and the music licence, printing, publicity, rosettes and prizes.

Income

This will come from the competitors' entry money, car-parking, admission of spectators, sale of frontage for trade stalls, sponsorship and profit from refreshment and sideshows.

Notes

- Arrange for a first-aid post (see page 16).
- Check on insurance (see Chapter 5).
- Make sure if you do play music that you obtain the necessary PPL Licence required to play music in a public location. See Appendix A (iv), page 113.
- Read Chapter 4 – an event of this kind, especially if it draws the crowds, offers plenty of opportunities for publicity. The local car sales firm or garage might be prepared to act as sponsors.
- It may be necessary for anyone working with children to have a Disclosure and Barring Services (DBS) check, see page 19 for more information.
- Appendix A (i), page 103 will tell you how to obtain a licence if you wish to run a bar or beer tent.

- If you intend to hold a car rally, treasure hunt or navigational scatter on the public highway there are useful guidelines issued by the Motor Sports Association. The MSA is the governing body for all motor sports in the UK. Further information on running these individual types of events can be found on their website www.msauk.org. General guidelines for events to be held on a public highway are reproduced in Appendix A (ii), page 106.
- A checklist for this event is given in Appendix H, page 135.

Carol Singing

Requirements

A choirmaster, members to sing in the choir, carol sheets, lantern and/or large torches, collecting boxes clearly marked with the name of your organization and transport.

Time to arrange

You should begin two or three months before Christmas.

Refreshments

Hot mince pies, hot toddy or soup to be served at the last house on your list.

Publicity

About a week before, put cards or small leaflets round the area where you intend to sing, saying:

> We hope you will be at home on ....
> at about .... p.m. when we will be in the area singing carols.
>
> A collection will be taken on behalf of ....

Method

Get someone who has handled choirs before to conduct your practices. Meet every week in different houses but get somewhere that has a piano in the early stages. Keep the numbers to about a dozen and ask each host to provide some simple refreshments. Work on some unusual carols as well as the more familiar ones. Decide on the number of evenings you will go out and plan a route that will avoid too much travelling. Be very firm about being lured into friends' houses for refreshments, however cold it may be. If you want to raise money you must stick to your schedule. Arrange for refreshments to be served to the choir at the last house you call at each evening you go out.

Expenditure

Practically nothing, unless you offer payment for petrol or refreshments. Most carols are out of copyright, that is when the author died seventy or more years ago, but do check in case your performance incurs a royalty fee.

Income

This will vary according to the area you are in and the number of houses you can fit in during an evening's singing, but you should be able to collect well over £100 on each evening.

Celebrity Concert

Provided that a celebrity with sufficient appeal can be found to ensure that all tickets are sold, this is not a difficult function to arrange. Some years ago, an internationally famous pianist gave a piano recital at the Queen's Hall Theatre, Barnstaple in aid of a well-known charity. Patrons had been found to help with the cost of putting on the concert, tickets and programmes were sold. The evening was a memorable one and a sizable cheque was handed over to the charity.

Requirements
A suitable venue, theatre, concert hall or school assembly hall and, preferably, one well-known artiste (although an enjoyable concert can be staged with two or three lesser-known stars).

Time to arrange
Six months to a year.

Refreshments
A licensed bar can be available during the interval for the sale of alcohol and coffee.

Publicity
By notices in the local paper, social media, posters, leaflets and car stickers.

Method
In a big association there is always somebody who is related to or knows someone famous, so the choice of a celebrity may not present much difficulty and negotiations can be done on a personal basis. Should you not be so lucky, get hold of a copy of *Who's Who* and write to the star of your choice, inviting him or her to give a guest appearance in aid of your cause. To be sure of getting a favourable

reply, give plenty of notice and let them choose the date (having first obtained a list of available dates for the venue). Once you have your celebrity booked and the date confirmed, the tickets can be printed, the programme prepared and the publicity campaign launched.

Expenses

The concert hall booking, the fee and expenses of the artiste, publicity and printing.

Income

Sale of tickets, sale of programmes, profit from the bar (if held) and income from sponsorship and patronage.

Notes

- The programme can simply be two photocopied pages containing a list of the works to be performed, a few facts about the composers, a biography of the soloist(s), some notes about the charity and, finally, acknowledgements to those who have sponsored the costs, arranged the flowers, loaned the piano, accompanied the artiste, etc.
- Find out from the artiste or the artiste's agent:
  - The fee required and whether expenses are to be paid for.
  - If accommodation, meals or transport will be required.
  - If the artiste has any likes or dislikes.
  - If they could supply some biographical notes for the programme.
- Make sure that the dressing room is suitable and has everything for the comfort of the performer.
- If your celebrity is a woman, arrange for a child to present her with a bouquet of flowers at the end of the concert.
- If you are running a bar on unlicensed premises, read Appendix A (i), page 103, about obtaining a Temporary Events Notice.
- Read Chapter 4, pages 15–20, if you wish to get the printing and publicity sponsored.
- Check that the location has all the necessary licences to cover playing music in public. See Appendix A (iv), page 113, for PPL Licence information.
- See the checklist in Appendix H, page 135.

Cheese and Wine Party

This is a very painless way of raising money, being easy to organize, most enjoyable to run and needing very little preparation.

Requirements
Someone with a fairly large house to agree to 'host' the party, preferably one who will allow you to run a bar in their house.

Time to arrange
Four or five weeks.

Publicity
Usually by the sale of tickets to those known to the host, and to members of your organization and their friends.

Method
Decide whether the drinks are to be limited to only one or two glasses of wine to be included in the price of the tickets or whether, additionally, to run a licensed bar. In the first case your income will be limited to the price of tickets whereas, if you decided to run a bar, the profits will keep rolling in as long as the party lasts. Having decided on a date and the price to be charged for tickets, get them printed and arrange for their distribution and sale by members of the committee. Apply for a bar licence (if needed) and choose a reliable person as bar tender. It is not a job for someone who is unable to keep a clear head.

Refreshments
Your hostess may be prepared to produce a cheese buffet herself but members of the committee usually agree to share the preparation of the refreshments. At the end of the buffet, serve tea or coffee. If you decide to apply for a licence to sell alcohol, allow for half a bottle of wine and one fifth of a bottle of spirits per person.

Expenditure
Printing of tickets, food and drink.

Income
Sale of tickets, profit from the bar and raffle if held.

Notes

- The committee should offer to arrange the tasks so as to leave the host and hostess free to circulate among the guests.
- See Appendix A (i), page 103, for application to obtain a Temporary Events Notice.
- If you intend to hold a raffle, see Appendix A (iii) page 108.
- Unless there is ample space for parking, it is advisable to station someone outside to supervise the parking of cars.
- If you will be playing music, check Appendix A (iv), page 113, for music licence information.

Coffee Morning, Coffee Afternoon, Devonshire Cream Tea

This is a very painless and a simple way of raising small sums of money, perhaps to provide a cash 'float' for a larger event.

Requirements
A private house with use of the kitchen, one large table for a bring-and-buy stall and three or four items suitable for use as a raffle.

Time to arrange
A few weeks.

Refreshments
Tea, coffee, squash and either biscuits or finger food.

Publicity
By notice in the local paper, parish magazine and posters in local shops and outside the house where the event is to be held. The sale of admission tickets prior to the event is well worth the effort as it results in better attendance.

Method
Ask someone with suitable accommodation to 'host' the event. Try to arrange for the use of all downstairs rooms and the garden, if fine, as guests need space to mill about and talk to their friends. Serve coffee after the guests have done their shopping at the stall (which ideally should be placed near the entrance). Arrange for members of the committee to be on the door, the stall and the raffle. This leaves the hostess free to circulate and to supervise the refreshments.

Expenditure
This should be minimal. People offering to hold these events usually give the refreshments without charge and, along with

members of the committee, donate a few items to start the bring-and-buy stall and provide prizes for the raffle.

Notes

- Order about six pints of milk for 100 cups of tea or coffee served with cold milk, but allow extra if you intend to heat the milk for coffee.

A Dance

There is no single formula for running a successful dance. Much depends on the suitability of the venue, the expertize of the band and the personality of the master of ceremonies. A disco will be popular with the teenager but tends to be altogether too much for older age groups who spend the evening trying unsuccessfully to get the volume turned down while waiting in vain to hear a tune they can recognize. So it is important to consider the age group of the people who are likely to buy tickets and to engage a band who will play a mixture of numbers to please both the mums and dads, the children, and the grans and granddads.

Attend a few local dances before you plan your own and you will soon find the dance band to suit your needs. Have a talk with the MC before the event; the band will do everything they can to make the dance go with a swing but they will appreciate a little briefing first to be able to 'strike the right note' with those attending.

Time to arrange
At least six months: but if you find a band you like, book them for your next dance as soon as you can, as good bands get booked up years ahead.

Venue
Check maximum capacity of the building and make sure there are adequate unobstructed fire exits.

Refreshments
These can vary from a finger buffet to a four-course, sit-down meal. Again, after you have attended a few dances you will be able to decide what is popular in your area. Run a licensed bar with spirits, wines, beer and soft drinks, etc. – see Appendix A (i), page 103, if applying for a Temporary Events Notice.

Publicity
By notices in the local paper, social media, posters and leaflets. For a small local dance, by the sale of tickets only.

Method
Decide with your committee the type of dance you intend to hold, the price of tickets and the maximum number of people you can accommodate without overcrowding (which will lose you support for next time). For further details on organizing the dance see the checklist in Appendix H, page 135.

Expenditure
Hire and heating of hall, band, refreshments, publicity, printing and decorations, cost of licences.

Income
Sale of tickets, profit from the bar and income from the raffle or tombola stall if held.

Dinner Party

Home Entertainment

Although it may seem distasteful to invite friends to come to a meal and then ask them to pay for your hospitality, when you are fundraising you must not shrink from using any legal means. If each member of your committee were to invite two couples to a dinner party, charging them a small fee, and if each of these couples were to hold a party to which they invited their host and hostess plus one other couple, and so on, the snowball effect would bring in a steady flow of money. The secretary or treasurer would have to exercise some gentle control over the proceedings to ensure that return invitations were made before everyone has forgotten what it is all about, also that money that has been collected by the hosts gets paid in before it is absorbed into the 'housekeeping'.

Banquets

If you can obtain the use of a large banqueting hall and recruit plenty of experienced helpers to prepare and to serve meals, you may consider holding a medieval, old English or Victorian banquet. Alternatively, if you are able to involve someone familiar with foreign cookery, why not arrange for them to present a series of overseas meals; Indian, Chinese, Scandinavian, Italian, etc. The choice is endless and people always seem to be prepared to pay for good food and drink, especially if you offer tempting and unusual menus.

Charity Dinner

A fundraising committee for a well-known charity holds a very successful annual dinner every year. They hire the banqueting hall of a local hotel and members of the committee and their friends supply the food for the buffet, which is always excellent. Tickets, which are not expensive, include a glass of wine and are limited to avoid overcrowding. It is found that the same people make up parties to attend this dinner year after year as it has, in the course of time, gained an excellent reputation.

The dinner is held in November and a stall for the sale of Christmas goods is an appropriate adjunct. An important source of cash comes after the meal from a professional auctioneer, who auctions a variety of gifts which have been donated by local firms and supporters for this purpose.

Pot-luck Supper

American fundraisers have an interesting way of providing either a hot or cold buffet meal for a large number of people who buy tickets for a film or show or similar entertainment that includes refreshments: they call it a 'pot-luck' supper. Everyone who buys a ticket is asked to arrive with four helpings of either an entrée, fish, main course or pudding. The food is laid out on the buffet table on plates or, if it is hot, left in a slow cooker, and guests help themselves. The organizers are left with the task of selling the tickets (which include wine), and providing cutlery and crockery, and the coffee after the meal.

Notes

- Check the section on food hygiene and safety, page 19.
- It may be necessary for anyone working with children to have a Disclosure and Barring Services (DBS) check, see page 19 for more information.
- If you play music, you should have a PPL Licence, see Appendix A (iv), page 113.

Donkey Derby

This is a very popular day out for the whole family, catering as it does for all age groups. The firm who hires out the animals for a donkey derby arrives with about a dozen donkeys. Some are made available for giving rides to small children while others are taking part in the races or enjoying a well-earned nosebag and stand-easy before being allocated other duties. Donkeys always come complete with saddles and racing colours.

Requirements

Find the name of a firm who hires donkeys from the internet. Recruit plenty of helpers to act as marshals, stewards, judges and donkey-hands. You will need people to sell refreshments and to run sideshows and attractions. You need a structure which can be used as a tote and people to man it. These people should have a good head for figures as they will have to calculate the payout on the winning ticket number at the end of each race. A tent or marquee for refreshments and a commentary box with PA system are also required. A commentator who has 'kissed the Blarney stone' is worth a lot to the tote takings.

Time to arrange

At least six months, but more if you want to invite a well-known person to attend.

Refreshments

Run a continuous buffet and a licensed bar in an open-fronted marquee and have a soft drink and ice-cream kiosk for the children.

Publicity

By billboards on the site where the donkey derby is being held, social media, posters, car stickers, leaflets, notices in the local paper and on local radio. By the sale of the racecard/programme in advance of the function.

Method

Telephone the donkey hire firm to discuss possible dates and to establish what they bring with them. (Some firms supply the tote paraphernalia and some bring four two-wheeler carts so that volunteers can compete in a 'Ben Hur' type of race as a finale.) Having established what props the firm intends to bring with them and how many races you can expect the teams of donkeys to run, you will be in a position to prepare the racecard/programme. Approach prominent citizens, asking them to act as sponsors to races or donkeys or to take part in the races. There is no doubt that the day is more fun and the tote takings higher when well-known figures take an active part in the proceedings. Then discuss with the committee what you can run in addition to the donkey derby – donkey races do not take very long to run (once you have got the animals off the 'start line') so it is important to have plenty of things for the punters to do between races. Fill the showground with sideshows, games, competitions, attractions, exhibitions and stalls and have cheerful music played over the public address system between the racing commentaries.

Expenditure

Hire of donkeys and equipment, tote, PA equipment, marquee, publicity, prize money and rosettes.

Income

From the sale of racecards/programmes, 'gate' money, car-parking, profit from refreshments and bar, takings from donkey rides, sideshows, stalls and attractions, etc., revenue from sponsorship, advertising in the programme, trade stalls, exhibitors and profit from the tote.

Notes

- When compiling the racecard, which in itself can be nearly as much fun as watching the volunteer jockeys trying to stay on during the races, make up appropriate names for the race, the donkey and its forebears, for example:

2.30 p.m. race – ***The Politicians Handicap*** **– sponsored by the president: Mr Manny Bags.**
4 runners.

No. 1.	'Snap Election' by 'Inflation' out of 'Control' Ridden by Mrs Talkemdown MP (Sponsored by Mr Green of Lime Green Custard Company)
No. 2.	'Propaganda' by 'Exaggeration' out of 'Panic' by Mr I. M. Keen, political agent (Sponsored by the 'Get It rIght' Printers)
No. 3.	etc. ...

- A list of sideshows and attractions which can be run in conjunction with this event is given on pages 92–98.
- It may be necessary for anyone working with children to have a Disclosure and Barring Services (DBS) check, see page 19 for more information.
- Instructions for obtaining a Temporary Events Notice are given in Appendix A (i), page 103, and the PPL licence information for playing music is in Appendix A (iv), page 113.
- The checklist in Appendix H, page 135, may be useful.
- For some reason, children frequently get separated from their parents during an event of this kind, so have a collecting point for lost infants which is clearly signposted.

Fashion Show

This is a popular and quite straightforward form of fundraising, since much of the organization is taken out of your hands once you have found a suitable venue and a fashion house, boutique or dress shop willing to cooperate.

Requirements
A room, series of rooms or a hall, where either rows of chairs or small tables and chairs offer guests a clear view of the proceedings. A catwalk is ideal in a hall but, failing that, a stage will do. A microphone may be needed in a large hall. A fashion house or boutique to supply the clothes and volunteers to act as models and/or dressers. The models will need a changing room. More volunteers will be needed to help with the refreshments.

Time to arrange
A few weeks, once the date has been agreed with the owner of the dress shop.

Refreshments
This will depend on the scale and location of the event and will vary from coffee and light refreshments in the village hall to a champagne buffet in a four-star hotel or stately home. A Temporary Events Notice is required from your district council if you want to serve alcohol.

Publicity
Posters, leaflets, social media and notices in the local paper, and also by the sale of tickets prior to the function.

Method
Your first move is to visit the owner of the dress shop and discuss the proposed event with him or her; they are sure to have put on

fashion shows before and will know how they would like it arranged. It is normal for the shop to supply a team of models to show the clothes, although additional talent might be welcome. You will probably be asked to supply a team of dressers who will be responsible for 'stripping down' and 'dressing up' the girls as they whizz in for a 're-fit'. Ask if they want to do the commentary themselves; if not, invite someone who is used to a microphone and can keep a cool head if things get a bit chaotic. Make sure that cards have been prepared in advance with the details of each outfit. If the event is being held in a private house, the models can circulate round several rooms, handing the commentator for each room a card containing the information about the outfit they are displaying. Gentle music in the background can help to provide a relaxed atmosphere.

Expenditure
Only what you spend on food, drink and publicity – unless you have to pay for the hire of the premises.

Income
From the sale of tickets and raffle or tombola if held.

Notes
- If you decide to have a raffle read Appendix A (iii), page 108.
- If needed, instructions for obtaining a Temporary Events Notice are given in Appendix A (i), page 103, and the PPL licence information for playing music is in Appendix A (iv), page 113.
- The checklist in Appendix H, page 135, might be helpful.

Film Show or Film Preview

Requirements
Any suitable hall, clubroom, theatre or cinema, a projector and someone to operate it, and the films.

Time to arrange
A small film show can be put on in a few weeks, but a film preview will take considerably longer. Much depends on the distribution programme of the film you wish to screen.

Refreshments
These will range from tea, coffee and biscuits in the village hall, or a licensed interval bar serving light refreshments, confectionary, coffee and alcohol, through to a buffet meal if supper is to form part of the evening's entertainment.

Publicity
Social media, posters, leaflets and notices in the local paper for a major film preview, or by the sale of tickets for a smaller show.

Method
A film show in a hall, club or private house is quite straightforward to arrange. Decide on the film you would like to show; these can be purchased or hired from any large supermarket or downloaded from the internet and you will require a laptop or computer, a projector, a screen and sound equipment. If, however, your aim is a prestigious event, a charity preview involving the first showing, locally, of a newly released film, you will hit a few unexpected snags. In the first place you will find that you are unable to hire or borrow the film of your choice for one single performance (the minimum period is for one week) so your best plan is to try to arrange with the manager of your local cinema to loan you a film he is intending to screen the following week. The choice of film

and the date of your charity performance therefore have to be keyed into the film distribution programme and you must call on the manager of your local cinema at the earliest stage of planning to discuss your ideas and aspirations with him. The loan of the film for charity may be free, or on condition that you pay a percentage of the profits from your show (after all your expenses have been deducted) to the Cinema and Television Benevolent Fund. Your plans will be further complicated when you choose the time and place for your event. Cinema performances usually run continuously from 2 p.m. until about 10.30 p.m. daily so, unless you intend to hold a midnight matinee, you will be unable to book the cinema and you will have to hold your function in a theatre or concert hall. In this case, remember to establish that the premises are licensed for this kind of entertainment and that the hall is equipped with projection equipment appropriate to the format of the film.

Expenditure
Hire of equipment, hire of premises, films, printing and publicity and licences.

Income
From the sale of tickets, profit on the refreshments and bar, if held, and in the case of a major film show, from the sale of programmes and of advertising space in the programme.

Notes
- See the chapter on dinner parties for an American pot-luck supper, page 52, which you might like to serve at the film show.
- Under UK Copyright law, you will need a STSL licence to show a film in public. See Appendix A (iv), page 113.
- If you plan to hold the function on unlicensed premises you should read Appendix A (i), page 103 which gives rules for obtaining bar and entertainments licences.
- A checklist for this function is given in Appendix H, page 135.

Fireworks Party

This event is run in very much the same way as a barbecue; in fact the only differences are that you hold the fireworks party earlier in the evening to cater for the younger members and, for reasons of climate and safety, the fireworks display should be where it can easily be viewed from the house. (Some very small children become upset by the noise and feel safer if viewing proceedings from behind a sheet of glass.)

Despite frequent broadcast reminders of the safety precautions to be taken by those organizing fireworks parties, tragic accidents still can, and do, happen. It is advisable to take some pains before the event to ensure that over-excited children will be excluded from the area of operations and particularly that the stock of fireworks will always be watched over by a responsible adult and protected from falling sparks or cigarette ends, as well as from the inevitable rain.

Notes

- For safety information for fireworks, check out: www.fireworksafety.co.uk and www.gov.uk/fireworks-the-law.
- You must not set off fireworks between 11 p.m. and 7 a.m. The exceptions are: Bonfire Night, when the cut off is midnight and New Year's Eve, Diwali and Chinese New Year, when the cut off is 1 a.m.
- It may be necessary for anyone working with children to have a Disclosure and Barring Services (DBS) check, see page 19 for more information.
- You may find the checklist, Appendix H, page 135, useful.

Flower and Vegetable Shows and Flower Festivals

Flower and Vegetable Shows

Most towns and villages have flourishing horticultural and gardening clubs or societies. Should you wish to run your own flower and vegetable show you should seek out the Chair of your local club and ask their advice on the best way to run it. They will probably accept your invitation to be the Chair of the panel of judges and will no doubt suggest the names of the people you should invite to assist him or her. Cash prizes, rosettes or vouchers (to be spent at a local garden centre) can be awarded to winners.

To make it an outing for the whole family you should arrange some sideshows, stalls or other attractions and have ice-cream and refreshments on sale.

Flower Festivals

If you are lucky enough to have a professional or very experienced flower-arranger in your area, invite them to direct your flower festival. This should only be undertaken by someone who has had experience in this sort of thing before. It is no task for a beginner, however enthusiastic he or she may be. Failing this, invite members of a flower club to undertake the project. Financial help over the provision of flowers must be offered and wide-spread raiding parties sent out to beg, borrow or scrounge from local gardens. Arrange for a strong back-up to deal with administrative details, such as car-parking, refreshments, sale of postcards, souvenirs and programmes. If your festival is being held in a church, abbey or cathedral, consult the priest in charge about the possibility of having organ recitals during the day or as a separate concert in the evening. Collecting boxes or plates should be placed in prominent places in places of worship but if the festival is being held in a private house, admission can be charged. There is an invaluable little book by Grizelda Maurice on flower arranging (Grizelda Maurice, *Flower Arranging and Flower Festivals in Church* (London:

Batford, 1982)) with special reference to flower festivals. This should be read by anyone interested in helping with this fascinating work.

Well Dressing

Those who have travelled in Derbyshire during the summer months may have seen the wonderful communal enterprises of certain villages in 'dressing' their wells with pictures and texts in flowers, grasses, seeds and other decorative materials, each one being a small work of art. Most of these arrangements are in the form of floral collages. A competition for the best work in this art form, usually from only natural materials, can be appropriate to any flower show or festival, with the valuable effect of involving large numbers of amateurs, often children, in your fundraising effort.

Garden Party, Fête, Fair or Bazaar

The *Oxford English Dictionary* states that a fair is a 'periodical gathering for the sale of goods, often with entertainment', a fête is a 'festival entertainment' and a bazaar is a 'fancy fête to raise funds for charity'. This leads one to conclude that the name for this type of function is unimportant, but don't advertise your function as an 'Olde English Fayre' unless you intend to make an effort to create an atmosphere consistent with the period.

Garden Party

An invitation to a garden party conjures up visions of sunlight on soft lawns and the leisure to stroll about and enjoy the company and conversation of friends and acquaintances. Of course a beautiful garden is an advantage but the main requirement is to lay on a good tea and groups of tables and chairs where the guests may sit in comfort. The addition of a few stalls or sideshows could be run with the intention of adding interest rather than making money.

Garden Fête

The distinction between a garden party and a garden fête, is that tickets for the latter do not include tea, and the stalls and sideshows are the principal money-raisers, so you must have as many as you can fit in. Bric-a-brac stalls are always popular and can be made to look decorative and interesting, but do exclude second-hand clothing as it always tends to make a stall look jaded. Teas and ice-creams are essential.

Fairs and Bazaars

The village or civic hall is an ideal location for these events. Tables, chairs and trestle tables are usually on the spot, and there are facilities for making and serving teas. For any event which is being held out of doors in our climate, you must of course have alternative plans prepared for wet weather. As in the case of the fête, do have as many stalls, sideshows and competitions as you can.

There are no fixed formulae for running all these events, like 'Topsy' they usually 'just grow', with people volunteering or being persuaded to run various stalls and sideshows. To get some idea about what can be held there, visit the place where the event is to be held before holding your first committee meeting and, in the case of a private house, find out what facilities the hostess can provide.

It is usual to co-opt a VIP if possible to open the event but it is somewhat doubtful that anyone less than a VVIP will have any significant effect on the attendance these days.

Notes

- For a list of sideshows and stalls which can be run at these events, consult pages 92–98.
- If playing music make sure you obtain a PPL Licence, see Appendix A (iv), page 113.
- You may find the checklist in Appendix H, page 135, helpful.

Golf Tournament

For many years charity committees have been using the goodwill of golf clubs to raise money, and most golf clubs may be already helping three or four local organizations on an annual basis. However, if you approach the secretary or manager of your local club he might allow you to hold a 'formal competition', especially if your organization will provide the prize money. With no overheads, except for that prize money and expenditure on publicity, you can expect to make a reasonable amount if you can get enough golfers to take part.

The junior members at our local golf club needed to raise enough money to equip a clubroom for themselves. They successfully reached their goal by getting sponsored 'per hole completed during fifteen hours of play'. A similar idea might be adopted by fundraisers with the cooperation of the club secretary.

If you are attracted by the thought of organizing a professional/amateur celebrity golf tournament you should be alerted to a few drawbacks; firstly, there are public rights of way through a large number of golf courses so it becomes impossible to 'cash in' on spectators by charging entrance money to those who turn up to follow their favourite stars round the course; secondly, both amateur and professional golf stars command very high fees, they also expect to be put into first class hotel accommodation with all expenses paid.

The good news is that golfers love to play golf, especially given an opportunity to play on a course that they would not normally have access to. If you are lucky enough to find a prestigious golf club willing to give you a reasonable rate or a split of profit to use their facility, it is a matter of working out the numbers: how many players you need to make a profit.

Requirements

A golf course willing to lease or donate their facility.

Time to arrange

As popular golf courses are usually booked up way in advance and only set aside three or four days a year for charity golf events, it is advisable to start planning at least a year ahead and remember to rebook for the following year if you plan on making it an annual event.

Refreshments

Find out what options are offered at the golf course; refreshments could be included or provided by the golf club, or they will allow you to provide your own refreshments. If they have a banquet hall and/or restaurant available, consider including an evening 'award ceremony' in the price of entry.

Publicity

Social media, local papers and radio, posters and flyers in other golf clubs and sports shops.

Method

Decide what size of event you are going to hold, remember the more you can offer, the more you can charge for the entries. Get local business sponsorship, either monetary or items for prizes or smaller promotional items for a goodie bag to hand out to the players. Check with the secretary or manager of the golf club and discuss how much they will be responsible for. It is usual, once all the entries are in, to group players into teams or 'foursomes' and let the golf club know how many groups will be playing. The golf club should handle setting up the play times and all the tournament arrangements on the day.

Expenditure

Hire of facility, printing of scorecards, prizes (if not gained through sponsorship), publicity and promotional material for sale, i.e. T-shirts, caps, water bottles, etc.

Income

Tournament entry fees, refreshments if provided, sale of promotional material.

Group Bookings

This is one of the ways to make a profit when you are short of time and helpers, there are many activities, e.g. coach trips, concert and theatre parties, river trips, day excursions and holidays abroad, that can be booked as a group and are fun to put together.

Requirements
Time to shop around for a good price or a trusted travel agent to work with you on the booking. A knowledge of your destination is a must; it a great disappointment to arrive at the hotel advertised as 'having wonderful sea views' to find that it is located right beside a busy motorway: the views are great but the road noise is so bad you are too tired to enjoy your holiday.

Time to arrange
Six months for a trip abroad or a month for smaller group booking.

Publicity
Local paper, internet and social media, but if you are planning a holiday or trip where you are going to be with the same people for an extended amount of time, it is best to keep it via word of mouth amongst friends, or advertised locally to a group of like-minded people, to ensure it a happy experience for all.

Method
Get a quote for a group booking from a hotel, travel bureau, coach company, etc. Work out the costs of the trip per head and charge people an additional percentage.

Horse Shows, Hunter Trails, Gymkhanas, etc.

Equestrian competitions are becoming increasingly popular and vary from one-day shows to three-day events. If you have never run a horse show before, start simple, e.g. a horse show and gymkhana run on one day only. When you have gained experience with a small show you can have a go at a two-day event, with trade stalls, exhibition sites, attractions and 'all the fun of the fair'. A true 'three-day event' is not normally tackled by local fundraising groups. The principal three-day events, which are held annually, usually televised and attract competitors from all parts of the world, have become established over the years and it would be hard to break into this highly professional field.

Requirements
The locations for the various types of equestrian events will vary according to the competitions being planned and the notes on pages 70–73 explain what is needed for each type. Remember to include a suitable area for exhibitors to warm up and school their horses before competing. If you are planning to run a horse show, the British Show Jumping Association (BSJA) publishes annually the *Member Handbook: Your Guide to Competition*, a tremendously helpful little book on organization, it also gives the names and addresses of the British show jumping representative, course builders, judges, etc., in each area. Once you have contacted your area representative and asked for their help and advice, you will find things falling nicely into place. Do ensure that the person who is taking on the job of show Secretary for a major horse event realizes that it will be a full-time job, especially during the last two months before the show.

Time to arrange
A year.

Refreshments

If you are planning to run a large show it is better to put the sale of food and drink out to a contractor. It will not make you a large profit but it will take a considerable amount of worry off your shoulders since it is always difficult to estimate the numbers to be catered for and your contractor will have the experience to ensure that this element runs without a hitch. On the other hand, if you are out for maximum profit and have the helpers (and they must be experienced at the job) you may decide, for a one-day event, to cope with the refreshments yourself – remembering that it is the spectators who produce your income and that you want them to come again if you run another event next year. You must cater for all their needs and those of their children, because a horse-show is a family day out. So for the catering side the least you need is a trailer supplying hot dogs, beefburgers, vegetarian options, tea, coffee, cold drinks, ice-cream and a selection of confectionery. You must, of course, make arrangements for your supplies to be replenished as necessary to ensure a continuous service throughout the day. Shelter should preferably be provided for those taking refreshments and, although tables and chairs are not necessary, an open-fronted marquee is a valuable asset, affording protection from the excesses of the British summer. A bar is virtually essential and you can run it yourself if you can find a team of experienced volunteers (see page 103 for information about bar licences, etc., and the section on page 19 on food hygiene). Again, an open-fronted marquee will provide a useful bolt-hole for the non-equestrian members of the public.

Publicity

By posters, billboards, car stickers and leaflets to be distributed to all the local equestrian centres, clubs, riding schools and establishments, also the local paper and social media. If you are planning a major show it is vital to see that an advertisement is put in the show number of *Horse and Hound* (the copy has to be in before either the last day of February or the first Thursday in March each year). This will ensure that your show gets wide publicity and it will also ensure that you get a good number of entries.

Method
If you are planning a small, one-day event, consult the secretary of your local pony club to get his or her advice about what is popular in your area. If you decide to go for a major show, invite the area representative of the BSJA to join your committee and use their local knowledge and expertise to help you plan the event and find a date which does not conflict with other horse shows in the area. The checklist in Appendix H, page 135, should be helpful.

Expenditure
So much will depend on the scale of the show you are planning but expenditure for most shows will include publicity, printing, prize money and rosettes, and hire of equipment including PA system, chemical lavatories, tentage, ropes, stakes, hire of jumps, water containers, etc.

Income
This will come from entry fees of competitors, admission charges for spectators, money from the sale of programmes, car-parking, profit from the refreshment and bar tents, and any subscriptions which can be drummed up from sponsors and patrons. At larger shows, significent revenue will come from the sale of trade stalls, exhibition sites and from any sideshows and attractions run in conjunction with the show (see pages 92–98). The profit from a small show should be in the region of a few hundred pounds but with good organization and a good attendance by the public, a two-day event should bring in a profit in the thousands.

Equestrian Events for Local Shows

Horse Show

Usually held in the summer months. To attract competitors for show jumping classes, at least one ring should be affiliated to the British Show Jumping Association. For affiliation you should consult the BSJA prior to fixing your date, to avoid clashing with other shows in your area. Once in their diary, no other shows will be arranged near to your date. To attract a particular breed or specialty-breed classes, contact the individual breed societies who are likely to be able to provide you a judge for the show or the specialty classes.

Classes include:

Show jumping

It is necessary to have two or more rings, depending on the size of the show, and a warm-up area. Each ring to be about 120 x 120 metres, one affiliated to the BSJA for scheduled show jumping, the other used in the morning for clear-round jumping (with a rosette being awarded for each clear round) and in the afternoon for non-affiliated jumping classes.

Showing

This is held in a third ring, which should be a flat area of about 120 x 80 metres.

Working hunter and working pony

Also held in the third ring, a small course of jumps consisting of brush fences, straw bales and gates will be needed (the sort of natural hazards one might find out hunting).

Gymkhana

Another third ring event, see entry below.

Dressage

Usually held in the spring and summer months. There are standard tests which are produced by British Dressage to test and demonstrate the obedience of the horse. A flat level surface of about 40 x 100 metres will be needed for this. Although one tends to associate dressage with the occasional rare snatches seen on the television screen of an expert performance, tests do also exist for the novice. Dressage tests are not held as frequently as show jumping and showing but they are gaining popularity. Schedules for these tests can be obtained at www.britishdressage.co.uk.

Gymkhanas and Mounted Games
Usually run in conjunction with a horse show. Events are run off in heats with the winners going forward to an eventual final with rosettes for the winners. There are many variations of these events but, whatever the programme, it is essential to make sure that the 'props' for each race are ready and that the judges and arena party know the order of events. There are no rules laid down by any society for mounted games so it is advisable for a few simple rules to be made by the organizing committee. For example: 'The use of whips and spurs is strictly prohibited', 'The Course Judge reserves the right to disqualify any animals which are, in his opinion, unfit to compete' and 'Protective headwear must be worn as well as suitable footwear. Plimsolls, trainers and sandals are not allowed'.

Hunter Trails
Usually held in spring and summer when the ground is most suitable. These require a cross-country course consisting of a number of natural fences and hazards over field and through woods. In most rural areas there are hunter trail courses already established which it may be possible to use but, if not, given a willing and cooperative farmer or landowner and with the assistance of an expert, it should not be too difficult to make a suitable course out of the natural features of an estate or farm.

Combined Training
This is a term for a show consisting of any combination of dressage, show jumping and cross-country.

Hackney and Driving Classes
Advice should be sought from the Hackney Horse Society or the British Driving Society before tackling these classes. Judging can be done in the main ring followed, perhaps, by a marathon drive of five to six miles. If you hold a marathon drive outside the grounds where the show is being held, discuss the route and traffic control with the police.

Useful addresses

The British Show Jumping Association (rules and year book), National Agricultural Centre, Stoneleigh Park, Kenilworth, Warwickshire CV8 2LR
Tel: 02476 698800 www.britishshowjumping.co.uk

The British Horse Society, Abbey Park, Stareton, Kenilworth, Warwickshire CV8 2XZ
Tel: 02476 840500 www.bhs.org.uk

British Dressage, Stoneleigh Park, Kenilworth, Warwickshire CV8 2RJ
Tel: 02476 698830 www.britishdressage.co.uk

The British Driving Society, 83 New Road, Helmingham, Stowmarket, Suffolk, IP14 6EA
Tel: 01473 892001 www.britishdrivingsociety.co.uk

Hackney Horse Society, Haydon Farm Cottages, Sutton Parva, Warminster, Wiltshire BA12 7AF
Tel: 01985 840717 www.hackney-horse.org.uk
(This office is not manned so keep trying.)

Info on course builders, hire of jumps, auto-timing equipment, rosettes and trophies can be obtained from your BSJA representative or from the internet.

Jumble Sale

Running a jumble sale is an excellent way of raising money. Amounts varying from fifty to several hundred pounds can be made with practically no outlay. It is important to select the date carefully, you don't want to discover that your jumble sale is the third one to be held in the area in the same month.

Requirements
A large hall, ten or twelve trestle tables, dress rails, hangers, a cash float, a tape measure for every table, plenty of jumble and bric-a-brac, and two helpers.

Time to arrange
A few weeks (no one is keen to give house-room to bags of second-hand clothing for more than a short period).

Refreshments
Tea, coffee and biscuits to be on sale and a few small tables and chairs should be available. Remember to have a bottle of squash on hand for children who don't drink tea.

Publicity
By notices in the local paper, social media, posters and leaflets (see the example given on page 129).

Method
Divide the area to be canvassed between members of your committee, each one being responsible in his own area for the distribution of leaflets and for calling back to collect items for the sale. On the morning of the sale, sort the clothing and bric-a-brac onto the trestle tables and hang the better-looking clothes on the dress rails. Don't put price tags on individual items, after you have been selling for a few minutes intuition will tell you how much you can

ask. On the whole it is better to keep the prices low and get rid of your stock. Do see that cashboxes are kept well out of the reach of the bargain hunters. A member of the committee should be detailed to stay at the door and collect a small entrance fee from those attending. Finally, arrange for a local dealer to call at the end of the sale to make an offer for, and take away, all unsold goods.

Expenditure
Hire of hall, printing and publicity.

Income
Entrance money, sale of goods and profit on refreshments.

Nearly New Sale, 50/50 Sale and Charity Shop

Newly New Sale

This event is run in much the same way as a jumble sale, but the goods must be in near-perfect order and, this time, much more effort must be given to sorting, sizing and pricing items, which should all be individually marked. Dress rails are a great asset in helping to display coats, suits and dresses. Persuade a member of your committee to design some simple rails or racks for the display of other items of clothing. (Go and see how Oxfam and Barnardo's shops do it, they are very good at showing clothes off to their best advantage.)

50/50 Sale

You frequently hear people say that they have unwanted clothes which are 'too good to give away'. This is where the 50/50 sale comes in. Here you offer the donors about 50 per cent of the price you get for the goods. This does involve you having to keep careful records, but it can be very lucrative. A 50/50 sale can be a one-day event but ideally you should find somewhere for the goods to be on display over a period of time, where people can come and try things on at their leisure. Arrangements should be made for the donors to call back to collect their goods if they have remained unsold for some time or their percentage of the sale price if they have been sold; this relieves you of having to send off postal orders or cheques for every item sold. Once it becomes known that there are bargains to be found you will have no shortage of customers. As sales may be made by various volunteers, do work out a simple but foolproof system of recording transactions. Make sure to issue receipts in a duplicate book for cash taken and get signatures for returned goods or for the money handed over to the donors. This should avoid recriminations at a later date.

Charity Shop

If you are interested in running a charity shop you are strongly advised to discuss the project with someone who has experience in this work. You will need a large and willing band of helpers to keep it manned during opening hours, also a constant supply of goods to sell. It is time-consuming and exhausting work. Most towns have two or three charity shops already but if you should find that you can get suitable premises at a low rental for a limited period, take some advice, then try and break into this popular form of fundraising. You may find Appendix E, page 129, helpful in the collection of goods.

Paying Guests

This is an easy and effortless way of raising money, especially if you are lucky enough to live in or close to a tourist area. All you need is a few large or historic houses with generous occupants willing to take in paying guests and donate all or part of proceeds to your cause. You might also have someone in your area who owns a holiday home on the coast, or in some exotic far away land, who is willing to donate a raffle prize of a week or weekend's 'getaway for two in romantic cottage by the sea'.

Requirements

A location which is nice enough to be a draw to the public and a gracious host who is willing to open their home to strangers and to make their visitors feel welcome.

Publicity

Use common sense and gear your publicity towards what is being offered. Keeping the publicity local and spread by word of mouth will help keep control of who you attract.

Method

Ascertain what amenities your host has to offer and any special requests they might have, e.g. no pets, unsuitable for small children, no smoking in the house or unsuitable for someone not able to climb three flight of stairs. Make sure these details are clear on all your publicity materials from the start to ensure it is a pleasant experience for all. Once you have successfully sold the bookings, all you have to do is keep your host informed of the number of guests, when they are arriving and if they have any special dietary needs.

Expenditure

There is minimal expense if you are selling the 'booking'. Guests pay an 'all in' fee for their holiday up front and the costs of the volunteer hosts can be refunded if they are not in a position to donate all the expenses. If you're offering the package as a raffle or auction item, there will be printing costs for raffle tickets and you should plan to spend a little more on publicity, especially if you have a desirable holiday location on offer.

Ploughman's Lunch

This is a simple way of raising small sums of money, perhaps to fund a larger event. The meal can consist of soup, followed by a plate of French bread, butter, cheese, pickles, onions, garnished with a salad, then tea or coffee. As you can see, there is not a lot of work in the preparation of the meal. Cider or beer can be served with the meal and included in the price of the tickets.

Let people choose where they wish to sit and eat. Don't hold a raffle or have a bring-and-buy stall and the event will probably turn into a pleasant, relaxed, conversational afternoon.

Sell the tickets in advance, as it is far easier to organize if you know how many 'ploughmen' you will be feeding.

Notes

- Instructions for obtaining a bar licence are given in Appendix A (i), page 103.

Street and House-to-house Collections

When an organization wishes to raise money on behalf of a charity by this means, an application for a Charitable Licence should be made to your district council. They hold the central register of charities who have been authorized to hold annual street or house-to-house collections. Not only is it a kindness to the public to space charitable collections throughout the year, but also it avoids any embarrassing tray-to-tray confrontations on doorsteps or in the high street.

Having first got outline permission from your district council and agreed a possible date, the promoter of the collection must apply for a Charitable Licence at least one month before that date. Those who organize collections are required by law to conform to the following regulations:

Street collections

- Street collectors should be responsible people, over the age of sixteen years, and should carry with them the written authority of the promoter. They must not receive any payment. Collectors must be told that they may not 'obstruct, annoy or importune'. They should remain static and should not be stationed less than twenty-five metres from one another.
- The tray and tins used must be clearly labelled to show the name of the charity or fund that is to benefit.
- The tins or collection boxes used for the collection must be sealed so that no one can get at the contents without breaking the seal. All money collected must be put into a box at once.
- If there is a sign that says 'No Cold Callers' – don't call!

After the collection

- All tins and boxes should be returned to their promoter unopened. Once all the boxes have been returned, the promoter should open them in the presence of another responsible person or bank official. Once the contents have been counted, the amount and names of collectors should be entered on a list which should be certified by both persons.

- Within one month of the collection, all required forms should be returned to the local authority, agreed and countersigned by a qualified accountant.
- Notice should be published in a local paper giving the name of the promoter, the area the collection was made, the name of the fund or charity, the date of the collection, the amount spent on expenses and the final amount collected.

From this it can be seen that the law on what is and is not permitted is precise. It may come as a shock to the promoter and collector to learn that the tin should not be shaken at people to attract their attention, nor should collectors approach members of the public to ask if they will subscribe to the cause by buying a flag, sticker, badge or ribbon. Promoters can make things easier for their team by arranging for tables to be put in shops or shop doorways in the principal shopping areas, where spare flags and tins can be held as a backup and posters can be displayed giving more details of the organization and the reason for the collection.

House-to-house Collections

House-to-house collections can be made either by tins or boxes (and these must be sealed) or by the delivery and subsequent collection of envelopes. The district to be covered should be divided into suitable areas. It is no longer possible to obtain a copy of the Register of Electors from your local council, so whenever possible select helpers who have a good knowledge of the area.

Few people really enjoy knocking on doors but the task can be made easier if they are able to address the householder by name when they identify themselves and the cause for which funds are being raised. It is usually found the best times to call are from 5.30 p.m. to 7 p.m. (except on elderly people who live alone) and at weekends. Where collectors have a local knowledge of the area it is better to leave the times of the collection to them. Collectors should be given a two or three week period to complete that task. They must carry with them the authorization of the promoter and the name of the charity should be clearly displayed on the tin, box or tray of flags.

Regulations governing house-to-house collections are as follows:

- The promoter must notify the police of their intention to hold a house-to-house collection and then obtain a licence to do so from the local governing authority, having first settled on dates agreeable to them. The application to the district council should be made at least one month before the collections are to be held. The licence usually covers a twelve-month period.
- The collection must be for charitable purposes.
- The promoter must be able to satisfy the council that:
  - The expense will not be excessive.
  - Both the promoter and the collectors he or she recruits are fit and proper people to conduct the collection in accordance with the law.
- Each tin or box used must be numbered and sealed with a label so that the contents cannot be extracted without breaking the seal. If envelopes are use they must have a gummed flap.
- The promoter should see that all collectors know where and when the collections are to be made and the date by which the unopened tins or envelopes must be returned. He must compile a list that gives the name of each collector, the number of the tin issued to that collector and the area to be covered, leaving a space so that the amount collected can be added at a later date.

After the tins or envelopes have been returned

- The promoter must open the tins/envelopes in the presence of another responsible person, count the contents and enter the sum on the list. On completion, the list must be certified by each person and within one month of the expiry of the licence, the authority concerned must be notified of the contents of the list.

Sponsored Activities

One has to admit with some reluctance that the modern trend, which almost amounts to a craze, for raising funds by sponsorship of individuals is sometimes a spectacular success. This reluctance stems from the knowledge that those seeking to fill their sponsorship forms with signatures are trading on the good nature and generosity of friends and relations who, regardless as to whether they care for the cause, would find it difficult to refuse to participate or to give less than other people who have already pledged support.

Sponsorship can be very successful when the participant is undertaking a challenge that most others wouldn't. For example, there are various companies that offer parachute training and jumps for charity. Those taking part need to secure a minimum pledge which can vary between £300 and £500, but they often raise much more. Another good moneymaker is a sponsored horse ride, which is described in detail in the next chapter.

There is a certain amount of advertising income potential in a good scheme in addition to the money raised in sponsorship. For instance, participants can wear T-shirts with the name of the product on them. Or how very satisfying, for the manager of a firm who has been generous in its sponsorship, to see the name of his product 'floating' down to earth on an intrepid parachutist whose deed gets coverage in the local press.

When sponsored events are undertaken by young children, the collection of signatures from people pledging their support does not present much of a problem. However their enthusiasm for the cause does seem to tail off after the event and unless the children are chivvied by someone to collect the money, the cash handed in seldom reaches the total promised. There are websites that have been setup to help with this, for instance www.justgiving.co.uk. Although they take a small percentage of each donation, the ease of donating and collecting can make it worthwhile.

The crazier the scheme, the more likely it is to attract participants and spectators, but also the more likely it is to attract unusual dangers. Think out all the hazards in advance and take precautions, don't leave safety to chance. Keep sponsored events off the public highways as much as possible, but when this is not possible, consult the police informing them of the special steps you intend to take to protect everyone taking part.

Sponsored Horse Ride

A sponsored horse ride is an excellent way of raising money. The route should, ideally, be wholly on private land but if this is not possible, discuss with the police the best places for the riders to cross public highways so as not to present any danger to pedestrians or motorists.

Requirements
A landowner who is prepared to permit competitors to ride over his land, plenty of volunteers to act as stewards and marshals, people to run a refreshment tent.

Publicity
In the local paper and by leaflet and entry forms distributed to schools, riding establishments, equitation centres, pony clubs, saddlers, tack shops and feed stores.

Method
Competitors should arrange beforehand to get themselves sponsored for a certain sum of money for each mile of the ride completed. The general conditions and instructions to competitors are set out in the specimen leaflet in Appendix D (iii), page 125. Invite a member of the riding fraternity to join your committee and together with him and the landowner who has agreed to allow the event to be held on his land, go over the route to be ridden. Invite a local doctor and veterinary officer to attend in an honorary capacity. Recruit and brief helpers to act as stewards and marshals on the course, and invite a team of the St John's Ambulance to be present.

Expenditure
Printing of leaflets and entry forms, publicity, provision of rosettes and competitors numbers and hire of tent or marquee if required. Donation to St John's Ambulance, if attending.

Income

Entry fees, sponsorship money and profit from bar and refreshments.

Notes

- Ask the secretary of your local riding club for the name of a supplier of rosettes and competitors numbers.
- Instructions for obtaining a bar licence are given in Appendix A (i), page 103.
- A checklist is given in Appendix H, page 135.

Subscriptions

Clubs and organizations which are able to offer their members social amenities, such as bars or sports facilities, are in the happy position of being able to rely on annual subscriptions for most of their income. Members understand that unless subscriptions are paid by the due date, membership will be withdrawn.

Associations that can offer their members little more than the satisfaction of giving to a worthwhile cause are not so fortunate. Though acceptance of 'membership' initially implies a promise of an annual donation, there is no incentive for members to pay up on the due date and collection of outstanding subscriptions can be a constant headache for the Treasurer.

It is important to check out all the information concerning the Data Protection Act 1998 when you are storing membership information, and ask members to sign that their information can be shared by members of your committee. Details of the act can be found at www.gov.uk.

Apart from the important advantage of providing a predictable annual revenue, experience has shown that payment by banker's order is the most satisfactory method as it avoids the embarrassment and expense of having to remind donors who overlook payments when they fall due each year.

This must be recognized from the beginning and the Treasurer must always be equipped with banker's order forms and try to persuade each new member to make one out in favour of the association when first joining (a specimen banker's order form is given in Appendix F, page 130).

This will not always be successful. It is probably fair to predict that not one in a hundred of the 'casual', though well-intending, subscribers will pay up by the date without prompting, particularly if the date has no other significance and is easily forgotten. When signing up a new member there is much to be said for adjusting the initial subscription proportionally so that the future annual payments will fall due on a date of some significance. The best date is that of the Annual General Meeting because reminders can be sent out without extra cost with the notice and agenda for the AGM. Even with this reminder there will be defaulters and the Treasurer is faced with the unenviable task of chasing them up.

Letters, even when accompanied by prepaid envelopes, do not ensure response and add considerably to administrative costs. The only really effective way of collecting overdue subscriptions is by personal contact. This means delegation, dividing up the area among dedicated individuals so that it is not too burdensome, for it is not a popular chore.

The essentials of such a method of collection are that the treasurer (or a specially appointed subscription secretary) should provide the local collectors with up-to-date lists of subscribers in their areas. The subscription list should include addresses, telephone numbers and the due dates. The collectors should keep the list under review and updated and initiate the action to call on defaulters within a week or two of the subscription being overdue.

'Wurdle Night'

'Wurdle Night' was the name given to a most successful evening of simple rustic entertainment held in Bedfordshire, on a fine summer night some years ago.

Requirements
A suitable outdoor location with an open-fronted marquee, plenty of equipment (in sets of four) for use in the games, straw bales (to mark out the race track and for spectators to sit on), small tables and chairs, outdoor lighting and a really good master of ceremonies complete with loud-hailer.

Time to arrange
Two months.

Refreshments
Run a licensed bar for the sale of wine, sprits, beer and soft drinks, and serve a buffet followed by coffee. Try to make the buffet *cordon bleu* standard.

Publicity
By sale of tickets only (you run this event in much the same way as a barbecue).

Method
A 'Wurdle Night', as it was run in Bedfordshire, consists of a programme of the most absurd sorts of races and contests that anyone can dream up, interspersed by eating, drinking and talking. Assemble as many children's toys as you can, the ones which grown-ups would love to try if they were not afraid of looking foolish, e.g. stilts, pogo sticks or space hoppers – children seem to master these, but your volunteer jockeys will find them impossible to steer if they have never ridden one before. Other contests might

be brushing barrels along the track with a besom or tipping straw bales end over end – a 'Wurdle' can be just what you want it to be after all!

Expenditure

Printing of tickets and hire of marquee.

Income

From the sale of tickets, profit from the bar, refreshments, and raffle or bottle tombola.

Notes

- Instructions for obtaining a Temporary Events Notice for the bar licence is given in Appendix A (i), page 103.
- A checklist for this event is given in Appendix H, page 135.

Attractions and Side Shows to be Run in Conjunction with a Main Event

The Showman's Directory is well worthwhile checking into as it is a useful resource for anyone planning a big event. It can be found on the internet at www.showmans-directory.co.uk and gives details of many outside attractions, e.g. where you can book a freefall parachutist or a circus clown. The cost of hiring one major attraction is usually justified by the extra people it draws to your show.

Attractions from your own local resources (especially if children are involved) will also help to bring in additional spectators, here are a few suggestions:

Baby Show

Get judges from another village, as disappointed parents have been known to create bad feeling in a close community if the judge, who is known to the contestants, does not select their little 'treasure'. Remember that a well-known personality might not be trustworthy around children; make sure the event is overseen by the person on your committee who has had a DBS check.

Book Stall

Second-hand books are always popular at any indoor sale, being easy to collect and store prior to the event. Since you should only expect to sell about a third of your stock, you will need to collect a lot of them, but those left over can form the nucleus for the next time! Leave plenty of space between tables or shelves as people take ages to select the books they wish eventually to buy.

Bottle Tombola

This is an excellent moneymaker, suitable anywhere there is space for the bottles – 200 donated bottles at 50p per ticket (and no blanks) will give you a profit of £100 with very little trouble (except for those who have to flog round collecting them).

Bingo, Housey-Housey

Always popular, takes very little organization but first read the regulations set out in Appendix A (iii), page 108. Find a caller who has done it before, as they will make it more relaxing and amusing.

Bowling for a Pig

The rules for this can be what you wish to make them but why not make the prize something easier to handle and store – like a side of bacon.

Boxing, Wrestling, Judo and Fencing

A chat with the sports master of a local school, the manager of a local sports club or sporting celebrity might provide you with someone who would organize a knock-out tournament for local clubs or schools.

Buy a Brick or Slate

This is a suitable fundraiser for a church or village hall restoration. Those buying a brick or slate can sign their names on it with a felt pen.

Children's Fancy Dress Competitions

Have a small gift (a bag of sweets or a lollypop) for each child taking part and additional prizes for the first three children placed.

Children's Play Area

There are many advantages for parents in being able to park their children (for a fee) in a safe playground, suitably staffed by a member of the community who has had a DBS and all the necessary licenses to be looking after small children. Toys and games can be borrowed or hired.

Coconut Shy

Try and borrow coconut stands from someone who has run this before (they must hold the coconuts firmly or you will lose every time). Have a plentiful supply of coconuts (if possible on sale or return), some hard balls and you can't fail.

Darts

Win a prize for the highest score with ten darts – but to avoid erratic players making unwanted holes in passing spectators, have your dartboard or numbered squares flat on the ground. There are many contests which can be devised with a dart board and a few darts; one popular game can be made by mounting the dartboard on the turntable of an old record player and throwing the darts when the board is spinning.

Dog Show

People who show dogs take it seriously, so if you decide to hold a dog show it must be done under the correct rules. Most areas have a local canine society who would be prepared to put on an 'exemption' dog show if requested. Your organization would then provide stalls and sideshows to capitalize on the attraction of the show. Before an 'exemption' dog show can be held, permission must be obtained from the Kennel Club. The local canine society would see to the entry forms, prizes and all the necessary publicity. If you wish to hold a small pet or dog show with 'fun' classes during some other event, no permission from the Kennel Club is needed. Get a local vet or well-known dog breeder to judge and award rosettes to the winners.

Donkey or Pony Rides

Borrow or hire the animals, then be prepared to heave children in and out of the saddle and walk for miles – it is no pastime for the frail! (And keep your feet away from the donkeys' feet, they are amazingly heavy.) Remember to ensure the children are safe, riding hats are a must and a trustworthy group of people helping the children on and off their mounts.

Five-a-side Football

If you have plenty of roped off space which can be set aside for this you can hold a knock-out competition throughout the whole afternoon. The coach of a junior football team could organize this for you.

Flower Arranging

This can only be held at an indoor event or in a marquee. Ask a professional flower arranger to 'set a theme' for the competition, then get him or her to come and judge on the day.

Fortune-teller

Get your fortune-teller to dress up and make herself attractively conspicuous at the entrance of her tent when not engaged. It is sometimes hard to get the first customer into the tent, so push a few of your helpers in to form a queue and get the ball rolling.

Gas-filled Balloons

There is an element of risk in this venture as a cylinder of gas is expensive. There is no refund on unused stocks and you will need to sell 500–600 balloons in order to make a good profit on a single cylinder. It is therefore only worth considering as an adjunct to a really large event, such as a county show, where you can rely on many thousands of fairgoers passing your stall. You should try to get a sponsor to advertise on the balloons to help to pay for the gas. The suppliers of the balloons will arrange for the overprinting.

Another risk is the environmental concerns of allowing balloons to float away on the wind. Balloons are harmful when ingested by animals and could even be fatal; you would not be invited back the following year if the neighbouring farmer lost his prize cow because it ate one of your balloons.

Have You Got a Steady Hand?

Get an electrical enthusiast to make up a box with two rods holding a 'live' wire, which will ring a bell if contact is made by the contestant, who is endeavouring to pass a ring along the length of the wire without touching. To make this more difficult, the wire should be bent in several palaces. Successful players get their money back.

Hoop-la

Not difficult to prepare and to run and should be a good money-spinner if you don't make it too easy for the competitors.

Lucky-dip or Bran-tub

Have two tubs, one for girls and one for boys. More popular for the very young at Christmas time, especially if you can get a jovial Father Christmas to do the 'Ho! Ho! Ho!' bit.

Putting or Golf Games

If digging holes to sink cups for clock golf is an unpopular move, an obstacle course can provide you with an interesting game without damage to the lawn. Another game can be devised by using a tennis marker or tape to form a series of rings (like a target) recording the highest score during the day and awarding a prize to the winner.

Raffles

There are no legal obstacles to running a small raffle during a dance, coffee morning or similar function if the sale of tickets and the draw takes place during the function and none of the profits go to private gain. No tickets may be sold in advance. A major raffle, when tickets are printed and sold to members of the public, must be run in accordance with the Gambling Act. Full details of this are given in Appendix A (iii), page 108. If you can find someone with 'winning ways' to scrounge interesting prizes and see to the distribution and sale of a large number of tickets you should be able to make a good profit. This is a useful way to fund a larger event.

Roll-a-penny

The props for this are not too difficult to make and, once you have the board marked out in squares and the grooved blocks down which you roll the pennies, you will have a popular game for many functions. The only snag is that new coins are too light so you will have to get hold of a plentiful supply of old pennies and make sure that your customers don't put them in their pockets, or get an engineering firm to stamp out some suitable discs.

Skittles

This can be set up in a variety of ways, either indoors or outside if you can find a bit of reasonably flat ground. Rolling balls through a series of numbered arches and recording the highest score made is also easy to set up and to run.

Steam-engine or Tractor Rides

Steam engine enthusiasts are usually delighted to bring their engines to a function, but don't invite them if they have to come from a distance – they are very costly to run and you must offer to pay expenses. Rides for children can be offered in trailers equipped with hay bales.

Talent Contest

Try to get a stage or TV personality to judge the competitors but, to avoid embarrassment on the day, do ensure that you will have plenty of contestants taking part.

Treasure Hunt

One popular way of doing this is for people to stick a pin in the place of their choice in a map of the world. A prize is given to the person with the pin nearest to the spot previously chosen. (A local travel agent might be persuaded to present a travel voucher as a prize.)

Tug-o-war

Invite teams to take part from the police, the local rugby club, Rotary Club, etc. You won't make any money from it but it will draw the crowds.

Wellie Throwing

A well-thrown wellie can take a child or dog off its feet, so make sure that the area is well cordoned off. Have a supply of pegs to mark the landing points and a surveyor's tape to measure the distance.

Notes

- It may be necessary for anyone working with children to have a Disclosure and Barring Services (DBS) check, see page 19 for more information.
- Useful addresses are:

Showman's Directory, Courtyard Office, The Courtyard, Parsons Pool, Shaftesbury, Dorset SP7 8AP
Tel: 01747 854099 www.showmans-directory.co.uk

The Kennel Club, 1–5 Clarges Street, Piccadilly, London W1J 8AB
Tel: 0844 463 3980 www.thekennelclub.org.uk

Stalls for Bazaars, Garden Parties, Fêtes, Fairs, etc.

Books and magazines
Bric-a-brac or white-elephant stall
Buttons and bows (haberdashery)
Cakes
Christmas decorations, cards, etc. (at Christmas time)
Costume jewellery and scarves
Groceries
Homemade and home produced
Men's stall
Nearly-new
Plants, flowers and vegetables
Raffle stall
Under 50p

PART THREE
Appendices

Appendix A (i)

Licences: Temporary Events Notice for the Sale of Alcohol at a Private or Public Function and Licences for Music and Dancing

Temporary Events Notice

The Licensing Act 2003 states that a Temporary Events Notice is required if drinks are to be sold at a social function. The Temporary Events Notice (TEN) can be obtained from your local council and you will need to apply at least ten working before the required date. When making an application, send a copy to the Licensing Authority with the current fee and also send copies to the police, the council's Environmental Protection Team, and one to the council's Health Food and Safety Team. Application forms can be obtained online and if made electronically the copies will be forwarded automatically from the Licensing Authority to the police and the other departments.

Before granting the licence, the licensing department must satisfy themselves:

1. That the officer is a fit and proper person to sell intoxicating liquor and is resident in the licensing district.
2. That the place where the function is to be held will be a suitable place for intoxicating liquor to be sold and is situated in the district.
3. That the sale of intoxicating liquor at the function is not likely to result in a disturbance or annoyance being caused to residents in the neighbourhood or that place, or in any disorderly conduct.

The legislation with respect of Temporary Events Notices stipulates that:

- The maximum length of time a temporary event may last must not exceed 168 hours.
- A minimum of twenty-four hours between events must be notified by the premises user in respect of the same premises.
- The maximum number of people attending at any one time

must not exceed 499. (It is important to remember that the above limit means the number of persons on the premises at any one time, this includes management, security, catering staff and any performers, so take this into account when you are to ensure you do not breach this limit.)
- An organization can only get five licenses in a year and the same premises cannot be used more than twelve times or more than twenty-one days in any calendar year.

The regulations are subject to change so it is advisable to check www.gov.uk/temporary-events-notice for up-to-date information.

Bar Equipment
The barman will need a plentiful supply of hot water, plenty of glass cloths and towels (you should check the glasses you have hired before the event as they may need washing), a pile of small tin trays, a couple of pails, a till and a float of at least £100. The more popular spirits should be served from optics which can be borrowed from a public house. Check them in advance as they can be evil things to operate if not in perfect working order. Borrow a spirit measure for the less popular spirits. A notice must be displayed stating the size of the measure being sold as a 'single' spirit, sherry, glass of wine, etc., and a measuring glass for dispensing the latter will be needed. A copy of the rules governing the sale of alcohol, which a publican may be able to lend you, should be on display together with a list of the price of drinks.

Notes
- It is illegal to sell homemade wine or beer.
- The above instructions for the Temporary Events Notice apply to England and Wales only. Instructions for other areas can be found at www.gov.uk.
- The full text of the Licensing Act 2003 can be found online. www.legislation.gov.uk.

Licensing Premises for Music and Dancing

Under the Miscellaneous Provisions Act 1982, responsibility for the issue of a licence for music and dancing is held by the premises' local authority.

Organizations raising money for charity, and not holding functions for private gain, are normally exempted from these regulations but you are recommended to consult the local authority when you wish to hold a function with music and dancing on premises which are not licensed. Each case will be referred to the committee of the district council which is responsible and they will decide any fee.

Appendix A (ii)

Guidelines for Events on Public Highways

The Royal Automobile Club Competition Authorisation Office

Guide To The Department Of Transport Regulations For The Authorisation Of Events On The Public Highway

The Motor Vehicles (Competitions and Trials) Regulations 1969 (amended) require that any motoring event which utilizes the Public Highway are subject to authorisation under the legislation. The Department of Transport has appointed The Royal Automobile Club & The Royal Automobile Club Motor Sports Association Ltd as the controlling agencies to undertake authorisation on its behalf in England and Wales. This legislation is handled by the Competition Authorisation Office (CAO). This function in Scotland is undertaken by the Royal Scottish Automobile Club.

The legislation requires that all events, the exception of those detailed below, are authorized by the CAO. Applications for such authorizations (except for specified major events, etc.) can be received a maximum of six and a minimum of two calendar months prior to the proposed date of the event.

The type of events which are authorized automatically, and do not therefore need specific authorization through the CAO are listed here.

a) An event in which the total number of vehicles driven by the competitors does not exceed twelve, no part of which takes place within eight days of any other part of any other event, where either the other event has the same promoter or the promoters of both events are members of the same club in connection with which the events are promoted (see Regulation 5a for full details).

b) An event on which no merit is attached to completing the event with the lowest mileage, and in which as respects such part of the event is held on the Public Highway, there are no performance tests and no route, and competitors are not timed or required to visit the same places, except that they may be required to finish at the same place by a specified time.

c) An event in which, as respects such part of the event as is held on the Public Highway, merit attaches to a competitor's performance only in relation to good road behaviour and compliance with the Highway Code.

d) An event in which all competitors are members of the armed forces of the Crown, and which is designed solely for the purpose of their service training.

Whilst the legislation grants automatic authorisation for the above events, it is recommended that organizers advise the local police of such events to ensure that the minimum inconvenience can be ensured whilst the event is in progress.

The Royal Automobile Club Competition Authorisation Office,
Motor Sports House, Riverside Park, Colnbrook, Slough, SL3 0HG
Tel: 0175 376 5075 Fax: 01753 682 938 e-mail: cao@msauk.org

Copies of The Motor Vehicles (Competitions and Trials) Regulations 1969, (Statutory Instruments 1969 No. 414) is available from the CAO. The report of the Advisory Committee for the Control of the Motor Rallies (Chesham report) is available from Her Majesty's Stationery Office.

For events in Scotland – organizers are requested to contact:
Jonathan Lord
RSAC Motorsport Limited, PO BOX 3333, Glasgow, G20 2AX
Tel: 0141 9465045

Appendix A (iii)

Gambling

The Gambling Commission was set up under the Gambling Act 2005 to regulate commercial gambling in Great Britain. Information about obtaining necessary licences is available on the Gambling Commission website at www.gamblingcommission.gov.uk.

Betting

If you want to run a race night, which is an event where participants stake money on the outcome of recorded or virtual races to raise money for a charity or another good cause, you can do so as long as you tell the players what the event is for and who you are raising money for, and you give all the money raised at the event to the good cause. This includes any entrance fees, sponsorship, fees for traders' stalls and other fees, although you can deduct any costs reasonably incurred from organizing the event, including the cost of prizes.

Players must not make more than one payment (whether as an admission or participation fee, stake or other charge, or a combination of those charges), and these payments must not exceed a certain amount and there is a limit to the total amount or value of prizes for all the games played at your event.

Bingo

Bingo is a most popular form of entertainment, enjoyed by many as an event on its own or run in conjunction with some other function. This, too, comes under the jurisdiction of the Gambling Commission, but there is good news on their website: http://www.gamblingcommission.gov.uk/gambling_sectors/bingo/getting_a_licence_what_you_nee/do_i_need_a_licence/circumstances_in_which_you_do.aspx

Fundraising

If you are organizing a fundraising or other non-commercial event you can run a bingo game (as long as it is not a remote bingo game) to raise money for a charity or good cause. You need to:

- tell the players the cause you are raising money for through the bingo game
- give all the money raised at the event (including any entrance fees, sponsorship, fees for traders stalls, and other fees) to the good cause, minus reasonable costs you have from organizing the event.

Reasonable costs include the cost of the prizes.

So it would seem that bingo can be played at fundraising events without incurring a liability to pay duty, but check with the Gambling Commission before arranging your event.

Gaming Machines

A gaming machine is defined by the Gambling Act 2005 as a machine that is designed or adapted for use by individuals to gamble (whether or not it can also be used for other purposes). Most gaming machines are of the reel-based type, also known as fruit, slot or jackpot machines. A licence is required to run these machines and there are set rules about where a gaming machine can be placed. You should definitely read the regulations if you are considering installing any of these money-eating machines so popular in clubs and pubs today.

You do not need any kind of licence to run gaming machines that do not offer a prize at all, or do not offer a prize worth more than the price you pay to play the machine.

Games of Chance

Baccarat, roulette, *vingt-et-un*, poker-dice, pontoon, *chemin de fer*, wheel of fortune, etc. Under the Gambling Act 2005, a casino operating licence must be held if any of the above or similar games are played. If you have not been put off by what you have read so far, read on – you soon will be: the price of the 2005 Act small casino operational licence starts over £28,000!

Careful reading of the website failed to reveal any exemption clauses for charities or fundraisers so you are recommended to leave this form of entertainment strictly alone.

Raffle and Lotteries

The Gambling Act 2005, Schedule 11, section 258 – Exempt Lotteries allows for four main types of lottery that do not need licences, these are:

1. Lotteries incidental to some other entertainment.
2. Private lotteries.
3. Customer lotteries.
4. Small society lotteries.

Raffles at Fêtes and Other Entertainments

These are lawful provided some simple requirements are observed:

- The raffle and other forms of gaming must not be the main attractions of the event.
- None of the profits of the event shall go to private gain.
- None of the prizes shall be money prizes.
- The whole of the raffle, i.e. issue and sale of tickets, draw and announcement of winners, must take place at the event; you are not allowed to sell tickets beforehand or outside the venue of the event.

Private Lotteries

These are those in which the sale of tickets is restricted to members of the society promoting the lottery. (In this case a local branch of a larger association constitutes a 'society', the association as a whole does not.)

For a private lottery to be lawful without registration with the local authority, the 'society' must either have some purpose other than gaming or must consist only of persons working on or living in the same premises and the following rules must be observed:

- The whole proceeds (after deducting expenses) must either be paid out in prizes or go to the purposes for which the society was formed or both.
- No written advertisement is allowed other than within the premises of the 'society'.
- The tickets all have to have the following printed on them:
  - The price (only one price for all).
  - The name and address of each of the promoters. (The promoter must have the written authorization of the governing body when the 'society' is one formed to pursue a specific purpose.)
  - A description of the 'society' to whom the sale is restricted.
  - A warning that no prizes will be awarded to anyone outside the 'society'.
- Tickets may only be sold for cash at the full printed value.
- No tickets may be sent through the post.

Customer Lotteries

These are not likely to affect you as they are essentially for use by businesses who occupy premises in Great Britain and must be set up in such a way as to ensure that no profits are made.

Small Society Lotteries

These are the sort for which you get tickets printed for sale to the general public. It may be promoted for any of the purposes for which the promoting society is conducted. The principal restrictions apply to:

- The price of each ticket.
- The percentage of proceeds allowed for expenses.
- The proportion allowed to be distributed as prizes.
- The value of the top prizes.
- The frequency in which similar lotteries are held.

The registration authority for the smaller lotteries is:

- In England: The district council, county council if the area does not have a district council, London borough council, the Common Council of the City of London or the Council of the Isles of Scilly;

- In Wales: The county council and county borough council.
- In Scotland, licensing board constituted under section 1 of the Licensing (Scotland) Act 1976 (c.66).

For the larger lotteries you will require a licence from the Gambling Commission.

Gambling Commission, Victoria Square House, Victoria Square, Birmingham B2 4BP
Tel: 0121 230 6666 www.gamblingcommission.gov.uk

Ignorance of the law is no excuse.

Appendix A (iv)

Music and Film Licensing

To Play Music

Licence fees are due from any business that plays recorded music in public. A shop, bar, office, restaurant, gym, community building, not-for-profit organization, charity – or even activities such as dance classes – are very likely legally required to have a PPL licence (formally known as Phonographic Performance Limited). More information about the legal requirements for a PPL licence can be found at www.ppluk.com. Licences can be applied for online or by phone: 020 7534 1070.

To Show a Film

The following information has been taken from the government information website at www.gov.uk/licence-to-show-a-single-film-title-in-public:

- To show a single film title in public on a commercial or non-profit basis, you need a licence, issued on a title-by-title basis, from the copyright owner.
- This includes films that are screened in DVD, Blu-Ray or video format.
- Filmbank Distributors Ltd (Filmbank) offer such permissions – in the form of a single title screening licence (STSL) – on behalf of a group of studios. [www.filmbank.co.uk – a licence application can be found on their website.]
- The Motion Picture Licensing Company (International) Limited (MPLC) also offers such a service to film clubs and societies via the MPLC Movie Licence. [www.themplc.co.uk]
- The licence you need depends on the film you are screening and the market sector your business operates in, such as event or festival management. You should check carefully with the licence provider to ensure you get the right licence for your specific needs.

- A licence fee is payable. For commercial events this is based on a minimum guaranteed per title, or a percentage of box office takings, whichever is greater.
- You can also obtain blanket licences from MPLC or Filmbank to show multiple film titles over the course of a year.
- If the film you want to show is not available through MPLC or Filmbank, you need permission from the individual distributor.
- Fines and penalties: If you show copyright films publicly without being licensed, you are infringing copyright and could be sued for damages.
- Note that, under the Licensing Act 2003, venues that show films may need a premises licence as well.

Useful websites
www.filmbank.co.uk
www.themplc.co.uk

Appendix B
Bulk Mailing

Here are some of the schemes offered by the Post Office to those dealing with bulk mailing:

Reply-paid envelopes

The Business Reply Service is a method of providing prospective clients, etc., with a response card/letter without them having to pay the postage. Annual licences are available – 1st or 2nd class. The organization pays the postage on each item received plus a small handling charge. Experience has shown that those who enclose a reply-paid envelope stand a better chance of receiving a donation than those who do not.

Freepost

This is the same principal as Business Reply but this system enables one to ask respondents to use their own stationery, using the word FREEPOST and a special postcode. Annual licences are available on 2nd class only. The charge on each item being normal postage plus small handling charge on each item received.

PO Box Number

There is an annual fee for this service and there seems to be little advantage in this scheme, unless the sender has no permanent address or he wishes to collect mail from the Post Office several times a week.

Bulk rebate service

Subject to a minimum of 4,250 items of the same weight and size being posted together, a rebate is payable if the items are pre-sorted into towns and counties. Having struggled to get out the first 4,250 letters, the next 750 are accepted free. As the number of letters increases, so does the discount and a really large mailing could be worth a 30 per cent discount on the postage.

For further details and to find out the costs of these services, go to postoffice.co.uk/contact-us or call their customer helpline on 08457 223344.

Appendix C

Layout of Minutes

Agenda

An example agenda to be sent to each member of the committee about a week before the meeting:

1. Chair's opening remarks.
2. Minutes of the last meeting.
3. Matters arising from the minutes.
4. Financial report.
5. Correspondence.
6. Project headings, e.g.:
   a) Poultry show.
   b) Coach outing.
7. Any other business.
8. Date, place and time of next meeting.

Minutes

The minutes should be a record of the proceedings in committee which is brief and pithy, but detailed enough a) to tell those members who were not able to be present what was decided, b) to remind members what they undertook at the meeting to be responsible for and c) to provide a starting point for the continuation of discussions at the next meeting.

The agenda provides the framework for the meeting and the minutes, naturally enough, mainly use the same headings as the agenda. The Secretary's problem is in deciding what to put in and what to leave out. Here are some thoughts on the subject.

Date, time and place

Only the date is really important. At some time in the future you may even regret having failed to note down the year.

Those present
This is important if decisions of past meetings are subsequently challenged. Apologies for absence by ... (which you sometime see as a separate item on an agenda) are merely a courtesy to the rest of the committee which it is quite unnecessary to record in the minutes.

Chair's opening remarks
Not everything the Chair says is worth recording but if it is of substance or you feel it would give anyone pleasure to read, not necessarily members of the committee, jot it down.

Minutes of the last meeting were read and agreed
This is the usual formula but secretaries are only human and this item gives Mr Fleece the opportunity to point out that he didn't mean that his wife would 'donate' the prizes, only that she would be pleased to 'present' them.

Matters arising from the last minutes
Most of these will be dealt with under specific project headings, e.g. 'Harvest supper', but it is important to sift through the last minutes and ensure that every item is going to be dealt with, even if it is only 'deferred until next meeting'.

Financial report
This should be condensed into a line or two.

Correspondence
Letters read out need only the briefest mention unless they require a reply or action. It is useful to highlight action responsibilities on the right-hand side of the page so that they may be seen at a glance, e.g.:

The Secretary reported the following correspondence received:
From Bussem: Coach hire charges for next year.
From Boutique: Offer of printed T-shirts.
Decision: NO requirement.

Southern area office: Offer of two places at seminar. Secretary to accept for Chair only.
Action: Secretary

Project headings
The real work of the committee will be the progressing of specific projects which should be listed separately. It is seldom necessary to report the discussion in much detail but it is essential that decisions and responsibilities for action should be clear and unambiguous (even if they are short to the point of being cryptic to others), e.g.:
Poultry Show – Exclude dogs
Action: Chair

All those at the meeting will remember that the Chair has promised to ask Mr Maulem to lock up his Alsatians on the day of the show to prevent a recurrence of last year's catastrophe.

Any other business
This heading may introduce new items which have to be described in rather more detail because they have not been previously discussed.

Date, time and place of next meeting
However weary, the Secretary should try to convert his meeting notes into draft minutes immediately after the meeting. Unlike a paid secretary, he will have been just as involved in the discussions as other members and unable to do more than jot down memory aids, which may be meaningless to him next morning.

Some Chairs like to discuss the contents of the agenda with the Secretary before they are typed and sent out to committee members, and some like to see a copy of the Secretary's minutes before the next meeting; both these points should be agreed between Secretary and Chair when a committee is first formed.

Appendix D (i)

Conditions of Sale of Exhibition Sites

This example Conditions of Sale of Exhibition Sites form is from a two-day equestrian event when an attendance of several thousand was expected. If only a few hundred spectators are expected, the range of spaces and prices should be drastically reduced.

Exhibition space is to be let in the following categories

			Per day
1.	Prime Sites Numbered on the plan: XXX	10ft frontage 20ft depth	£xx
2.	Prime Sites Numbered on the plan: XXX	10ft frontage 20ft depth	£xx
3.	Open Sites Numbered on the plan: XXX	10ft frontage 20ft depth	£xx
4.	Open Sites Numbered on the plan: XXX	10ft frontage 40ft depth	£xx
5.	Covered Sites 40 available in Arcade and Craft Exhibits hall	10ft frontage 10ft depth	£xx
6.	Hard Standing 20 available	10ft frontage 10ft depth	£xx
7.	Hard Standing 20 available	10ft frontage 20ft depth	£xx
8.	Extra Depth 2 available	Numbered on the plan: XXX	£xx
9.	Ringside Display Per Foot	Ringside display boards up to a max of 4ft high, sign-written and erected by the exhibitor, can be erected at the following fee:	
	a) Ring one (2 day exhibit)		£xx

b) Ring two (2 day exhibit) £xx
c) Ring three (2 day exhibit) £xx

10. Voluntary Organizations — May book sites from Items 4, 5, 6, 7 and 8 above at 50% discount.

Adjacent sites may be booked for all exhibition space.

Electricity and Wi-Fi is available, at a connection charge of £xx plus a unit used charge of £xx.

All sites must be paid for at time of booking.

Exhibitors will automatically receive membership of the show and two passes to the members' enclosure. Further tickets are available (see booking form).

Three free admission passes to the site will be issued per exhibition space per day. Additional passes are available from the show secretary at the time of booking at 10% discount.

No exhibitor will be allowed on site without an admission pass per person for the dates of the show.

All cheques should be made payable to ....

In the event of exhibition space having already been allocated before your application arrives with the Secretary, the Organizers reserve the right to allocate another site of equal worth.

All correspondence should be addressed to – The Secretary, Mole Cottage, Upper Slade, Lumpshire.

ARRIVALS AND DEPARTURES: The showground will be open for the reception of trade exhibitors and industrial exhibits five days prior to show opening. Stands must be ready to receive the public from 9.00 a.m. on both days of the show. Stands may not be dismantled before 5.00 p.m. on either day. Exhibitors who do not arrive until the morning of the show would be well advised to ensure that the site is available and prepared before the day.

ADMISSION: Admission cost £xx per adult and car-parking is free. Three free passes, exhibition space and additional tickets may be purchased from the Organizers.

CANCELLATION: If any exhibitor cancels space reserved for him for any reason, all fees paid will be forfeit and the Association reserves the right to re-let the space.

SECURITY: The Association will not be responsible under any circumstances for any articles exhibitors may have brought to the Showground, but will require the Exhibitors to take charge of their own property.

FIRE PRECAUTIONS AND DAMAGE: Exhibitors are required to take all necessary precautions against fire and a damage to their own exhibitions and to ensure that due respect is paid to the property of the Association, the visitors and in particular, our host, Briar Lodge Farms Ltd.

SITE CLEARANCE: Exhibitors must replace turf, fill holes and make good any damage to the ground occupied by them and clear away any materials, metal, glass, plastic and rubbish. The Association reserves the right to charge for reinstatement if such work is not carried out by the Exhibitor.

DISCLAIMER OF LIABILITY: In this clause the terms 'Exhibitor' shall include persons taking part in any competition or display arranged by the Show Committee and the owners of any animal, plant, machinery or other thing involved in any such competitions or display or otherwise exhibited on the Showground. Save for death or personal injury caused by the negligence of the Committee, its servants or agents, the Committee will not be responsible for death, injury, disease, damage or loss caused to any Exhibitor or to his or to her servant or agent or to any animal, article, plant, machinery or thing of whatever nature brought on to the Showground by the said Exhibitor from whatever cause, death, injury, disease, damage or loss, arises. Save as aforesaid, the Exhibitor shall indemnify the Committee against all claims, damages and expenses whatsoever in any way arising out of the presence of the Exhibitor, his servants, agents, exhibits, vehicles or equipment on the Showground and shall assume full responsibility therefore. Acceptance of the foregoing provisions shall be a condition of entry. Exhibitors are advised to insure against fire and other appropriate risk, not only as regards their own property, but also against any third party claim.

CONDITIONS OF ADMITTANCE: Persons are admitted to the Showground at the discretion of the organizers and at their own risk and, while every endeavour is taken to ensure their safety, the Committee will not (save for death or personal injury caused by negligence of the Committee, its servants or agents) be responsible for personal injury (whether fatal or otherwise), loss or damage to property and any other loss, damage, cost and expense however caused.

CAR-PARKING CONDITIONS: Persons are admitted entry to the Show Car Park at their own risk and, while every endeavour is taken to ensure the safety thereof, the Committee will not (save for death or personal injury caused by the negligence of the Committee, its servants, or agents) be responsible for personal injury, whether fatal or otherwise, loss of or damage to property and any other loss, damage, cost and expense, however caused.

N.B. A plan of the show site and a map of location is included with this leaflet and application form.

Appendix 'D' (ii)

Equine Event Exhibition Application

This is an example application form, which can be adjusted as needed.

LUMPSHIRE ASSOCIATION HORSE SHOW
18 and 19 July 20XX

Name of Exhibitor

....

Address

....

....

Telephone numbers

....

Email address

....

Name of person in charge of stand

....

Mobile number for person in charge

....

Type of stand/stall/exhibition

....

....

The site space that I/we require is as follows:

Site No./Nos ....

I/We require .... additional passes onto the Show site @ £xx each

I/We require .... additional passes to the Members Enclosure @ £xx each

I/We enclose £ .... for Exhibition Space Saturday 18th*/Sunday 19th* and for additional passes on to the show site*/Members Enclosure*.

(*Delete where applicable)

I/We have read and agreed to abide by the rules and conditions laid down by the Organizers.

Signed

....

Printed name

....

For and on behalf of

....

Appendix D (iii)

Sponsored Ride Flyer and Entry Form

Here are examples of both the sponsored ride flyer and entry form which can be adjusted as needed.

South Lumpshire Association Sponsored Horse Ride

From WOODHALL PARK on SUNDAY 11 APRIL,
starting at 10 a.m.

By kind permission of Mr and Mrs B. Wise,
Honorary Doctor: Dr I. Makewell
Honorary Veterinary Surgeon: Mrs G. Upp BVetMed
Entry forms may be obtained from the Ride Secretary, Mrs V. Welly, Mudd Farm, Lumpton. (Tel: XXXXX XXXXXX)

The sponsored ride is being held in aid of Association funds and a donation will be given to the Riding for the Disabled Association.

The idea of the sponsored ride is that competitors should arrange beforehand to get themselves sponsored for a certain sum of money for each mile or the course which they complete. Any number of sponsors may support each rider.

It is hoped that Mr I. Talkemdoun MP together with Master of Foxhounds Colonel I. Headthefield will lead the ride. It will take place over farmland and bridle paths and it will give riders a wonderful opportunity to view some of the Woodhall Park's most delightful scenery. The ride is approximately 20 miles.

Awards

- Rosettes will be awarded to all riders taking part.
- There will be an award for the rider who raises the largest sum of money through sponsorship.

Classes

- Over 18 years on the day of the ride.
- Under 18 on the day of the ride.

Entries

Entries will close on Saturday, 3 April. They must be made on the accompanying form and sent to the Ride Secretary, or Treasurer: Mrs B. First, Bridge House, Lumpton. (Tel: XXXXX XXXXXX)

Entrance Fee

If any entrant raises £XX or more through sponsorship the entrance fee will be refunded.

Sponsorship

A sponsorship card is enclosed and additional cards can be obtained from the Ride Secretary. Completed cards must be handed in to the Secretary's tent on the day of the ride, prior to the start.

General Conditions

1. Riders must wear hard hats and be appropriately dressed.
2. Riders may retire their horses at any checkpoint, should they wish to do so, but they must report to the Steward so that the mileage can be recorded for sponsorship purposes.
3. Stewards will be authorized to ask a rider to withdraw or to await veterinary opinion at the start or at any checkpoint on the route should they think it necessary.
4. The Association will not accept liability for any damage, accident or injury to any animals, persons or property.
5. Riders must check in at the Secretary's tent whether they complete the ride or not.
6. A rider may dismount and proceed dismounted but must go through the start and finish mounted.
7. Riders must keep to the course and strictly observe all signs on the route.

Notes

- The ride is not intended to be a race and no speed factor is involved.
- The starting time will be 10 a.m., but the field will be open from 8 a.m. onwards.
- The event will start and finish in the same field. There will be ample parking provided for cars and boxes.
- The course will be well marked and stewarded; the police will be informed of the points where the ride crosses a road.
- Groups of riders will leave at intervals.
- Identity numbers must be worn by all riders; these will be provided and issued prior to the start and must be collected from the Secretary's tent.
- All sponsorship money is to be sent to the Treasurer not later than Saturday, 8 May.
- There will be a marquee where light refreshments will be available. A bar licence has been applied for. Free orange squash for all riders will be provided by kind permission of Mrs Wise. Spectators are welcome at the start and finish but are requested to keep off the course. Only official cars will be allowed on the course.

South Lumpshire Association
Sponsored Horse Ride Entry Form

20 Mile Sponsored Horse Ride from Woodhall Park
Sunday, 11 April at 10.00 a.m.

Please use block letters

Name and address of rider

....

....

Over 18: (Y/N) ....

Name and address of owner if different from above

....

....

Name of horse

....

I wish to take part in the Sponsored Ride and enclose my entrance fee.
I agree to stand by the rules and conditions as stated.

Minors need consent of an adult – e.g. if under 18, parent or guardian's signature is required.

Signature

....

Entries close on Saturday, 3 April.

Send to: Mrs B. First, Bridge House, Lumpton.
Tel: XXXXX XXXXXX

Adults (18 years and over)	£XX
Under 18 years	£XX

FOR OFFICIAL USE
Number allocated: ....

Appendix E

Leaflet for the Collection of Goods for Sale

Example of card or leaflet for use in the collection of goods for jumble sales, furniture and antique sales and auctions, book sales, nearly new and 50/50 sales.

(Front of card)

> **Lumpshire Community Association**
>
> A jumble sale, furniture and antique sale/auction, book sale, nearly new sale/50/50 sale
>
> is being held
>
> on .... at ....
>
> Starting at ....
>
> If you have anything which you think would be suitable for this sale please fill in the back of this card and place it in your window, and a member of the committee will call to collect your donation.

(Back of card)

> **Lumpshire Community Association**
>
> I have a donation.
> Please CALL after .... /anytime.

Appendix F

Example of Direct Debit Form

DIRECT Debit

Company logo
or name here

Instruction to your bank or building society to pay by Direct Debit

Please fill in the whole form using a ball point pen and send it to:

Address here

Eight lines only

Service user number

Name(s) of account holder(s)

Reference

Bank/building society account number

Instruction to your bank or building society
Please pay (A N Company) Direct Debits from the account detailed in this Instruction subject to the safeguards assured by the Direct Debit Guarantee. I understand that this Instruction may remain with (A N Company) and, if so, details will be passed electronically to my bank/building society.

Branch sort code

Name and full postal address of your bank or building society

To: The Manager — Bank/building society

Address

Postcode

Signature(s)

Date

Banks and building societies may not accept Direct Debit Instructions for some types of account

DDI2

This guarantee should be detached and retained by the payer.

The Direct Debit Guarantee

DIRECT Debit

- This Guarantee is offered by all banks and building societies that accept instructions to pay Direct Debits
- If there are any changes to the amount, date or frequency of your Direct Debit (insert your organisation name) will notify you (insert number of) working days in advance of your account being debited or as otherwise agreed. If you request (insert your organisation name) to collect a payment, confirmation of the amount and date will be given to you at the time of the request
- If an error is made in the payment of your Direct Debit, by (insert your organisation name) or your bank or building society, you are entitled to a full and immediate refund of the amount paid from your bank or building society
  - If you receive a refund you are not entitled to, you must pay it back when (insert your organisation name) asks you to
- You can cancel a Direct Debit at any time by simply contacting your bank or building society. Written confirmation may be required. Please also notify us.

Appendix G

Websites and Social Media

A wealth of opportunities have been opened up with the expansion of the internet and social media. It is growing so quickly that it is difficult to keep up to date with the latest popular sites, but it has rapidly become a low cost and efficient way to share information with members of the public and friends. Smartphones and tablets are becoming such common appendages that it is not uncommon, while waiting at the bus stop, in the checkout line at the local supermarket or walking along the street, to see someone with a phone glued to their ear or their nose glued to the screen. Take advantage of this, social media is here to stay.

Websites

Setting up a website does not need to be a daunting task. The first step is to decide on the website name. Ideally choose a name that closely matches your organization's name or the goals of your organization or fundraising event, e.g., www.lumpshirehorseshow.org.uk. This will make it much easier for the public to find your website if they don't already have the address, but be careful to choose a name that is not too similar to another, to avoid confusion.

Once you decide on a potential name, perform an internet search for 'domain name registration' to find a list of sites that allow you to check availability of a website name. You can compare the costs and other features offered. They all charge a nominal fee for a given period and usually have the option to renew automatically. Remember, if you do not choose this option and forget to renew your registration, it is possible that your website name may be snatched up by someone else next year, so make sure to mark the expiry date in your calendar.

When selecting the website name, you will notice there are a number of different extensions available, but it is usual for non-profit or charitable groups to use the name extension .org.uk or just .org, and usually these options are less expensive than some of the other choices.

If there is not enough money in your budget to have your website professionally designed, there are many options on the internet available which guide you through designing a simple website on your own. www.wordpress.com is a popular site that is free and has a large number of templates to get you started. A simple layout that provides easy access to the pertinent information about your organization, the goals, contact information and a list of upcoming events, etc., is much more effective than a lot of animated graphics and coloured backgrounds that take an age to load and are unreadable when they do. For smaller events or organizations, a Facebook page might be all you need (see below).

Be clear on who your organization serves and provide valuable content for those people. It is much more important to keep the website simple and the information current. There is nothing worse when checking for the opening time of the local village flower festival to find the 'Schedule of Events' page is titled 'Below is a list of the upcoming events for 20XX(two years previously)'.

Once your website is designed, it is possible to link your website with social networking sites such as Facebook, Twitter and Pinterest, allowing you to share the information quickly and easily between them. The days of a phone tree are gone – when a news item is manually posted to your website, it can automatically feed through to other social networking sites in one easy step. Social media also means others can 'like', comment on, and 'share' or 'retweet' your item, which means that your news can be carried further very quickly.

Posting a Blog

The term 'blog' comes from 'web log' and is usually a written commentary, information or discussion, but can also be a photographical account, that is posted on the web. Blogs can be used by organizations and societies to inform members or other interested parties about membership activities and events. The most popular websites include Tumblr and WordPress, offering an easy-to-use interface to post your 'blog' and there is no charge to do so. Once a blog has been posted, a link can be added on your website and Facebook page to lead members to the information.

Social Networking Sites

Social networking sites are constantly evolving. The following have demonstrated some staying power and can have real benefits for marketing and membership development for your organization or fundraising event.

Facebook

Originally developed as a way for college students to interact, Facebook has now become a common platform for individuals, businesses and organizations to share news and list upcoming events. Facebook offers different types of user options, an organization, non-profit group or individual can set up a Facebook page on which it can share local news, post information or photographs of prior events and a calendar of any upcoming events. Facebook also provides an option to set up a group and invite members to join. A group offers more privacy and control of who can view the information posted, so is a quick and easy place to send out membership information or allow a discussion group or forum amongst the members.

Twitter

Twitter is another popular social networking site for short text-based posts called 'tweets'. These are limited to 140 characters and can be useful to push upcoming events, breaking news, publish links to other online sites, blogs or interesting videos and articles, and is a quick way to spread the news. The best use of Twitter is the addition of a hashtag to a key word or your organization name, e.g., #savebadgers, which allows all conversation on that topic to be collected into a single thread.

YouTube

YouTube is a site that allows video clips to be uploaded and shared on the internet for all to see. Not all that are uploaded are worth watching, but if you have a budding videographer with clips of a prior event or a short promotional video that you would like to share, there is no charge to do so. Once uploaded to the YouTube site, links to the video clips can be added to the website, forwarded to members via email, Twitter and on your organization's Facebook page.

Pinterest

Pinterest has a similar format to a bulletin board and has caught on like wildfire. It allows users to bookmark or 'pin' images and create unlimited numbers of topic boards, where each pin on the board links back to the original internet location. Setting up a topic board with articles of interest, can be assigned with privacy options to be viewed by members only or made available to the general public, and is another way to share information that may be of interest to your members.

Appendix H
Checklists

Checklist for Amateur Dramatics, Celebrity Concert, Antique Valuation, Film Preview or Fashion Show

Before your first committee meeting

Inspect all possible venues (theatre, village hall, concert hall, civic hall or school assembly hall) to establish the following:

- Seating capacity and approximate size of stage.
- Dressing room accommodation or, in the case of antique valuations, suitable rooms that lock up.
- Is there stage lighting or points for footlights, spotlights or floods. (Dimming controls can be useful but not essential.)
- State of curtains. Do they draw? Do they meet?
- Is there any scenery? Are there any scenery 'flats'?
- Are the acoustics good? Is there a microphone, record player or PA system?
- Are there bar and refreshment facilities? Are the premises licensed?
- Does the establishment hold a current licence for entertainment, music, dancing or film shows?
- What is the capacity of the car park?
- Make sure there are adequate fire exits and adequate signs and emergency lighting.

Points for subsequent meetings

- The Secretary must confirm all bookings in writing. It is vital that there should be no ambiguity about dates and locations.
- The Secretary must also establish from the artist or agent whether he or she expects to receive a fee, expenses or both. This applies equally well to models at a fashion show, antique valuers and their staff.
- The Treasurer must produce an outline budget of expected income and expenditure to help determine the price of tickets, duration of show, etc.

- The Catering Officer should be given outline plans of the refreshment required and be prepared to give costings, prices to be charged and estimated profit at the next meeting.
- The Bar Officer should be given the outline requirements for the bar and be prepared to report his/her estimates to the next committee meeting. He/she should acquaint themselves with Appendix A (i), page 103, in case a Temporary Events Notice is needed.
- The Publicity Officer should be prepared to outline and cost his publicity campaign, to include the distribution and sale of tickets. (If the show is to be held on more than one day it is advisable to have tickets printed in different colours.) Seating plans should be kept to indicate the number of tickets sold. Try to get firms and shops to buy advertising space in the programme. Try to find a sponsor to cover the costs of the publicity materials.
- If holding a concert, someone should be made responsible to make sure that the piano is in tune, all necessary music licences have been applied for, the sound equipment is working properly and has been PAT tested and that there are people available to move the piano if necessary.
- The Secretary should ensure that anyone who will be working with children has had a DBS check.

Helpers required for stage productions

Producer

Stage manager

Assistant stage manager (stage sets, props, special effects, etc.)

Lighting and sound technicians

Electrician

Scenery painter

Wardrobe mistress and make-up artist

Prompter (Usually the ASM)

Helpers required in the front of house
Box office
Programme sellers and ushers
Refreshment and bar tenders
Cloakroom attendants

Checklist for Barbecue, Fireworks Party, Garden Party or 'Wurdle Night'

Before the first committee meeting

Call on the owners of the property where the event is being held to find out:

- If your host can provide:
  - Fairy lights or any other outdoor lighting.
  - Flags or bunting.
  - Barbecue equipment (if required).
  - Any covered accommodation or rainproof area for use in a sudden downpour.
- To what extent the host and hostess wish to be involved, both in the planning stages and on the actual day.
- If the hostess is prepared to surrender her kitchen to a gang of helpers or if she would prefer to make her own domestic arrangements (with, perhaps, help from members of the committee).
- If there is a lavatory accessible without having to let people wander about inside the house.
- If an area can be earmarked for the parking of cars, big enough to take the number of cars anticipated.
- Are there any unprotected ponds or lakes which could be a hazard to small children.
- For firework parties, check the following websites for current guidelines:
  www.fireworksafety.co.uk or www.gov.uk/fireworks/thelaw

First committee meeting

Allocate tasks to members of the committee and recruit other helpers if necessary:

- If you are running your own bar, see about obtaining a Temporary Events Notice and secure the services of a reliable barman, see Appendix A (i), page 103. Arrange for the hire of glasses and the purchase of drinks.
- Decide what refreshments you are going to serve and appoint a catering subcommittee to do the job.
- Discuss your plans for publicity, the price of tickets and any printing necessary and arrange for the work to be done.
- If there is no accommodation available for wet weather, discuss whether to hire a marquee. (If you need additional tables and chairs, these can also be hired from the same firm.)
- Discuss the programme and, if fireworks, games or competitions are involved, list the 'props' or requirements and decide who will be responsible for borrowing, hiring or buying them.
- Discuss the distribution and sale of tickets and decide who should be sent a complimentary one.
- The Secretary should ensure that anyone who will be working with children has had a DBS check.

Last committee meeting

This should be held shortly before the event. For discussion:

- Check on the sale of tickets and iron out any last minute problems that may have arisen.
- All electrical equipment should be safety checked for hazard from tripping and make sure if being used outside they are weather proof. See PAT testing on page 19.
- Also re-read the food safety and hygiene section if food preparations are being done by volunteers or members of the committee on page 19.
- Arrange for a 'fatigue party' to clear up the garden after the event (the provision of waste bins will help to keep the mess to a reasonable level), and see that all borrowed items are returned to the rightful owners.

- Arrange to write a letter of thanks to your host and hostess, remember to let them know how much you have raised. Check also to find out that they have not suffered any loss or breakages.

Checklist for a Dance

Before your main committee meeting

- Inspect various venues, village halls, school assembly rooms, hotels, large private houses, club rooms, etc., to establish the following:
  - Capacity for dancing, allowing for seating accommodation at small tables and space round the bar. Check on the maximum number for which the hall is licensed and that it has adequate emergency fire exits.
  - If the premises is licensed for music and the sale of alcohol.
  - Cost of hire and available dates.
  - Fitted stage, bar, kitchen and serving facilities, fire precautions, car-parking facilities and cloakrooms.
  - Possible routes of access for gatecrashers.
- Get a list of dance bands and disco operators and find out their cost and available dates.
- Establish which is the best day of the week to get people to turn out for a dance in your area (remember that Saturday bar licences always expire before midnight). Check to see if there are any conflicting attractions due to be held on the date on which you wish to hold your function.

At a preliminary meeting (about six months before the dance)

- Agree the date, then confirm in writing the venue and the band or disco.
- The Secretary should ensure that anyone who will be working with children has had a DBS check.

At the next committee meeting (about two months before the dance)

- Agree the price of tickets and arrange for them to be printed.
- If necessary, apply for a Temporary Events Notice (see Appendix A (i), page 103).
- Check on need and apply for PPL Licence. Your facility may already have the necessary licence needed to play music, if not, see Appendix A (iv), page 113.
- Draft publicity material and agree how best to sell tickets.

At the third committee meeting (a few weeks before the event)

- Check on the sale of tickets.
- Decide on supporting attraction (i.e., raffle or bottle tombola, etc.).
- Agree on the allocation of complimentary tickets and arrange for them to be sent to those invited.
- Invite two experienced and reliable people to run the bar.
- Arrange for the purchase of wines and spirits, etc., and the hire of glasses.
- Discuss the menu and arrange for members of the committee to be responsible for the provision and serving of the refreshments.

Final meeting before the dance

- Telephone the band to check the booking and make sure that they know the venue for the dance.
- Check the heating in the hall and make sure that the power points for the stage are in good working order for the band's electrical equipment.
- See that there are sufficient tables and chairs for the numbers attending.
- Are there tablecloths, or will you have to supply these yourself?
- Have you got spot prizes and (if they are volunteers) some small gifts for the barmen.
- Ask someone to provide and arrange some flowers – small dishes on each table, some on the buffet table and a large flower arrangement on the stage. (If this is arranged in a basket, the whole thing can be auctioned at the end of the dance.)

- Check on the availability of crockery and cutlery for the buffet, including cups and teaspoons for the coffee.
- Have all the prizes for the raffle or tombola been collected? Have you got enough books of cloakroom tickets for use as raffle tickets?
- Have you mustered the following for the bar? Pressure gear, glasses, tea towels, hand towels, small trays, buckets, bottle openers, optics, spirit measure and a till.
- Make sure all electrical equipment that will be used has been PAT tested (see page 19).
- You will need a substantial float for the bar and a smaller one for the person who is selling raffle tickets or running the tombola.
- Nominate people to be responsible for:
  - Switching on the lighting and heating before the dance and receiving the band (who usually arrive early to set up their equipment.)
  - The reception and seating of guests who have complimentary tickets.
  - The parking of cars.
  - The cloakroom.
  - Taking the tickets on the door, and to remain on the lookout for gatecrashers (particularly at the time when the pubs close).
- Finally, arrange for a party of helpers to see to the washing up, clearing up the hall after the dance and for returning all borrowed equipment as soon after the dance as possible.

Checklist for Equestrian Events, Donkey Derbys and Car Rallies

Items marked † are for horse shows only.

Event minus twelve months

If possible, before the first committee meeting obtain information on the following:

- Suggested date(s) († having consulted the show programme in the *Horse and Hound* and talked to the Secretary of the local Pony Club or Area Representative of the British Horse Society for advice on dates of local shows and the best places where your show might be held).

- If you wish to run a Donkey Derby, search the internet for the names of local firms who hire donkeys for this sort of event.
- Call the farmer or landowner of proposed site and ask if they are prepared to have the show on their land and, if so, ask if the following are available on site:
  - Electricity.
  - Water.
  - Lavatories, or suitable place for Portaloos.
  - Suitable firm ground for a car and horsebox park, with turning space and gates wide enough to cater for all size of vehicles.
  - Office for Secretary.
- Invite a specialist in the field of the event you are proposing to run to join your committee.
- †The name of someone willing to take on the equestrian side.

Event minus eleven months

Call your first committee meeting and:

- Appoint your key helpers (recruiting others if necessary), making sure they know their responsibilities.
- Agree date and type and scale of event to be run.
- Consult Appendix B, page 115, on bulk mailing.
- Discuss with your committee additional fundraising ideas which might be incorporated.
- Make arrangements to hire or borrow if required:
  - Generator for electricity.
  - Water carrier or stand pipe.
  - Portaloos or chemical lavatories.
  - Tent, caravan or other suitable office for the Secretary.
  - PA system, commentary box(es) (†one per ring for a horse show) with telephone/radio connection to the Secretary's office. † Remember to check that the PA system can be heard in the stable and horse box parking areas.
  - A set of three or four kiosks for use as tote (donkey derby only).
- † Apply to the appropriate body for your show or individual classes to be affiliated.

- Make arrangements for the date of your show to be published in appropriate publications such as horse or car magazines, local parish magazine and 'what's on' section in the local papers and websites.
- In conjunction with the expert, engage the services of the following as required:
  - † Course builder.
  - Judges, marshals, stewards and arena parties.
  - Commentator(s).
- Write to the local branch of St John's Ambulance asking if they will attend.
- Write to a local doctor and veterinary officer inviting them to attend in an honorary capacity.
- † Invite a farrier to attend.

Event minus six months

- Working with the expert, draft out the schedule for the show. † If horse show send a copy to the appropriate affiliating body for their approval.
- Write to local firms and traders, asking them if they would like to take advertising space in the programme or set up a trade stall or exhibition on the day(s) of the event. See Appendix D, page 119.
- Invite local people to become vice-presidents, sponsors or patrons of the show. (Find out if they intend to attend, as the sponsor usually presents the awards.)
- Invite tenders from two or three catering firms for the provision of a bar and refreshment tent. (If you decide to run refreshments yourself, consult Appendix A (i), page 103 for licensing information and check the food safety and hygiene rules information on page 19)
- Plan your publicity campaign and appoint a member of the committee to carry it out.
- Make application to a recognized insurance company for third-party legal liability cover. †If your show is to be affiliated to one of the larger horse associations, enquire if insurance is included.

Affiliation to the BSJA carries with it automatic insurance, check with the appropriate association to see what their current maximum coverage for accidents is arising through fault or negligence of the show committee and for which the show is liable at law, but additional cover is recommended.

- Draft out the entry forms and †send for the score sheets and judges' cards from the relevant association.
- Consult the schedule to calculate the number of rosettes and other trophies you will need (always add on a few extra ones of each colour – in the event of a tie judges may call for additional awards). Order the rosettes and/or trophies. (You will find the names of firms who supply these advertised in the *Horse and Hound*).
- Invite people who are used to using a microphone to 'man' the commentary boxes. A clear voice is essential and, when more than one commentator is being used, it is helpful to choose speakers with distinctive voices. †In the case of a horse show, select someone who has had experience in this type of commentating. Remind the commentator to mention and thank the sponsors.
- The Secretary should ensure that anyone who will be working with children has had a DBS check.

Event minus four months

- Call on the landowner with your draft site plan and check that:
  - Your plan is workable from his point of view.
  - Ambulances can get to every hazard on the course.
  - Certain areas of grass will be rough-cut before the event.
  - You have selected the best places to site the trade area, refreshment tents, lavatories, water containers or standpipes, generators, litter bins and the main litter skip.
  - A tractor and driver can be spared to stand by all day in case of emergencies.
  - The public address is sited so that it can be heard by competitors in the practice areas and car parks as well as the main arena.
  - They will be able to help with materials or labour in roping off competition areas, show rings, or barriers separating spectators from race tracks, etc.

- They have no objection to large posters, billboards or hoardings being placed on the land to advertise the event.
- Inform the police of your plans and discuss with them the problems that may have to be faced over congestion on the roads at a time when the bulk of competitors will be arriving or leaving.
- Agree tenders for the bar and refreshments and confirm in writing.
- Arrange to hire walkie-talkie radios for your ring stewards.
- Having got the agreement of the landowner to your site plan, you can begin to set out the programme. The general layout should include:
  - A list of officials, sponsors, patrons and vice-presidents, judges, commentators and show officials.
  - The timetable of events, times of races, competitions, etc.
  - A list of classes giving the names of sponsors and the prizes to be awarded.
  - Advertisements, advertisers, trade stalls and exhibitions.
  - Acknowledgements to the St John's Ambulance, the doctor and the veterinary officer.
  - Rules for the conduct of competitors.
  - A plan of the site and a map showing the location of the show ground, including secretaries office, car parks, stable blocks, lavatories and show rings.

Event minus three months

- †Once your schedule has received appropriate association approval, get the schedule and entry forms, printed.
- Compile the programme and send it to the printers.

Event minus two months

- Send out the schedules and entry forms. † The BSJA recommend that no entry form should be accepted unless the entry fee is enclosed with them, and that a closing date for the acceptance of entries should be stated. The entry forms should show if entries may be accepted in the field. A self-addressed envelope must accompany all requests for schedules to be sent by post.

- Follow up your advance publicity in the local press, on local radio, by hoardings, leaflets, social media and any other means you can devise. Send small posters, with some copies of the schedule and entry forms, to schools, riding establishments, saddlers and tack shops, garages, driving schools, car sales rooms, etc., as appropriate.

At your final committee meeting before the show

- Check with the landowner that they are quite happy about the arrangements both for the day and for clearing up after the show.
- Make sure that you have enough helpers for the car park, programme selling, etc., and arrange to have at least two really reliable 'runners' on station at the Secretary's tent at all times.
- Check with members of the committee that they are quite happy with the responsibilities they have taken on and have encountered no major snags.
- Make arrangements with the bank for night safe facilities and arrange to collect the night safe bag, together with a selection of moneybags and bands which the bank will supply. Work out with the Treasurer how much float you will require and make arrangements for this to be collected in suitable denominations the day before the event.
- Assign the task of putting up clear directional signs to the show, leading cars and horse vans to the appropriate entrances and be responsible for removing the signs after the event.

After the function

- Arrange for a fatigue party to:
  - Clear up the show site.
  - Return all borrowed items.
  - Take down all publicity materials, banners and notices.
- Remind the Secretary to write letters of thanks to all who contributed to the success of the function.
- Check to see that all outstanding bills have been paid and that all claims for expenses have been met.

Acknowledgements

This book would never have happened without the support of my late husband, Vincent Russell, who tirelessly worked beside me through the organization and running of all the forms of fundraising events mentioned in this book.

When it came to putting it all down in writing in a first draft, it was a project we worked on together and had a lot of fun doing so. While I typed and collated, he supplied me with cups of tea and corrected numerous spelling mistakes (these were the days before computers could do all that with a click of a button) although there were times I had to curb his enthusiasm, when he started to rewrite some of the paragraphs. His writing style was so different than mine that I got my first taste of writer's block and quietly had to put it back the way it was before being able to continue. The memories that go along with this book are of the many happy hours we spent together, not only while putting the book together but on the journey that led us to that point.

The addition of illustrations to the first draft by my elder daughter, Gillian Russell, added some fun to the rather mundane subject matter about fundraising. Although her cartoon illustrations were not sophisticated enough to be used in the finished book, they were used as guidelines for the professional graphic artist.

It was Gillian also who resurrected the project after a number of years of the almost finished 'book' being put out of sight and out of mind after the death of my husband. With renewed enthusiasm she took the moth-eaten photocopy of the original hand-typed manuscript, complete with the faded illustrations that she had drawn some years before, and transcribed it. Researching and updating to the most current rules and regulations, she seamlessly added new paragraphs where needed.

Simon Riemersma should also get a mention of thanks, as his background in printing and his good eye for proofreading, found mistakes that everyone else had missed.

In the final stages my younger daughter Eleanor lent her expertise and added some important legal changes and requirements that were not even in existence when I started on my fundraising adventures.

Special thanks to Noah Johnson and Gillian for leading me down the hitherto unexplored territories of 'social media'.

Finally, I would like to thank all the hard-working members of the various committees, volunteers, friends and neighbours that I worked with over the years, who all made the fundraising ventures 'fun' enough to inspire me to write this book.

Index